SCOTTISH BATTLES

SCOTTISH BATTLES

John Sadler

BIRLINN

This edition first published in 2010 by
Birlinn Limited
West Newington House
10 Newington Road
Edinburgh
EH9 1QS

www.birlinn.co.uk

ISBN: 978 1 84341 047 8

British Library Cataloguing-in-Publication Data
A catalogue record for this book is available from the British Library

Typeset by Hewer Text UK Ltd, Edinburgh
Printed and bound by Bell & Bain Ltd., Glasgow

To David Winston Eggleston
A brave Douglas and a true friend

Acknowledgements

I am grateful to all those friends and colleagues from whom over the years I have had the opportunity to learn, by discussion and by reading, of the many aspects of Scottish military history. As to the opinions and interpretations and, of course, in respect of any mistakes contained herein, however, I remain entirely responsible.

Acknowledgement should also be made of the assistance given by Dr David Caldwell of the National Museums of Scotland; Miss Catherine May of the National Galleries of Scotland; Mr Joseph Wright of Historic Scotland; Mr Brian Moffat of the Johnnie Armstrong Museum of Border Arms & Armour; Ms Alyson Rhodes of the Art Department and to John Ferguson for sharing his researches into Flodden. Thanks are due also to Dr Richard Oram for providing me with an insight into exciting new lines of enquiry with regard to the Agricolan campaigns in Scotland; Mr Charles Wesencraft for allowing me to use photographs of his superlative models; to my agent, Duncan McAra, for his indefatigable assistance and encouragement; to Neville Moir and Hugh Andrew of Canongate Books for their support and enthusiasm; to Glenda-Gill for her patience and forbearance in typing and re-typing the manuscript and enduring my appalling handwriting; and lastly to my wife, Ruth, for her support throughout.

J.S.

Contents

List of Battle Plans

Preface

It is possible to view Scotland's history as a chronicle of battles from the defiant stand of the Caledonians in AD 84 to the last charge of the clans over Drummossie Moor, the final vestiges of that tribal society pelting through the sleet towards oblivion. The object of this study, therefore, is to provide for the general reader a military history from the Iron Age to the defeat of the Jacobites in 1746.

At a number of key points in the nation's history its development was decided by a clash of arms. The fateful encounter at Nechtansmere (Dunnichen Moss), in the distant spring of 685, determined that the kingdom would no more be a mere Northumbrian client; later the carnage at Carham in 1018, when another Northumbrian host was decimated, resulted in acceptance of the banks of the Tweed as marking the border. Wallace and Bruce, by their prowess, threw off the English yoke in the early fourteenth century and, of the first four Stewart kings, none died in his bed.

With each of the battles described I shall attempt to sketch in the general political and social background and expound, where appropriate, on the weapons and tactics employed. Obviously, and especially with earlier encounters, the details may be scanty and the existing accounts not infrequently contradict one another. Medieval chroniclers were apt to gild the horrors of battles with poetic licence and certainly tended to exaggerate the numbers involved. As a rule of thumb and when trying to assess the size of forces deployed it is prudent to divide the chroniclers' estimate by ten.

An understanding of leadership is always vital to an assessment of any battle or campaign; on paper Montrose's forces, available at the outset of 1645, were paltry yet that was to be the Year of Miracles when successive armies sent against him would reel in defeat. It is certainly possible to say that without Bruce there could have been no Bannockburn and equally without the ostensibly reckless and misplaced ardour of James IV, no Flodden Field. Lord George Murray would never have willingly fought a battle on Culloden Moor, and the Jacobite cause might have triumphed half a century earlier if Dundee had not fallen in his moment of victory at Killiecrankie.

The often bloody trail of Scottish history is strewn with myths. The celebrated nineteenth-century Prussian strategist Von Moltke is credited with the belief that to sustain morale boosting myths 'is a duty of piety and patriotism'. The employment of myth as a tool of propaganda is not uncommon but it is not history and the historian has a duty to consider the romantic fiction of the past in a more objective light. Hollywood burlesque such as Mel Gibson's *Braveheart* has added a new veneer of romantic fiction which plays to a Nationalist sentiment, fuelled by romance ahead of history.

Battles can be described in a variety of ways; one form of treatment is described by the eminent military historian John Keegan as the 'general staff approach' – a purely objective, often sanitised view, aimed at reducing the uncertain horrors of conflict to a scientific study, where battalions advance as pieces on a chess board and whereas troops may be 'badly mauled' or 'suffer casualties' the agonies and the all too frequent waste are considered irrelevant. In this approach battles are classified by type – battles of encounter, attrition, envelopment – conducted on the basis of set principles, concentration, offensive action, surprise.

This dissection has a role to play, but I believe the study of war cannot evade the stark realities of conflict or ignore the fact that blind chance is frequently an arbiter on the field. War is essentially nasty, battle the antithesis of civilised behaviour, where ruthlessness, brute force, low cunning and deception march alongside valour and idealism.

There is also the 'great man' approach, a tendency to view history as being moulded by the actions of outstanding characters. Napoleon Bonaparte may have remarked, 'History is but a fable agreed upon,' though I am uncertain if this utterance came before or after Waterloo. I believe war is best seen, as far as possible, through the eyes of the embattled, 'allowing the combatants to speak for themselves', though this route, too, is fraught with peril, as frequently those engaged in battle see only a limited position and that, not unnaturally, distorted by stress. Any attempt to see early battles through the eyes of the warriors engaged is frustrated by the fact that most, if not all, were illiterate and many early writers, Tacitus being a good example, are less than impartial in their approach.

Surprise, facilitated by sound intelligence, has always been a significant factor in victory. It was not uncommon in the Saxon era for commanders to agree to meet and do battle at a certain location at an appointed time, like a rather boisterous picnic, but given the difficulty of terrain, the relative smallness of forces and the lack of efficient communications, armies could easily miss one another which would make for bloodless, if frustrating, campaigning. Fear should never be underestimated, terror fuelled by propaganda leading to atrocity, as exemplified by Cumberland's fatal order in the wake of Drummossie Moor:

> A captain and 50 foot to march directly and visit all the cottages in the neighbourhood of the field of battle, and to search for rebels. The officers and men will take notice that the public orders of the rebels yesterday was to give us no quarter.[1]

In fact, no such order had ever been given but an eyewitness reported the deadly earnest of the redcoats, acting in pursuance of their general's bidding:

> 'the poor men made a shift to get up and went along with the party with an air of cheerfulness and joy, being full of the

thought that their wounds were to be dressed'. But an instant later a volley of shots rang out and the twelve 'poor men' were poorer still.[2]

No study of battle can ignore horror and degradation, nor, however, should it dwell upon these. Moral judgements, too, are best avoided; it is difficult in the comfort of one's own chair to ponder upon what so and so should have done but battlefield decisions are usually made in the heat of the moment, amidst smoke, dust, confusion and not infrequently with shot and shell raining around – factors which can dominate even the coolest of minds.

This history is therefore an attempt to look at a series of battles which were significant in terms of scale and/or consequence. It will endeavour to place each encounter or series of encounters in the context of the period and also look at the tactics, weapons and fortifications of the era. It will try to explain the combat in clear tactical terms whilst seeking to relate how it might have felt to be a combatant. In any event, this work celebrates the rank and file of Scottish armies throughout history, and their present descendants, who through triumph and disaster have never failed to add valour to their country's name.

'We are not Yet Subdued'

Evening on the fringe of the Highlands. The four-square marching camp, distinctive playing-card shape, a fresh scar upon the landscape, green-timbered palisade and fresh thrown earth, a raw intrusion. It bears the imperial stamp of Rome and the cutting edge of empire crowds the tented hides.

The attack comes with an appalling swiftness, stillness rent by strident cries, great host swelling unseen, a ragged steel-tipped avalanche. The mad exultant rush carries the outworks, gasping sentries overwhelmed, men from distant Spain vomiting blood onto Caledonian soil. Beneath the slashing swords and stamping feet of the tribesmen many of the *Legio IX* (Ninth Legion) are falling, no time for triple ordered ranks and wall of shields.

Men struggling with harness, fingers clumsy with fright, mouths dry, but yet they are not children these men of Rome, they are the legions, pride of the empire. Singly, in twos and threes, in groups, centurions screaming obscenities, they stand and fight, a soldier's battle, no general's hand or genius guiding. Every man for himself, rally to the standard, painted faces hideous in the near dark. They twist and dart, no room for manoeuvre, no space nor time to cast a javelin, parry clanging on shield, thrust into naked belly, skittering back, clutching entrails.

Across the clear and darkened air the sound of conflict carries to the tent of the Roman general, dread chance already half-anticipated. The camp's alert sounds, cohorts formed, orders bawled and curses shrieked. Armoured men stumbling through the short summer night across the trackless wastes. The forced march continues through the night till dawn's first grey light.

Exhausted, depleted, but not yet beaten the *Legio IX* is still fighting. Discipline begins to tell, the wild charge of the clans has leaked its fury through the savage night. The host seeks refuge in flight, crowding into sheltering mosses, denying serious pursuit.

The Caledonians

By the time the Roman legions, under Gnaeus Julius Agricola, invaded the area now called Scotland in the latter part of the first century AD, the people of Caledonia had a social system which was capable of offering large-scale resistance, able to raise an army to face invaders. Such a force could be maintained in the field and they could produce leaders competent to develop a coherent strategy.[1]

This strategy manifested itself in the cautious approach adopted by the Caledonians. The tribes respected the armoured legions and did not rush headlong into a pitched battle but sought to probe the Roman columns for weaknesses, to attack supply lines and disrupt communications. As a race the Celts have often been accused of throwing themselves into battle and dissipating their resources in a usually fruitless rush to death and glory. The defeats the southern tribes had suffered at the hands of Rome appear to have taught their northern neighbours wariness.

At this period, some 120 years after the Romans had first attacked under Caesar and 40 years since the Claudian invasions of southern England, the area now called Scotland was a forbidding fringe on the northern frontier of a mighty empire whose southern flank rested on the Euphrates.

Tacitus describes all territory north of the Forth as 'Caledonia' but distinguishes the particular tribe called the *Caledonii* (who were a Highland tribe living round the Great Glen, north and west of the *Creones*) from others such as the *Vacomagi*, who seem to have occupied Angus and the Mearns, the *Taezali* of Buchan, the *Decantae* of Ross, the *Lugi* and the *Cornovii* of Caithness and the *Venicones* south of the Tay. In the regions to the north-west lived the savage *Cereni*, *Smertae* and *Carnonacae*, who were said to smear their faces with the blood of the slain.[2]

Celtic Warriors

In their descriptions of the people Roman writers tended to associate the chieftains of Caledonian tribes with the fair-headed warriors from Germany. According to Tacitus, the 'reddish hair and large limbs of the people of Caledonia ... speak of German origin'.[3] Calgacus, the great hero of Agricola's war, is more properly known as Calgaich, the Swordsman, a name not unknown in Ireland.

In addition to this warrior élite Cassius Dio[4], writing of Severus's Campaign, mentions a more primitive people, nomadic hunter-gatherers who had no agriculture and went naked and barefoot. We may thus envisage tall, redhaired chieftains with their distinctive helmets, enamelled shields and proud spears. The peasant levy were distinguished by lime-washed hair and skin tattooed with woad. Leaders, chariot-borne chieftains, clothed in fine tunics and breeches with leather sandals, their distinctive oval, hexagonal or rectangular shields might be decorated with symbols of animals or geometric designs.

As a race the Celts were renowned as horse warriors and, throughout antiquity, had been used as mercenaries by both Greeks and Romans. Indeed, horse and rider were a favourite theme of Celtic art and the horseman seems to have possessed a fairly high social status. Their tactics were often based on the principle of hit and run, combining speed and firepower. It has been suggested that Celtic cavalry may have fought in small tactical units not unlike the medieval lance, in which the heavily armed horse warrior was supported by his more lightly armed followers and groom.

Only chiefs and proven warriors were armoured, with iron helmets and shirts of mail. The long Celtic sword which was worn slung from the hip also appears to have been a badge of rank. The Romans appear occasionally to have been disconcerted by a swaggering propensity for theatrical flourishes of sword-play. Although there is some suggestion that many Celtic swords were of poor temper and often had to be unbent or straightened

in the course of battle, some undoubtedly were of fine quality.
Examples have been found varying in length from 55cm to 77cm
and a particularly fine example dating from between 50 BC and
AD 100 was found at Embleton in Cumbria.

Celts were noisy fighters; accounts speak of the huge din
their hosts created, a great undisciplined mob of men, horses
and chariots, war chiefs resplendent as Homeric heroes and
the sinewy horde on foot. There are many representations of
Celtic accoutrements, their standards, horns and trumpets. The
commonest form of the latter was the Carnyx, a good example
of which was found at Deskford.

There appears to be a continuity of identity between the
Caledonians and the Picts, or *Pictii*, first mentioned by a Roman
writer in the later third century AD. The description 'painted
people' has come down as a somewhat disparaging term although
the name may have derived from a confusion to Roman ears
with the Celtic *Pretani* mentioned by an earlier traveller, Pytheas
of Masillia. Possibly the Caledonians carried on the older Celtic
tradition of applying blue-shaded body colouring which appears
to have continued north of the Wall some time after it died out
in the south. Caesar, in his commentaries on the invasions of 55
and 54 BC, mentions the southern Britons decorating themselves
in this way. The more primitive northerners, less tamed by the
civilising hand of Rome, may have clung to the old ways.

It has been suggested that the Caledonians, despite their physical similarities to the Germanic tribes, are more likely to have
originated in Ireland though there is no real evidence of this, and
the nature of their forts or duns suggests a non-German origin. It
may be that the western fringes may have been settled by immigrants from the south-western corner of present day England.
North and west of the Great Glen there are examples of hill
forts timber-laced in the Germanic fashion. The language of
the Caledonians also suggests a non-Irish origin, Brythonic as
opposed to Goidelic (Irish).

Agricola, General and Governor

Gnaeus Julius Agricola was a member of the Roman governing class and we are fortunate to have a formal biography written by his son-in-law P. Cornelius Tacitus. The general served his apprenticeship under the redoubtable Suetonius Paulinus and was blooded in the fierce campaign against Boudicca and her Iceni. Later he was promoted legate of the *Legio XX Valeria Victrix*. By the time he began to cast his eyes northward he was already imperial governor of Britain, probably in his early forties and at the height of his considerable powers. He was appointed in AD 77 by the Emperor Vespasian. Earlier in that same decade Q. Petillius Cerealis had conquered vast tracts of northern England and subjugated the hitherto independent Brigantes. His successor Julius Frontinus hammered the wild Silurians and Ordovices of Wales. This policy of expansionism was continued by Agricola, who, within the first two years of his tenure, completed the conquest of Wales and set a firm grip upon Brigantia.

To provide logistical support for his ambitious policy he established a line of frontier forts between the Firth of Forth and the Firth of Tay, supported by a typically efficient road system.[5] An early expedition penetrated as far as Strathmore and created a forward outpost at Ardoch near Dunblane. Later, in his subsequent campaigns, he sought to block the main exits from the Highlands by constructing forts at Fendoch, Dalginross and Callander. At Inchtuthil, near the junction of the Isla and Tay, he built a major fort, intended to serve as a legionary base.

The first expedition in AD 80 required a force of some 20,000 – 25,000 legionaries, 5000 auxiliary horse and 10,000 foot. The shock troops were drawn from the four British-based legions: *Legio II Augusta*, from Caerleon, *Legio XIV Adiutrix*, from Gloucester, men of the *Legio IX Hispana*, marching out of Lincoln and his old legion, *Legio XX Valeria Victrix*, based at Wroxeter.

He first advanced into Scotland in AD 79 and overran the country as far north as the banks of the Tay. He consolidated his gains behind the Forth/Clyde line but in AD 81, spurred on by Domitian's hunger for glory, he began an ambitious and aggressive exploration of the west coast. The following year he made the strategically important advance beyond the Tay and in the final storm fought his great battle which we know as Mons Graupius (the Grampian Hill).[6]

For the campaign of AD 83 he used a striking force whose cutting edge was comprised of detachments from three legions – *II, IX* and *XX* – though all of these appear, particularly *Legio IX Hispana*, to have been under strength due to overseas commitments. In an auxiliary role he used the fleet which sailed up the length of the east coast, thus exploiting a significant military and naval advantage whilst also securing a line of supply. The Romans always made good use of intelligence and understood the value of detailed reconnaissance; Agricola was clearly master of his trade.

The offensive involved the building of what were, in effect, forward battalion posts which were to be used for aggressive patrolling and further reconnaissance. The Highlands, west of Perthshire, must have appeared unattractive to a heavily armoured conventional army of the time though the Romans had campaigned successfully in even more difficult terrain.[7] It made far more strategic sense to make use of the broad valleys running roughly parallel to the east coast.[8]

The cornerstone of this sustained advance was to be the great legionary fortress at Inchtuthil. His strategy clearly appears to have been to advance northward by this eastern route securing the seaward flank with the fleet and blocking, with a fort, or battalion post, every passage to the Highlands on his exposed left, creating a coastal corridor and securing his otherwise extended lines of communication. By these means he would seek to reach the gateway to Scotland's granary, the land along the south side of the Moray Firth, west of the Spey, whilst the wild tribes of the west remained confined to their mountain fastnesses.

The Roman Legions

The basic tool the imperial governor proposed to use in achiev-
ing this victory was the Roman heavy infantryman, the legionary, a man who trained for ten hours a day for five years. Such
a soldier was led by a professional officer core of tribunes, all of
whom were Roman citizens and usually young men of eques-
trian or patrician rank, careerists or political opportunists on the
first rung.

The legions marched beneath their fabled standard, a silver
eagle carried high upon a tall shaft, the loss of which in battle
was the greatest dishonour any legion could suffer. In Agricola's
time the armour and accoutrement of the legions had nearly developed to its full extent. Possibly not all were armoured but wore a
leather cuirass with an iron helmet, flanged to protect the neck. At
the waist a metal-studded belt from which hung six weighted rows
of iron beads, on their feet thonged sandals finished with heavily nailed soles. Each shoulder was covered with an epaulette of
double thickness, beneath the chaffing leather a close-fitting tunic
and breeches which reached down usually to mid-thigh.

The figures marching in worn relief on Trajan's mighty column
show clearly the rounded helmet with its distinctive cheek-guards
and knotted sweat-cloth worn around the neck to prevent chaffing. The shirt beneath the cuirass is kilt length and has sleeves
ending at the elbow. These legionaries, though obviously dating
from a later period, wear the classic armour which consists of
a series of five iron strips or loops around the torso, jointed to
allow lateral movement, topped off by hinged shoulder plates
and known as *lorica segmentata*. As this armour is believed to
have been in service by AD 75–80 Agricola's legionaries may
have looked very similar to their Trajanic descendents. Officers,
gorgeous in ornamental plumed helmets and encased in moulded
and chiselled breast plates, also sported torques and plaques cast
in bronze and gold.

The distinctive curved, legionary shield, or *scutum*, was
rectangular in elevation, framed in wood, covered with hide.

Each legionary carried a heavy seven-foot *pilum* or javelin and short stabbing sword, the *gladius*, auxiliaries carried the heavier *lancea*. The legionary javelin had a sharp, well-tempered point connected to its shaft by a long shank of soft iron. Should this, when thrown, strike an enemy shield it would become embedded, the soft shaft bent and the enemy, virtually unable to withdraw the weapon from the shield, was forced to discard it as useless. Thus, when the fighters clashed hand to hand, the short and lethal *gladius* could do its deadly work beneath the enemy's upraised sword arm.

The essential tactical formation was the legion itself which, at full strength, would comprise 5280 foot divided into ten cohorts of 480 men each. The cohort was subdivided into six centuries or three maniples. The first cohort, double strength and comprising the fittest and most experienced soldiers, was commanded by the general or legate. The post of adjutant belonged to the camp prefect and each cohort was commanded by its own tribune. To assist them in the realities of military life these young noblemen had a nucleus of senior NCOs, the redoubtable centurions. Of these the most respected and most grizzled carried the honoured and hard-won title of *pilus prior*. Each century was loosely divided into ten squads each of eight men commanded by a junior NCO, or decurion. Despite his high level of morale and physical fitness the legionary could fight for only 15 minutes at peak efficiency and thus the cohort of 600 was divided into ten 60-men waves so that each soldier fought for no more than the allotted quarter and rested for a full hour; this system thus ensured that the front line was constantly manned by fresh troops.

Battle of Mons Graupius

It was with such a force that Agricola marched north from Inchtuthil in the summer of AD 84. His advance had by now brought him almost to the granary of the northern hill tribes. This was a prize the Caledonians could not afford to let slip.

To do so would be to invite defeat through starvation and the martial temperament of the hill tribes was such that they would not suffer humiliation without offering resistance.[9]

The location of Mons Graupius is uncertain – the word 'Grampian' derives from a setting error in the text of Tacitus's biography of Agricola when it was printed in Milan in the 1470s – but on a warm day in that distant summer it was thronged with 30,000 or more determined warriors led by a chieftain/general called Calgacus. The foot, it appears, were marshalled in ranks upon the slope of the hill which, though it appears to have risen quite steeply in places, was free of forestation or scrub.

In front and occupying the more level plain stood the chariots. This may be somewhat inaccurate, as Tacitus says 'in the midst', which probably means the chariots stood in the centre of the Caledonian force rather than to the fore. He later goes on to state that 'it was the foot who clashed first' which would imply that the chariots were stationed on the flanks. It is quite possible that Mons Graupius was not really a single hill at all but a series of undulating ridges. We have an impression that the Celtic forces may have crowned a succession of low hillocks, which could help to explain how a division was deployed to menace the Roman flanks, even though the main body was already hotly engaged.

Although the use of chariots in warfare had virtually died out by this time these remote clansmen, far to the north of the civil-ised centres of the Mediterranean countries, and even of south-ern England, still clung to the old ways. Outdated as they have been, such chariots none-the-less commanded some respect from the Romans. In construction they were very light and elegant, riding upon two spoked wooden wheels, bound, as were the hubs, with iron and the wheels themselves secured to the axle by means of iron linchpins. The body of the vehicle was open front and back, constructed of a light ash frame, finished with wicker-work panels. Usually the chariots were pulled by no more than two horses or ponies, perhaps similar in appearance to modern Welsh hill ponies, 12 or 13 hands in height, but harnessed with splendidly crafted and enamelled rein rings and flexible bridle bits.

Each chariot had a crew of two; one a driver, the other a warrior. We know from contemporary descriptions that the chariot warriors were capable of running along the pole as far as the yoke whilst travelling at full speed and then turning to run back. The chariot seems to symbolise the very spirit of the Celt, its design embodying practicality and superb elegance in perfect harmony. In all probability the chariots prowled the dead ground between the armies, the warriors hurling Homeric challenges.

The day prior to the main engagement the Romans advanced towards the foot of Mons Graupius but Agricola was determined to rest his troops before committing them to battle and the men dug, ditched and palisaded a marching camp in their habitual manner. On that next and fateful morning the imperial army drew up beyond the camp in line of battle; 8000 auxiliary foot in two lines of almost equal strength, with 1500 light horse on either flank, faced the foe. The legions themselves were held in reserve; Agricola appears to have been determined to let his auxiliary troops bear the initial brunt. To avoid being outflanked by the superior numbers of the Caledonians the Roman line was spread quite thinly and their front probably covered a distance of some two miles or so. As a further reserve were four brigades of cavalry covering the legions' flanks.[10]

It may be that Agricola exaggerated the size of the force which confronted him; a fine victory is never spoiled by higher odds and 30,000 appears a very high figure for a Celtic army though we must remember that he was facing a coalition of tribes, the *Caledonii* having been joined by men of the *Taezali* and *Vacomagi*. Before the battle Tacitus has each of the commanding generals addressing his troops. He puts a fine anti-imperialist speech into the mouth of Calgacus, though this should be treated with some degree of scepticism:

We, the most distant dwellers upon earth, the last of the free, have been shielded till today by our very remoteness and by the obscurity in which it has surrounded our name ... But there are no more nations beyond us; nothing is there but rocks and waves now, before us more deadly still than these – the Romans.[11]

Agricola, as befits a true professional, kept his address brief and to the point. He warned his troops that to suffer a defeat whilst engaged so deep in enemy territory would be an irreversible disaster, and with this pragmatic advice the general sent away his horse and took up position, on foot, in front of the legions, beneath the proud glare of the eagles.

With the formalities thus concluded the business of the day could begin in earnest and presently the air was filled with a deadly rain of missiles as each side loosed their barrage. Although many of the Roman javelins must have found their mark their impact failed to shake the ranks of the Caledonians. They stood their ground, dodging javelins, deflecting them with their long-bladed swords. Agricola ordered four of his Batavian and two of his Tungrian cohorts to close with the enemy, these Batavians, from the Rhine delta and the Tungrians from Tongres in the Ardennes were first-quality fighting troops. With commendable *élan* they swept into the ranks of the Caledonians thrusting with their short swords, jabbing shield bosses into screaming painted faces. So decisive was the shock of impact that the Celts on the lower level began to give way and the cohorts pressed forward.

Although Tacitus is quite emphatic that the Celtic chariots were in the centre of their army, it is certainly not impossible and, in fact, would appear more logical, if these had been positioned on the flanks; it may have been that the opening moves in the battle also involved a brisk cavalry action between British chariots and the Roman horse on the auxiliary wings. Quite possibly it was the Celts who, with the reckless bravado typical of their race, began the attack by charging the Roman squadrons.

At some point, however, horse and foot appear to have become intermingled in one desperate mêlée. The weight of numbers which the tribesmen were able to dispose and the nature of the ground began to slow the otherwise inexorable advance – well-ordered lines shaken and disordered by broken chariots, the mangled bodies of horses and men.

The next initiative came from the Britons. Several bodies of foot had descended from the further ridges and made their way around to outflank the embattled cohorts, a bold move but one which Agricola had already anticipated. He rushed his four reserve mounted brigades, or *alae*, to the front and threw them against the massed Celtic foot. Thus it was the Romans who triumphed on the flanks as the Britons were driven in some disorder back upon their lines.

Under constant pressure in the centre and hemmed in on both flanks the Caledonian line began to dissolve. Many were cut down as they sought refuge in flight. The Roman cavalry on their flanks were ideally poised for relentless pursuit. A few isolated pockets of *Gaesti*, or berserkers, continued to hold out, at great cost, but the majority withdrew as best they could towards sheltering woods to the rear.

Though defeated, the tribesmen had some fight left in them, and a body of foot rallied at the woodland fringe and turned on their pursuers. This tactic might have cost the Romans dear as their own jubilant infantry pounded pell-mell after the fleeing Britons. Agricola, though, was master of the situation. The infantry pursuit was checked, the ranks reordered, and the line advanced steadily against the diehards. The Britons melted into the cover of the enveloping trees.

> The open plain now presented a grim awe inspiring spectacle
> ... equipment, bodies and mangled limbs lay all around on
> the blood stained earth.[12]

As the last echoes of combat died away Agricola was able to report that some 10,000 Caledonians lay dead upon the field. Their army, or what remained of it, was in full retreat. As for casualties on the Roman side he reported 360 dead including one tribune, Aulus Atticus, who, according to his commander, 'was carried away by his youthful bravery and by his spirited charge into the midst of the enemy'.

The next day awful silence reigned on every hand, the hills were deserted, houses smoking in the distance . . .[13]

Although he had won a great victory Agricola was not able to follow it up due, at least in part, to the lateness of the season. The victorious Romans withdrew into the territory of the *Boresti*, an unknown tribe whose lands must have lain somewhere around the Moray Firth. By stages the great army dispersed into winter quarters.

The battle of Mons Graupius may have marked the furthest northward advance of any Roman army, prompting Tacitus, with a certain measure of poetic licence, to claim that Britain 'was completely subdued'. Calgacus himself seems to have survived the battle though his credibility as a general would have been severely if not fatally damaged by the magnitude of defeat. Obviously, the loss of so many young men to a tribal society together with the inevitable damage to their crops must have been a major blow and the survivors would spend a miserable and demoralised winter.

It is fair to say, however, that the larger portion of the Celtic army had escaped and the Romans denied any effective pursuit. Calgacus, as a general, is to be commended for the manner in which he chose his position and for the manner in which the withdrawal was effected.

Despite this seemingly glittering victory Agricola's forward policy had many opponents in Rome, who asked whether a major expedition into such harsh and unproductive territory was really worthwhile. Whatever the reason Agricola was recalled soon after the battle and his role in the affairs of north Britain came to an end.

The actual site of the battle has exercised scholars and enthusiasts ever since. The discovery of a large marching camp near Inverurie to the north-west of Aberdeen has been used as the basis for suggesting that a hill, known as Bennachie (1073 ft), may have been the location. Other historians, notably W. F. Skene, thought the site lay beyond the Isla at the hill of Blair. A Roman marching camp has been found at Meikleour in the peninsula at the junction of the Isla and Tay, and between these two points there is a flat plain known as the Muir of Blair.[14]

More than a dozen possible sites have been suggested for the location of Mons Graupius, including the Pass of Grange near Keith and Durno, under the lee of Bennachie near Inverurie in eastern Aberdeenshire. The most plausible is perhaps a site south of the Mounth, where the Bervie Water flows below Knock Hill near Monboddo in the Mearns, a district which in the tenth century was known as 'the Swordland', and which, even in the turbulent years of the early medieval period saw more than its fair share of conflict.[15]

After this bloody interlude Scotland north of the Tay sinks back into obscurity.[16] Yet Rome had not finally done with this vexatious northern province and the eagles returned in force in the summer of AD 140 when the governor, Lollius Urbicus, began building the Antonine Wall, completed five years later, stretching for 37 miles and including 18 forts.

Though still impressive the Antonine was a lesser work than Hadrian's Wall to the south. Though it spanned the narrow Forth/Clyde isthmus it was open unless covered by a strong naval presence to amphibious raids on both flanks, it carried neither mile castles nor turrets and the forts were considerably smaller. It has been suggested that Hadrian's Wall had, in effect, a dual garrison, a 'police' force and a mobile field force ready to take the fight to the enemy. The smaller garrison of the northern bastion had to fulfil both roles.[17]

The total complement probably never exceeded, say, 7000 men, of whom perhaps a third were legionaries.[18] The wall itself was of an altogether more utilitarian construction, turf ramparts with timber palisades. Even the forts were built of wood.[19]

There has been much speculation as to why the Antonine Wall was ever thrown up in the first place as the earlier wall was certainly not abandoned. The answer most probably lies in the growth in the population and power of the Lowland tribes, many of the hill forts scattered through the present border counties date from the second century AD and it may be that Rome felt the need to lay a restraining hand on these virile and likely quarrelsome neighbours. It could be further suggested that this pacification involved the slighting of numerous of the native forts and some forcible relocations of the inhabitants.[20]

The dissipation of manpower resources between the two lines of defence may have contributed to a crisis which arose shortly after the completion of the Antonine Wall. The *Brigantes*, the powerful tribe of north-east England, rose in revolt and the flames seem quickly to have spread to the Lowlands. The northern wall may have suffered and there is some evidence of rebuilding at this period. Late in the century, however, in the ill-fated reign of Commodus,[21] a major uprising occurred in the Lowlands and the wall was overrun:

> Of the wars waged by Commodus the greatest was in Britain. The tribes in that island crossed the wall which divides them from the Roman fortresses, and did great harm. They slew a [Roman] general and the men under his command. Commodus, greatly alarmed, sent Ulpius Marcellus against them.'[22]

A good choice, a tough martinet with previous experience in Britain, defeated the rebels and restored order, obviously not without cost. The tribesmen appear to have overrun the Antonine Wall and inflicted serious casualties. Quite clearly, however, Hadrian's much stronger bulwark to the south held out. Marcellus proceeded to rebuild the northern wall but there is the sense that this was largely a face-saving exercise, for the structure was abandoned before the century was out and the works dismantled. Rome had won another battle but the initiative seems to have passed to the native tribes and the frontier rested on Hadrian's Wall for the remainder of the occupation.

When Commodus's unedifying reign was terminated by an assassin's knife the empire reeled in the wake of civil war and bubbling internecine strife as rival claimants scrabbled for the purple. Not till the rise of the dour 'African' Septimius Severus, the former governor of Upper Pannonia, was order restored. Clodius Albinus, his British counterpart, was one of those who threw his hat or rather his sword into the ring – unsuccessfully; he was trounced near Lyons and chose the well-tested option of falling on his own sword.

In launching his abortive enterprise Albinus stripped the northern garrisons and the wall, hated symbol of imperial domination, was thoroughly slighted with a most unbarbarian thoroughness. So total was this epic of destruction that many later scholars believed that Severus had actually built the wall rather than restored it.

Particularly active were the *Maeatae*,[23] who capitalised on Rome's aberration and weakness to despoil and pillage at will. So powerful were these raiders that Severus at first did not feel strong enough to engage them in the field but relied on bribery and subsidies to buy them off. The emperor spent ten years from 198 to 208 in reconstructing his shattered defences. Once secure he launched a series of punitive raids which occupied him until his death at York in 211.

The effect of these campaigns in Scotland has been the subject of much debate; it has been suggested that this resumption of an aggressive 'forward' policy was a failure – no great battles were fought and won, the tribes relied on Fabian and guerilla tactics. In the end Severus died, the northern tribes unimpressed and unsubdued. His son and successor abandoned his father's policy and Scotland was left alone thereafter.

Conversely it can be argued that Severus's policy was never aimed at conquest or even permanent pacification; his intention was to intimidate and overawe, to impress with the might of Rome's long arm. In these limited and more realistic objectives he may well have been successful for the frontier did remain quiet for several generations. It is possible that he did carry out some further forcible resettlement of particularly troublesome clans.

Amidst all of these alarums Scotland did enjoy some of the many benefits of Roman civilisation; the military occupation provided a network of good roads and a boost to the local economy – forts such as Trimontium[24], were large manufacturing and distribution centres in their own right. Others such as Inveresk, near Musselburgh, fuelled the development of a civilian settlement or *vicus* beyond the walls.

The large native hill fort or *oppidum* at Tap o' Noth near Rhynie in Strathbogie may be contemporary with the Roman occupation – a major site enclosing about 50 acres and which may have been the focus for a tribal grouping north of the Forth/Clyde line. If so then its inhabitants must have been able to co-exist with the Roman garrisons for there is no evidence that the place was ever stormed or slighted.

As the legions finally withdrew southward the land we call Scotland must have appeared little touched by the Pax Romana and certainly far less so than England. To what extent the Roman occupation influenced the later history of Scotland is a constant, and likely never ending, source of debate. The land was fought over, wasted and patrolled but never finally subdued or dominated. And yet no one who has seen the majestic and still awe-inspiring sweep at Hadrian's Wall can deny its impact; in the words of another writer – 'Hadrian drew the line'[25] – he created a frontier. Though the line moved north and then south again the eagles were there for over four centuries and the imprint of their culture cannot have entirely failed to leave a mark.

The Four Peoples

The disaster which a confederation of Picts and Scots and Britons from Strathclyde inflicted on the hitherto almost invincible Northumbrian host at Dunnichen Moss (Nechtansmere) amongst the Sidlaw hills in the spring of 685 was a momentous victory. The defeat of the Angles put an end to their systematic inroads onto Scottish soil which had threatened to turn the Pictish kingdom into a mere Northumbrian province. On the occasion of the 1300th anniversary of the fight in 1985 it was hailed as the most decisive battle in Scottish history.

These tough descendants of the Anglian Chief Ida had begun to exert pressure on their Celtic neighbours after they had established themselves on the north-east coast of England. Aethelfrith, aptly named the 'Destroyer', had clashed with the Scots of Dalriada led by Aedán mac Gabrain in 603 when the latter attempted to push back the tide of Anglian encroachment.

A great battle was fought at Degsastan, which may be Dawston in Liddesdale, though sites as far distant as Dissington, near Ponteland, just north of Newcastle upon Tyne, have been suggested.[1] The Scots came on full of impetuous valour and in the first clash the Northumbrian van, led by the king's brother, Theobald, was overcome and its chieftain killed. Aethelfrith countered with his main body and for a space the field was hotly contended as both sides held their own and casualties mounted. The discipline and staying power of the better drilled Anglian warriors began to tell and the Scots host, at length, disintegrated, Aedán fled for his life but counted most of his followers amongst the fallen. 'From that day until the present,' wrote Bede in 731, 'no King of the Scots in Britain has dared make war on the English.'[2]

This should not imply, however, that the Angles had it all their own way; this influx and expansion were not uncontested. Relegated to the land of bardic myth is the principality of Rheged whose capital may have been Carlisle and whose kings claimed descent from Magnus Maximus. Even the boundaries of this Celtic state remain a mystery. None-the-less its most celebrated ruler, Urien, was a favourite hero whose praises were sung by Taliesin and Llywarch Hen. He defeated the Angles in a series of battles and succeeded in penning them up in their coastal fortresses.

> Hussa reigned seven years, against whom four Kings made war, Urien, and Rideric, and Guallian and Morcant ... and he shut them up three nights in the island of Metcaud [Farne Island]: and during that expedition he was slain, at the instance of Morcant, through envy . . .[4]

Disunity, the tragic flaw of the Celt, jealousy and the assassin's blade ended Urien's brilliant reign. He was treacherously struck down at the mouth of the Low Burn near what is now Beal, presumably at the instigation of his supposed ally Morcant.[5]

With Urien slain the mantle of chieftainship was passed to Owain his son, 'Chief of the Glittering West' and a worthy hero to succeed his father. Owain, too, became a favourite of the bards, whose noble verses chronicle the death-throes of Celtic Britain.

Owain is credited with a great victory over the Angles at Argoed Llwyfain, when the Saxon prince of Fflamddwyn is said to have suffered defeat and death. Ultimately he too failed to stem the tide and fell at the battle of Catraeth (Catterick?) around 593, an end made glorious by the poet Aneirin's epic of the 'Gododdin'.[6]

The Rise of Pictland

Though Rheged vanished the other British kingdoms survived. Saint Patrick wrote to the *Damnonii*, secure in their rocky fastness at Dumbarton, ruled by one Coroticus or Ceredig, who was roundly lambasted by the saintly traveller for trafficking in slaves.

North of the Britons lay the kingdoms of the Picts and Scots. The former, who comprised the majority, were the descendants of those who had rallied to Calgacus. Their origins were obscure; Irish legend chronicles the Picts' first arrival as invaders from distant Scythia, an interesting if unlikely conjecture. It does appear that there were two distinct Pictish kingdoms, for as early as 310 Cassius Dio refers to the *Caledonii* as living north of the *Maeatae*, who so disturbed the reign of Commodus. In 565 Columba visited the Pictish king, Bridei, in his dun near the future site of Inverness.

Several centuries later Bede distinguishes the northern from the southern Picts, early kings, who could be graded in the Irish manner: *rí tuaithe* – a petty king or tribal chieftain; *ruirí*, overking and the *rí ruirech* or King of overkings – and who were little more than local warlords with power shifting on the thrust of a spearpoint.

It may be that in this early period the balance of power lay more with the northern Picts but seems to have finally swung in favour of the more southern province of Fortriu which originally covered what is now Strathearn and Mentieth. Gradually a series of aggressive *ruirí* extended their sway over, first, the Mounth and, finally, the whole of the north. The chief hold of Fortriu was at Scone, a site that in the reign of Kenneth mac Alpin in the ninth century began to acquire its deep religious and mystic significance.

Bridei mac Bile, who slew Ecgfrith, brought all of the Picts beneath his own potent banner, and carried it against the Scots of the western seaboard, attacking their formidable capital at Dunadd. His descendant Oengus MacFergus (752–61) finally defeated the Scots and achieved a Pictish supremacy.[7]

The Scots of Dalriada

These Scots were immigrants who had filtered across the Irish Sea in relatively small numbers, probably not beginning to arrive before the fall of Rome. By 500, however, their chieftain Fergus Mor and his two brothers had established toeholds in Kintyre, Lorn, Islay and Jura.

Their principal hold was that splendid fortress of Dunadd, a site which even today remains heavy with the scent of legend. Columba built upon the faith of these invaders and religion appears to have strengthened the infant kingdom which sturdily maintained its independence from its numerous and warlike Pictish neighbours.

Aedán mac Gabrán was the great-grandson of Fergus Mór; he established himself king of the Dalriadic Scots in 573 and was crowned by Columba. He pursued an aggressive policy towards his Pictish neighbours but was first repulsed by them and then crushed by the Northumbrians. Further disasters followed: Aedan's grandson, Domnall Brec Aedan, fell in battle against the British King Owain of Strathclyde in 642. Thereafter the Scots were beset by internecine feuds leading to an epic sea battle in 719 when a cadet branch emerged triumphant. Even this could not stop the rot and a new breed of warlike kings of Fortriu battered Dalriada; in 741 Oengus led his Pictish warriors to victory over the Scots.[8]

The Art of War

Skirmishes between these uneasy neighbours were frequent affairs, swift and bloody encounters opened with swarms of lightly armed horse warriors, mounted on sturdy garrons, deluging their opponents with a shower of lances. When the foot closed they massed in solid formations, phalanx-like, armed with strong, heavy-bladed spears and square shields. Stone carvings suggest that these formations may have been quite well organised with rows of pikemen protected by a separate rank of

shield-bearers, perhaps suggesting the origin of the later medieval schiltron.

The rank and file would not be likely to possess fine weaponry,
armour or accoutrement; such as was to be found would be the
reserve of chieftains, who carried long-bladed swords, possibly
of Irish origin, and wore rounded iron helmets. Casting spears
were undoubtedly also in use by the foot and the *Irish Annals*
speak of javelins propelled by attached thongs, the grip retained
by the thrower who could thus recover the dart if the cast missed
its mark.[9]

Naval warfare was also important at this time; we have
already seen how the sub-kings of Dalriada fought at sea and
Pictish kings also maintained substantial fleets of swift galleys,
each typically having seven benches, 14 oars and a crew of
twenty-odd.

The *Annals of Ulster* also record the fury of the attack on
Dunadd by Oengus MacFergus in 742 when the fortress fell to
the Picts and the kingdom thereafter survived only as a client of
Pictish kings.

Despite this bloody feuding there was a great deal of inter-
marriage, for example of Dalriadic kings bearing Pictish names
and vice-versa. By a strange twist of fate it was a Scots chieftain, Kenneth mac Alpin, who took the Pictish throne in 843
and who began the business of unification, though this business
took some four centuries to complete. Exactly how this coup
was achieved is uncertain. The Picts were wearied and battered
by Viking raids and Kenneth's lightning campaign appears to
have succeeded without any major battle. As Pictish Kings ruled
afterwards, it appears possible that the two peoples may have
been closer to unity than was previously supposed.

The Angles

When Aethelfrith, the pagan victor of Degsastan, himself fell
beneath the blade of his successor Edwin, the heroic age of
Northumbria could be said to have begun. The emerging power

of the northern Anglian kingdom began to reach into Lothian. This pattern of conquest was far from consistent. Northumbrian kings were frequently diverted by bloody squabbling with their powerful southern neighbours from Mercia. Edwin himself is credited with giving Din Eidyn (Edinburgh) its name. Anglian armies frequently pushed northward to the Forth/Clyde line and Dunbar became the stronghold of a Northumbrian Ealdorman.

The late seventh-century king Ecgfrith had developed a considerable contempt for the Picts borne out of earlier and easier victories. Apparently, quite early in his reign, a Pictish confederation had rebelled against the Northumbrian yoke, only to be decimated when the Angles stormed their redoubt. Ecgfrith's cavalry, possibly aided by Pictish allies, slaughtered the lightly armed Celts in a lightning attack, 'filling two rivers with the corpses', according to the Anglian Chronicler Eddi.[10]

In his spring campaign of that fateful year he pushed up to the Forth without meeting any serious opposition and crossing at Stirling drove up through Perthshire to the Tay. It may be the expedition was less than popular with his own subjects, some of whom viewed this aggressive stance as pure warmongering for little practical gain.

Bridei mac Bile was no mean opponent and the Northumbrian's overconfidence proved his undoing. Bridei had come to preeminence early in the decade when he had established himself as ruler of all Fortriu.[11] A formidable confederation was arrayed against Ecgfrith, memory of the Angles' prowess temporarily blotted out internecine rivalries and the Picts may have been joined by Scots from Dalriada and Britons from Strathclyde.[12] The same Fabian tactics that had, generations earlier, foiled and frustrated the emperor Severus, served well for the Anglian host, which was led onto broken and difficult ground amidst the Sidlaw Hills. Respect for the well-armed Northumbrians kept the tribesmen at bay but, already, the killing ground had been chosen.

The Northumbrians

The Anglians were a warlike race, sprung from that virile Saxon stock which first reached these shores as mercenaries in the service of the British chiefs they were soon to supplant. Chiefs of renown attracted a unit of hardened warriors to their banners, a retinue of house-carls who were expected to follow their leaders to victory or death – for one to return home when the chief had fallen was the greatest dishonour.

The Northumbrian host would comprise a hard core of these seasoned veterans gathered around the person of their king with a more motley array of levies, latterly called the 'fyrd'. These commoners would be scarcely better armed or accoutred than their Pictish foes.

Few would boast any form of armour other than leather jerkins and simple iron skull-helmets. Swords were a rarity and most would carry the cruder sax and heavy thrusting spears, long leaf-shaped heads socketed onto seven-foot ash staves. Shields were rounded and slightly convex, of wood covered with hide and stiffened by a metal rim and bands.

Chieftains and their retainers could present a far more martial appearance – protected from throat to thigh by a short-sleeved mail shirt or *byrnie*, the 'ring woven corselet' or 'woven breast nets' of bardic lays. The head was covered by a helmet framed in iron and finished with plates of horn perhaps surmounted by the warrior's crest, say, a bronze boar, such as the example found in a burial at Banby Grange in Derbyshire. It was not unusual for helmets of this period to come with sculpted facepieces, giving the wearer a degree of bizarre anonymity.

Swords were rare and precious things, the true emblem of a warrior elite, given as prestigious gifts or handed down through families. A yard-long blade, straight, double-edged and shallow-fullered, short functional quillons, grips of wire-bound wood. The distinctive, angular or 'cocked hat' pommels might be mounted with gold and bejewelled. Particularly prized samples were often given names such as Egils' Dragvandil.[13]

Nechtansmere

South-east of Forfar, at Dunnichen Moss on 20 May 685, the Pictish confederation was waiting and as the Northumbrian host lumbered into view they struck. A storm of missiles poured from the hills dropping unarmoured levies by the score. The traditional fighting formation of this period was the unwieldy but often redoubtable shield wall – the chieftain and his warriors in the centre, lesser mortals massed on the flanks. Bridei had chosen his ground well; the terrain did not favour a regular deployment and the suddenness of the onslaught appears to have caught the invaders totally unaware.

If the Northumbrians were ever able to form a line of battle they did not long retain their ranks. The levies, stunned, bruised and now a very long way from home, broke and ran – a fatal error, it may be supposed, for most, however, as their retreat was hampered by the presence of a small lochan called Nechtansmere. It was here around the banner of their king that the Northumbrian élite paid the full price for his headstrong folly. The lochan itself, located somewhere between Dunnichen and Leithen, no longer exists nor is there any trace of the contemporary settlement which may have stood on the south side of Dunnichen Hill and whose presence further hindered the invaders' attempt to deploy.

Any attempt to ascertain the numbers involved in the battle would be purely speculative – we may certainly assume that they were not great. It is not improbable that the Picts and their allies outnumbered the Northumbrians. It may be that the mere fact of a confederation suggests warbands from each kingdom rather than the mass array of Calgacus's day. Ecgfrith's warband numbered a few hundred at most, a total force of perhaps 500 or 600 men.

The victory was total. The threat of Anglian dominance declined and the country moved a definite step towards nationhood. It may be possible to speculate that without the defeat of Northumbria the union of Picts and Scots might have been delayed and Kenneth mac Alpin's overlordship may not have occurred when it did. By uniting, even temporarily, in the face of a common foe, the disunited peoples of Scotland began to function as a race. Even without this defeat it is probable that the Anglian threat would have diminished. Ecgfrith was the last of the easy 'heroic' kings of Northumbria and his death marked the advent of a more cautious age,[14] though some of his successors such as Eadbert in the mid eighth century won great renown.

An interesting postscript to the battle concerns the discovery of a stone relief in Aberlemno churchyard, which appears to depict a battle scene in a narrative memorial:

> If the Aberlemno stone bears the most splendid representation of a Pictish battle, and if, in that battle, the Picts are seen defeating the Northumbrians, then what better battle to commemorate than their greatest victory, that won at Nechtansmere.[15]

The House of Canmore

From the early ninth century Scotland suffered increasingly from the predatory attentions of the Norsemen. Recent consideration has led to a more moderate view of the Vikings and a reappraisal of their achievements as explorers and traders. Yet to any inhabitant of Scotland at that time the sight of those great square sails crowding the horizon spelt terror and bloodshed.

The Vikings' weapons were heavy stabbing spears, which, like their swords with yard-long tapering blades and distinctive pommels, often carried names: 'Odin's Flame', 'Battlesnake'.[1] A favoured arm was the mighty battle axe with a heavy trumpet-shaped blade mounted on an ash shaft of sufficient length to allow the weapon to be held in a double-handed grip. In the heat of battle, men of the lower classes, landless, often outlaws, would be gripped by that strange and terrible bloodlust and frothing at the mouth, gnawing at the rims of their shields, tearing off helmet and mail, would fling themselves at the enemy line – certain death the berserker's due reward.

The Norse menace was both potent and immediate; in 839 Oengus's son Eogan fell in battle as, in 877, did Constantine I. In 903 the Vikings swept the length of the kingdom laying waste to Lothian. Rallying behind Columba's sacred banner the Scots fought back and roundly thrashed their oppressors the following year at Strathearn.[2] Ten years later, in 914, the Scots were on the offensive but were defeated by Ragnall of York at Corbridge in Northumberland. Four years after that Constantine II routed Ragnall with a tidy irony, also at Corbridge.

The west coast, with its long sea lochs and sandy stretches, proved a favourite hunting ground, though the east coast suffered equally.[3] Ironically the very fury of the Vikings so weakened the ancient Anglian kingdoms that expansion from the south was checked and the relentless pressure of Norse raids drove the Picts and the Scots into alliance, a tortuous process and one which took generations to finally accomplish. The dominant Picts shared a common tribal heritage with the Britons of Lothian, both relatively untouched by Romanisation. Their way of life, centred on the tribe with its chieftain at the apex of a structured social pyramid, was broadly similar. From the sixth century onwards the spread of Christianity became an increasingly important factor. The earliest contact had been established through the mission of Ninian, a Briton trained in Roman traditions, to the southern Picts from his church at Whithorn around AD 400; later, Columba crossed the narrow waters of the Irish Sea in 563 and established his seat on Iona.

Columba was a born zealot, so fervent and uncompromising that his preaching led to civil war in his native Ireland. Nonetheless, by the time of his death in 597 Iona was the heart of a spreading faith which spawned a series of communities. This Celtic Church was pastoral and for a time there was a taint of schism but the apparent gulf with Rome was healed, in Rome's favour, at the Synod of Whitby (663–4).

Kingship in early Scotland was frequently a hazardous business and those who died in their beds were fortunate. To those who fell in battle against the Vikings must be added more who died in internecine strife or by the assassin's knife. Throughout the period 850–1050 there was a gradual, if at times imperceptible, 'coming together' of the kingdom. The Pictish state assumed the mantle of nationhood though its core lay at the heart of the old kingdom of Fortriu.

The accession of Kenneth mac Alpin is seen as the first major step towards unity, though Kenneth's reign is probably better viewed as a step in the process begun by his predecessor and carried through by his descendants. It was, in fact, Kenneth's grandson, Donald, who was the first to call himself *ri Alban* – king of Alba.[4]

As the powers of the Anglian kingdoms of Northumbria and Mercia crumbled beneath the Viking onslaught Scottish kings used their growing power to interfere in the affairs of northern England. Constantine II (900–43) penetrated as far south as Corbridge early in his reign though he profited little from this incursion. The situation was reversed when the virile rulers of Alfred's line, having tamed the Norse, extended their sway northwards.

The fall of Northumbria meant that the old northern province of Bernicia once again was distinguishable from the Viking principality based in York. Predatory as these Norse neighbours may have been, they came to constitute a useful buffer between the Scots and the swelling power of the West Saxons. Edward the Elder, son of Alfred the Great, brought all England south of the Humber under his sway; his son, Athelstan, a brilliant and aggressive ruler, clearly perceived York as ripe for shaking.

The death of Sihtric of York in 927 gave Wessex the opportunity to intervene and Athelstan ruthlessly drove out the Norse pretender Olaf Guthfrithson, who fled to his compatriots in Ireland, normally no friends of the York Vikings. With the north-east of England apparently secure Athelstan, in 934, conducted a *chevauchée* through Scotland, an enthusiastic show of strength that saw an English fleet penetrate as far as Caithness. Constantine, thoroughly alarmed, clearly decided that a buffer state in northern England was needed to insulate Scotland from the rapacity of the West Saxons.

In 937 he formed an alliance with Olaf and the Strathclyde British: Scots, Norse and Celts driven by fear of Wessex. Olaf, with a fleet of 600 keels, sailed boldly up the Humber to reclaim his lost kingdom. His ranks swelled by Norse and Britons from the west and by Scots from the north, he posed a substantial threat to Athelstan.

Unfortunately the Saxon king was not easily daunted and, raising his own forces, confronted the allies possibly somewhere on Humberside. A fearsome battle ensued, a combat begun at dawn that raged till dusk. Mercians against Norse, Saxons pitted against Scots. Constantine's son was amongst the dead and this defeat, with such great effusion of blood, seems to have broken the king's spirit. Any hope of Scotland creating a 'buffer zone' or of even annexing Bernicia outright perished on the field and in 943 the king withdrew to monastic life.

Some time later, however, there was a resurgence of Danish power centred on York, and Malcolm I (943–64) was able to conclude a treaty with Edmund of Wessex, whereby the Scots effectively 'leased' Cumbria from the English, thus, hopefully, from Edmund's view, closing the 'back door' from Ireland.

Steadily the English influence increased. In 973 King Edgar steered on the River Dee a ceremonial barge at the oars of which were six client kings, including Kenneth II of Scotland (971–95)[5]. The reign of Aethelred provided an opportunity for the Scots to reassert themselves and the warlike Malcolm II proved equal to the challenge. He annexed Strathclyde and in 1006 swept through Northumbria with fire and sword terrorising the ineffective Earl Waltheof. Dismayed at his father's weakness, Uctred, Waltheof's son, fought back on his own initiative, first raising the siege of Durham and forcing Malcolm's forces back across the Tweed. Newly created earl in his father's stead, Uctred went over to the offensive, driving Malcolm north almost to the Tay and asserting Northumbria's ancient grip on Lothian. In 1016 the earl's career was cut short by an assassin's blade and his less aggressive brother Edwulf, who succeeded to the title, withdrew.

The loss of substantial revenue from estates in Lothian outraged the Northumbrian clergy who in 1018 swore to protect such income by force of arms. A great levy of warriors was raised, amply blessed and commanded by prelates, which clashed with a Scots army led by Malcolm at Carham on the Tweed, probably at a location, quarter of a mile north-west of the spot now occupied by the Norman motte at Wark. After a savage battle the Scots were victorious and many of the English fell, including a fair score of Northumbrian nobility and no less than 18 leading churchmen.[6] The fight proved – with time – decisive, for the line of the Tweed finally became the accepted border and the English claim to Lothian passed finally into history. (Carham was the site of a later extended skirmish in 1370 when Northumbrians under Sir John Lilburn fought a long and bitter fight against Scottish riders led by Sir John Gordon – again Scottish tenacity won the day.) The victory at Carham raised the question of the annexation of Bernicia once again to create a buffer zone between the Scots and English but the late resurgence of Northumbrian power under Siward forestalled any such attempt.

By the 1040s the power of the crown was firmly established though by no means either universal or particularly secure. The monarch ruled through his nobles or mormaers,[7] who, like later medieval barons, controlled their territories, collected their own taxes and administered justice in the name of the king. These relationships were not always congenial and the problem of the 'overmighty subject' was a familiar bane.

The method by which a new king was chosen relied upon the old Gaelic custom of election from within an eligible group or 'derbfine' – this could include a claimant from a certain class whose great-grandfather had been a king and success was determined by suitability. The term 'Tanaiste'[8] appears to have been restricted to one designated as the ruling monarch's heir during his lifetime. Perhaps not unsurprisingly, this system led to bitter and sanguinary feuds. Two principal lines of royalty emerged and claims were frequently decided on the battlefield. Once successful the monarch, in order to maintain a clear field for his own progeny, might feel justified in butchering any potential rivals.

Malcolm had no immediate male heir but intended his grandson, Duncan, to succeed. The obvious male challenger was summarily killed but not before he begat a daughter (or possibly a granddaughter) who, by her second marriage, wed MacBeth, mormaer of Moray and himself of royal blood. This Duncan who succeeded his grandfather in 1034 was not, as Shakespeare would have us believe, an old and wise king, but a young and rather stupid one, whose six-year reign was characterised by rash and spectacularly unsuccessful military adventures. Finally, and in open field, he was slain by MacBeth who, far from being a tyrant, ruled well for 17 years and felt sufficiently secure during that time to undertake a pilgrimage to Rome.[9]

Before his death Duncan had bowed to a resurgence of Northumbrian power under the formidable Siward, a Danish freebooter who won the title of earl in 1041, by ceding Cumbria. Duncan's death created an opportunity for Siward when his young sons fled to England. First, he championed the dead man's brother Maldred, whose foray into Lothian in 1045 was sponsored by Siward. Unfortunately, the pretender was slain and Siward had to wait until Malcolm, Duncan's bastard, came of age. The boy had spent most of his formative years at the court of Edward the Confessor and the king supported his bid for power by allowing him a force of his own house-carls.

In 1052 the allies first invaded and in a series of hard-fought campaigns pushed MacBeth beyond the Tay. At the start of the campaigning season in 1054 the Northumbrians, who had apparently mustered on Tayside, crossed the river and inflicted a defeat on the Scots at the battle of the Seven Sleepers [hills]. MacBeth was still not finally defeated and the ageing Siward retired southward and died the following year. Malcolm meanwhile remained on the offensive and in 1057 after a flanking march through the hills cornered MacBeth, apparently accompanied by only his household warriors, at Lumphanan in Aberdeenshire. Despite being outnumbered the usurper is said to have attacked, and fell gloriously with his followers around him.

In addition to the fame conferred by Shakespeare, MacBeth is credited as being the first Scottish ruler to import Norman warriors as mercenaries.

Malcolm III, once victorious, began to consolidate the power of the monarchy. It is not surprising that he was influenced by his upbringing at the English court and that his reign should see the development of the feudal state. After Malcolm's death in 1093 at Alnwick there was some manoeuvring for the vacant throne. For a while the King's brother, Donald Bane, held sway whilst Malcolm's son Duncan fell in combat at Mondynes in the

Mearns. In 1097 the eldest surviving son Edgar gained the crown though he also acknowledged the King of England as overlord.

King Henry I married a daughter of Malcolm's widow, Queen Margaret, and the girl's younger brother David secured an advantageous match, bringing with him wide revenues from English estates. On his death in 1107 Edgar was succeeded by Alexander I though David enjoyed virtual independence as ruler of Lothian and Strathclyde. When, in turn, Alexander died in 1124, David, who was to rule until 1153, became the obvious successor. England, after 1136, was racked by civil war as the barons ranged themselves behind Stephen or Matilda.

The Normans

Prior to his succession David had encouraged Norman immigration and it was under his patronage that such families as Moreville, Soulis, Lindsay, Somerville and Bruce made their first appearance north of the border. These knights found ample employment for their martial skills when David, once secure upon the throne, looked to stamp his will on the turbulent northern fringes of his dominion. This pacification of the north was a task ideally suited to the incomers and the distinctive motte-and-bailey type of fortification began to appear – at Duffus near Elgin, Inverurie in the Garioch and near Braemar at Invernochty.

Duke William's decisive victory in 1066 had confirmed the superiority of the mailed and mounted knight over the traditional Anglo/Norse warrior. The Norman horse soldier was protected by a mail shirt or hauberk which reached to the knees with splits to facilitate movement. The hauberk was worn over a long woollen undergarment to ease chafing. The mail hood or coif was, in all probability, an integral element and further protection to the head was afforded by a conical helm fitted with a reinforcing rim and nasal bar. His weapons were the lance, generally carried couched for thrusting, and the sword, similar in design to the Viking type, but with longer downswept guards or quillons and the distinctive 'Brazil nut' pommel. The sword was carried in the scabbard, hung from a wide, rather loose belt around the waist strapped beneath the mail slit to allow the blade to hang freely on the left hip. To protect the knight's unguarded flank he carried a kite-shaped shield, rounded and gradually curving to a point.[10]

Formidable as the mounted warrior might be the battle at Hastings had been won by a judicious use of missile power and shock impact. Repeated charges had failed to dislodge the stubborn defenders whose packed ranks continued to defy the cavalry until the archers, firing into a massed target, opened gaps for the horse to exploit. The Normans relied upon the shortbow, the famed longbow remained undiscovered as a battle-winning tool until the Welsh wars of Edward I. The crossbow, which had been in use since the days of the Romans, in its early form consisted of a bow fixed at right angles to a wooden stock. When loaded, or spanned, the bowstring was held taut by a catch which, upon release, powered the dart or quarrel, previously placed in a horizontal groove in the wood.

As the Normans infiltrated Scotland, rather than invading, castle building came relatively late though the proliferation of petty lordships and years of strife ensured that fortified dwellings were still being built well into the sixteenth century. As the Anglo-Normans filtered into Galloway, Lothian and the northeast they threw up their motte-and-bailey constructions that had appeared, like a plague, over many an English acre following the conquest.

Battle of the Standard

The dynastic squabbles south of the border afforded David a golden opportunity to intervene and extend his own territory. The autocratic Matilda had alienated many of the barons and Stephen of Blois had moved quickly to seize power, though his grip was never strong. David was Matilda's maternal uncle though his exertions were restricted to capturing the key border fortresses of Carlisle, Wark, Alnwick, Norham and Newcastle.

Stephen hurried north to repair the damage and though David withdrew he won extremely generous terms. Thus encouraged he forayed south in 1137 and again the following year.

Stephen reciprocated but his invasion proved a farce and the Scots harried him southward. The king led a force towards Newcastle whilst a flanking division under his nephew William swung westward through Lancaster. Bowing to the inevitable one of the leading northern magnates, Eustace Fitzjohn, defected to David opening the gates of Alnwick and Malton. Capitalising on this unexpected bonus the Scots poured over the border, their numbers swelled by ferocious Gallgaels.

Archbishop Thurstan of York, despairing of help from Stephen, enmeshed in his fratricidal problems, mustered the northern gentry who marched beneath the puissant banners of St Peter of York, St John of Beverley and Wilfrid of Ripon. Moving upon Thirsk the English offered terms, but secure in numbers, King David replied with contempt. The northerners pushed on to Northallerton and by the early morning of 22 August 1138 were deploying on two undulating hills on the right flank of the Darlington road.

The standard of each saint fluttered from a mast on a carriage placed at the highest point. A body of dismounted archers and men-at-arms formed the van with a solid phalanx of knights clustered around the standard. The shire levies covered both flanks and provided a mounted rearguard.

The Scots army drew up on the more northerly hillock. Initially, the better-armoured foot soldiers and archers were deployed to the fore with the Gallgaels and Highlanders behind. The tough and eager Gallgaels bitterly resented what they saw was a deliberate humiliation and vociferously demanded the honour of leading the attack. Though the king may have doubted the wisdom of committing lightly armed troops to mount an assault against mailed opponents he gave way and altered his dispositions accordingly. Now the Gallgaels formed the van; in the centre, Earl Henry with a force of mounted knights, warriors from Lothian and the Borders took the right flank, the Highlanders the left. The king led a reserve comprising the men of Moray and the eastern shires.[11]

Storming forward in a spirited charge the Gallgaels fell in droves brought down by a storm of arrows. So furious was the onslaught that the survivors leapt forward over piles of their own dead, driving the van back on the main body. The English knights and men-at-arms fought back savagely, the Gaels retired, reformed and charged again and again as the archers continued to take a heavy toll. A contemporary chronicle has left this vivid picture of the valour of the Gallgael.

> Like a hedgehog with its quills, so would you see a Pict bristling all round with the arrows that had pierced him, yet still brandishing his sword and in blind madness rushing forward, now smiting a foe, now beating the air with vain blows.[12]

As the Gallgaels faltered Earl Henry spurred forward with his mounted knights cleaving a bloody path through the English centre. This was the crisis of the battle, if the Scots men-at-arms had followed up this success the day would have been theirs, but the English recovered and closed ranks. Earl Henry and his survivors found themselves isolated and played no further part in the fight, regaining their own ranks with difficulty. The attack was stalled and though a large part of the army remained uncommitted the king saw little point in continuing the offensive and the Scots began to filter from the field, an orderly withdrawal covered by a mounted reserve. The English made no effort to pursue, but the victory was theirs and the Scots retreated across the border. Though defeated, King David remained potent and his sway still extended over much if not all of northern England.[13]

The Last Norsemen

The end of the eleventh century witnessed an upsurge in Norwegian aggression when the tough warlord Magnus Bareleg sought to realise his vision of a Norse empire. Between 1098 and 1103 he stamped his seal firmly upon Orkney, the Hebrides and

Man, compelling King Edgar to cede the Western Isles. The pressure from the north eased only when Magnus was killed leading an expedition to Ireland, but the Jarls of Orkney remained powerful, one of their number, Harald, in 1192–4 being strong enough to invade Norway itself.

Alexander II was able to gain ground in the north and west, finally dying on campaign at Kerrera in 1249. Twelve years after the death of his father Alexander III sought to purchase the Western Isles from Hakan. IV of Norway, whose daughter Cecilia had been wed to Harald, king of Man, both bride and groom perishing at sea – and Alexander sought to capitalise on the King of Norway's loss. To reinforce his bargaining power the earl of Ross laid waste to Skye in 1262. Alexander's ambassador returned from Bergen empty-handed. Hakan, though ageing, was not a man to be so easily intimidated and resolved to spread a little terror of his own. He had, during his reign, consolidated his hold over Orkney and Man whilst adding Iceland to his empire. In July 1263 he had put to sea with a great fleet, the sleek ships crammed with fighting men – the greatest host that ever left the shores of Norway, according to the annals of Iceland.

From the outset, the expedition was continually dogged by foul weather, and having reached Orkney, remained harbour bound till 10 August when the fleet made sail for the Hebrides. Potent as the Norse army was, the island chiefs were wary of committing themselves. Scottish power had obviously left an impression and most sensibly opted for cautious neutrality. Magnus, king of Man, however, came out in full support and swelled the fleet with his own galleys. The winds seemed to have declared for Scotland early on and the great fleet languished through weeks of frustration and by the time the sails rounded Kintyre the season was well advanced.

Cruising down the Firth of Clyde the invaders seemed to fritter away their time in pointless parleys.[14] Waiting for the autumn gales to win the battle for him, Alexander simply sought to delay. His envoys, a party of Dominican friars, proved skilful in the art of prevarication. Tiring of the game Hakan issued an ultimatum and moved his fleet up the Firth to an anchorage between the Bay of Largs and the Isle of Bute. A squadron of 46 hulls swept up Loch Long, pillaging and foraging supplies, particularly fresh drinking water, which was running low. As the laden keels tacked down the loch they were buffeted by strong winds and on 30 September a gale struck the main fleet causing much damage and driving several vessels onto the shore.

And this was a hostile shore. A Scottish force had been shadowing the invaders' progress. What numbers were involved and who, if anyone, commanded is uncertain, but as the Norse ships ran aground the Scots set to plundering. Stung by this impudence Haken sent a force of 700–800 warriors ashore to recover the vessels. A skirmish developed along the shoreline as more Scots joined in. Hemmed on the narrow beach the Vikings were definitely worsted and retired in some disorder. The 'battle' of Largs was fought on 2 October and Scottish propaganda quickly created a great victory with the Norwegians decimated. Though he had suffered a reverse Hakan probably did not register a defeat, and the following day, when the battered galleys had fought their way back down Loch Long, he sent out several shore parties to burn the abandoned keels. Thereafter the fleet weighed anchor and withdrew, stripping Arran bare to provide desperately needed supplies.

Though Largs was not a great battle, the episode was decisive. Hakan's vaunted expedition had proved futile, the fleet racked by storm as it edged its way back to Orkney. This was as near home as the ageing king would manage, for in December of that year he became ill and died. The Norse menace was at an end. Bowing to the inevitable Hakan's son and successor agreed to the Treaty of Perth in 1266 whereby Norway ceded all of its claims over the Western Isles, retaining only Orkney and Shetland for a settlement of 4000 marks and an annual retainer of 100 marks. As time passed the Norse inhabitants of the north and west were absorbed into the cultural fabric of Scotland, enriching its society with their own proud traditions.

Developments in the Art of War

The thirteenth century has been classed as the golden age of castle building in Scotland with many of the nation's mightiest fortresses dating from this period: Dirleton, Kildrummy, Bothwell and Caerlaverock. From the bare essentials of motte-and-bailey, castle design had progressed to curtain walls of finely dressed ashlar, studded with compact drum towers, castles of *enceinte*.[15] The great square keep was no longer a prominent feature, but more a first amongst equals, a larger more expansive tower, placed in the remotest corner. The domestic offices were ranged against the curtain with an open central courtyard, the more important hall, solar and kitchens being a discreet distance from the entrance.

One of the noblest and most original examples of thirteenth-century work is Kildrummy, near Alford in Aberdeenshire, the curtain stiffened by four great towers. The gatehouse is a late feature belonging to the period of Edward I's occupation, designed by the Englishman's master mason, James of St George, a native of Savoy and builder of some of the finest Edwardian castles. The change in emphasis, which such additions represent, indicates a shift in philosophy from the purely defensive to the potentially offensive, utilising the features of the building as a spring-board for counter-attack.

The spread of royal power through the Norse enclaves in the west produced, as previously discussed, a rash of castle building. Dunstaffnage, on the shore of Loch Etive, north of Oban, is a prime example, the chapel a particular gem, the first in the pointed Gothic style to be seen in Scotland. Mingarry, seagirt and remote in Ardnamurchan, and Castle Tioram both belong to this confident expansion.

The mounted knight was still the dominant force on the battlefield; mail the principal protection; sleeves now extended to the wrist with mail mittens, leather palmed and secured with thongs. Beneath the hauberk was a padded tunic stuffed and quilted, a legacy of the Crusades and called an 'aketon'. Scale armour, comprising plates of horn and iron riveted to a leather lining, was an alternative to mail.

Additional protection to the legs was afforded by mailed leggings or hosen secured by laces to the waist belt, the old conical helm was strengthened by a protective neck guard and, in some cases, earflaps. Latterly a more cylindrical flat-topped model came into use, the wearer's face more covered than before, with the old straight nasal replaced by a shaped panel, slitted to allow vision and perforated to facilitate the passage of air. The mail coif was now extended to cover the throat by means of a flap or 'vantail'. Lesser mortals were obliged to rely for bodily protection on a stuffed doublet or gambeson and the ubiquitous 'kettle hat', forerunner of the infantryman's headgear through both world wars.

The cumbersome kite-shaped shields of the Norman period became smaller, with a flat leading edge, and secured to the wearer by a neckstrap. As he charged the knight relied primarily upon his lance, drawing his blade only when engaged in mêlée. Swords of the period were becoming longer and stiffer, increasingly intended for thrusting. To distinguish friend from foe combatants began to paint distinctive devices onto their shields, the beginnings of heraldry.[16]

The feudal levy was never an efficient means of raising an army and its profound shortcomings were amply demonstrated at the outset of the war of independence when the Scots host was pitted against an English army. This army had been raised by a king who issued commissions to experienced commanders or captains who raised regular companies, usually of experienced warriors, and continued to serve for the duration of the campaign.

By the end of the thirteenth century body defences of plate armour were beginning to supplement mail, initially in the form of small plates at the shoulder and elbow; garments reinforced by sections of plate were sometimes worn beneath the surcoat. Religion or religiosity was undoubtedly important. Both sides would hear Mass before being committed to the fight and armies always numbered priests among their ranks.

Once battle was joined the commitment was irrevocable, the enemy was the man directly in front, victory was the only guarantee of survival. Flight would be fatal, more men died in a rout than ever fell in combat. When the lines joined there was little control a commander could hope to exercise, morale was largely uncertain, motivations many and varied – fear, hunger, the desire for ransom and loot. A poor crofter might earn his fortune in a heartbeat if he could capture a man of rank, if he distinguished himself by some feat of arms or conspicuous act of valour. Life was cheap and for all the moral and religious overtones attaching to knighthood the benefit of chivalry was reserved for those of the appropriate standing. It was not unknown for armoured knights to ride down their own foot, as did the French at Crécy, so total was their contempt for those outside the ranks of the élite.

In short, medieval warfare was savage, bloody, frequently clumsy and always uncertain; most wounds were fatal and promised a lingering death in excruciating pain; the foot soldier was usually hungry, verminous and racked by dysentery and other ills. Disease stalked armies more certainly than any foe and a multitude of fevers, spurred on by malnutrition, together with an absence of sanitation and little or no personal hygiene, killed or disabled far more men than enemy action.

Armourers, sutlers, farriers, wives, children, tapsters and whores struggled in the wake of armies and like the men they followed were as welcome as the plague. Looting, rape and slaughter were commonplace; civilians fled at the approach of armed men, regardless of whose side they appeared to be on. Standards of discipline varied enormously, frequently lax, often non-existent. Some captains hanged or flogged looters, others turned a blind eye, some even encouraged. Warfare is essentially a dreadful business and every era produces its own brand of nastiness. The Middle Ages were no exception.

The Battlefield

Warfare in the twentieth century has produced such an abundant crop of horrors that the medieval battlefield seems almost tame, veneered with a superficial gloss that has persisted from Malory to MGM. The reality would have been less cosy. Hand-to-hand combat is a relative rarity in contemporary warfare, field surgery a highly organised, skilled and sophisticated business.

Although we know that the English army of Henry V carried a corps of 20 surgeons in its train,[17] medicine was, at best, embryonic, surgery in its infancy. There is evidence to suggest that if clean wounds were dressed quickly a wounded man had a chance of survival. Simple fractures could also be treated. Penetrating wounds from arrows were frequently fatal and gave an agonising death, none of the merciful numbness of a high-velocity bullet. If a shaft pierced the intestines spilling the contents into the abdomen, death was inevitable; if, say, the chest was pierced and a fragment of dirty clothing carried into the wound, sepsis was likely if not also inevitable.

Head wounds were probably the most common cause of death – when, in the nineteenth century, the floor of Elsdon church in Redesdale, Northumberland, was lifted, the bones of what were presumed to be the English dead from the battle of Otterburn were discovered. The skeletons were mostly those of young adult males and many had died from blows to the head.

The field was always the province of the victor and the wounded of both sides must have suffered terribly. Men of rank may have had their personal surgeons and, if left alive, had some ransom value. Other ranks, of no pecuniary worth, would be left to die slowly of blood loss, shock, exposure or a slit throat as scavengers flitted over the field. The dead were usually buried in pits without any due ceremony.

Heavy drinking often preceded battle, perhaps not altogether surprising. Most combatants fought probably without knowing, or even caring, why. They followed their captain or their lord, and sometimes their king. The presence of royalty was a factor in morale, the religious symbolism of kingship giving an edge of moral certainty.

'Not for Glory . . . but for Freedom'

*For as long as a hundred of us are left alive, we will yield in no
least way to English dominion. We fight not for glory, nor for
wealth, nor honour; but only and alone we fight for freedom,
which no good man surrenders but with his life.*[1]

Alexander III was, according to certain of his contemporaries, a
man of healthy appetites, especially where the opposite sex was
concerned: 'Neither storm nor floods nor rocky cliffs would
prevent him from visiting matrons and nuns, virgins and widows,
by day or by night as the fancy seized him.'[2] In March 1286 he
had been married, for the second time, for a mere five months, his
new bride being Yolande, daughter of the Count of Dreux. On 18
March the king, having presided over his council at Edinburgh,
decided to return to his new wife at Kinghorn in Fife.

Though the day was blustery and inclement and getting late,
Alexander chose to brush aside the cautious murmurings of his
courtiers to delay his trip. It was snowing heavily and a cold
wind whipped the Forth as the king reached the crossing at
Queensferry. Ignoring further warnings, this time from the boat-
man, a perilous passage brought the royal party to Inverkeithing.
The road passed along the foreshore and in the darkness the king
became separated from his guides and some time on that fateful
night, he met his death, a fall that plunged his country into a
deeper abyss than any who discovered his mangled body on the
foreshore next day could have possibly imagined.

England was ruled by Edward I, whom history was to christen
Malleus Scottorum, 'Hammer of the Scots', a strong and vibrant

ruler who had earlier crushed the English barons under de Montfort on the bloody field of Evesham. Edward had systematically conquered the hitherto independent Welsh principalities and now, seeking new horizons, cast his eyes northward. A peerless knight and accomplished commander, Edward was a force of almost elemental power, single-minded to the point of obsession, austere, utterly ruthless. When Alexander took his fatal tumble his only direct heir was a child, his granddaughter, the Maid of Norway, and Edward was quick to propose a marriage alliance with his own young son, the first Prince of Wales. Unhappily the little girl died in Orkney on her way to Scotland, leaving an empty throne.

There was no shortage of candidates, including scions of the powerful families of Bruce and Baliol, already at each other's throats in Galloway. The regency council appealed to Edward as judge. John Baliol and Robert Bruce 'the Competitor' were the main contenders. The final judgement favoured Baliol, whose claim in law was undoubtedly the stronger.[3] Edward went home well pleased, having by cunning and diplomacy effectively added Scotland to his titles without striking a blow. Eventually, however, King John reached the limit of malleability and rebelled, carried along by a wave of anti-English sentiment. From Edward's point of view the war that followed was no chivalric contest, but a squalid revolt to be put down swiftly, effectively and without mercy.

Baliol was scarcely cast in the heroic mould. Though the Scots drew first blood by raiding south Edward was swift to retaliate and stormed northward; on 30 March 1296 he overran Berwick-upon-Tweed in a day, brushing aside timber palisade and ditch. At this time Berwick was a major port, one of Scotland's largest towns, far outshining its Northumbrian rival Newcastle, with an established and wealthy bourgeoisie grown rich on trade.[4] As a dread herald of the carnage to come, Berwick was systematically sacked, its merchants ruthlessly slaughtered, its mercantile tradition burnt out in an orgy of destruction. Thereafter the town would be rebuilt as a fortified outpost in a hostile land like the *bastides* of Gascony and the castles of Wales.

Whilst Berwick burnt the Scots were still north of Dunbar and on 23 April Edward dispatched John de Warenne with a mounted contingent to secure the castle. In theory this should not have been difficult. Patrick, earl of Dunbar, had remained loyal to the English crown but his wife, a patriot, duped the earl's mesne knights and opened the gates of the fortress to King John's army.

De Warenne, however, was not dismayed and, leaving a skeletal force to man the works and counter a sally, drew up in battle array to face the Scots as they came over the brow of Spottismuir. The English commander did not intend to fight on the defensive and pushed his men downhill towards the crossing of the Spott Burn, which flowed across the front of both armies. The Scots, assuming that the English were about to flee, abandoned their vantage to mount a precipitate charge. Counter-attacking in good order, de Warenne drove the Scots back, amongst the foot hundreds were cut down and many of rank made captive.[5]

The débâcle demonstrated with chilling clarity the weaknesses of the Scottish host, hopelessly outfought by the English. Edward's campaign became a triumphant march, the king simply overawed the Scottish nobles with the terrible lessons of Berwick and Dunbar still fresh. The English king confronted his abject puppet at Montrose where Baliol was ritually humiliated, his coat of arms torn from him and flung to the ground, the sacred Stone of Destiny pillaged from Scone, along with the most treasured relic in Scotland, the Black Rood of St Margaret. Tired of local surrogates Edward chose to ignore the claim of Bruce, or any other, and appointed an English viceroy to govern. Scotland was a kingdom no more, the defeated must learn to bend to the yoke. As Edward recrossed the border into England he is said to have summed up his feelings towards Scotland in a simple, pithy, sentence: 'A man does good business when he rids himself of a turd.'[6]

Though her army had been shattered, her pride broken, her nobles enfeebled, the flame of liberty was not extinguished and one man at least would never surrender Scotland's freedom but with his life.

The origins and antecedents of William Wallace are uncertain. He belonged to the minor gentry, a younger son of a tenant of the Steward, Sir Malcolm Wallace of Elderslie. He certainly appears to have been outlawed and hid out in the forest of Selkirk, a northerly Sherwood infested with broken men and desperadoes. Legend relates that his mistress and her family perished, burnt out by an English patrol full of vengeance after a skirmish with the hero and his merry men. Wallace is said to have sought out the perpetrators and dispatched them all.[7]

A thread of savagery marks his career thereafter, physically powerful, utterly fearless, a born leader, a dark warrior for a dark time.[8] His harrying of the English, which he carried into Northumberland, was merciless. Wallace was not alone in fomenting resistance. In Moray, Andrew Murray, son of Sir Andrew Murray of Petty, who had suffered capture after the débâcle at Dunbar, raised the flag of rebellion.

As the rebels gathered support their example rekindled defiance, prompting the former governor of Berwick, Sir William Douglas, and James Stewart, a leading landowner, to throw off the English yoke. The nobility, tied by their oaths to Edward and fearful for their estates, vacillated. The king even sent Bruce to lay siege to Douglas's hold, so confident was he of loyalty – overly confident, for Bruce experienced a change of heart and threw in his lot with the rebels.

By the summer of 1297 Wallace was becoming more than an irritant. In August his partisans fought a running battle with the English garrison of Glasgow led by Anthony Bek, the fighting Bishop of Durham, who was driven from the streets and obliged to seek refuge in Bothwell Castle.

Stirling Bridge

John de Warenne, earl of Surrey and victor of Dunbar, commanded the English forces in Scotland, though this responsibility appears to have been shared with Hugh Cressingham, Edward's chief tax collector and a man for whom the rebels reserved a particular hatred. Surrey had been a leader of proven ability, a veteran of the barons' war and Welsh campaigns, though now somewhat past his prime. His reactions certainly appear sluggish and neither he nor Cressingham seem to have taken the threat of Wallace seriously.

In the first week of September the English forces had reached Stirling to find Wallace, now joined by Murray and the men of the northern shires, strongly posted on the far side of the River Forth. It would appear that the Scots were deployed in a position roughly a mile north-east of the wooden bridge which probably stood 50 yards or so upstream from the later sixteenth-century crossing. In front of their position, on the lower south-facing reaches of the Abbey Craig, a raised causeway ran down to the bridge, flanked on either side by waterlogged meadow pasture. The Scots were, on their own left flank, protected by a loop in the river. Surrey was in no hurry to fight and Cressingham, grumbling over excessive expenditure, even sent a contingent back. Stewart and Lennox offered their services as intermediaries, though Wallace would offer the English nothing but defiance.[9]

Surrey had proposed leading an assault across the river, but gave way when Cressingham took fright at the likely expense. By the morning of 11 September he had resolved to fight but confounded his own plan by oversleeping. The bridge, which the English knights and men-at-arms would have to cross, was barely wide enough for two horsemen to ride abreast and the inherent risks appeared obvious. What coherent strategy existed swiftly degenerated as men received conflicting orders. Finally a force of knights and men-at-arms were allowed to cross and debouched onto the causeway. Seldom has any army been presented with such a heaven-sent opportunity and, timing the moment to perfection, the Scots swept to the attack. The English army was effectively cut in two; the lightly armoured Welsh foot, judging the situation, dropped weapons and took to the water, a few knights hacked a path to safety but many more were unhorsed and killed. At some point, and to compound the disaster, the bridge itself gave way. Whether destroyed by one side or the other or simply collapsing under the weight of fugitives, the ruin of the English on the far bank was complete.[10]

How many fell is uncertain. Cressingham had written earlier to the king advising that he and Surrey mustered some 300 horse and 10,000 foot. Perhaps as many as 100 knights and over 1000 men-at-arms lost their lives. The hated tax collector never lived to make a final audit; he perished with the other victims of his own folly, his gross carcass flayed by the jubilant Scots.[11] Surrey retired southward with the shattered remnant leaving Sir Marmaduke Tweng, one of the few to fight clear, to hold Stirling Castle. Lennox and Stewart cannily maintained their neutrality till the day was won, then, suddenly overcome by a rush of patriotism, they plundered the English baggage.

It is difficult, if not impossible, to estimate numbers on the Scottish side. Casualties seem to have been few. Murray, nevertheless, was amongst the injured and died soon after. With the victory Wallace's prestige soared. At a stroke the shame of Dunbar had been wiped away and the myth of English invincibility punctured. National pride was restored, resolute men had squared up to armoured knights and won. In the forest of Selkirk, in the spring of 1298, Wallace was entrusted with sole Guardianship of the realm.[12] Throughout the autumn northern England met the full bill for the blunder at Stirling Bridge and the horrors of Berwick.[13]

Falkirk

Edward had meantime become entangled in his difficult relations with France and in quarrels with his own barons, but matters in the north were not to be avoided and by the following year he had planted the royal standard at York and was preparing to deal with Wallace. His army was formidable: 2500 horse, as many as 12,000 foot, a heterogeneous force with archers from Wales and crossbowmen from Gascony.[14]

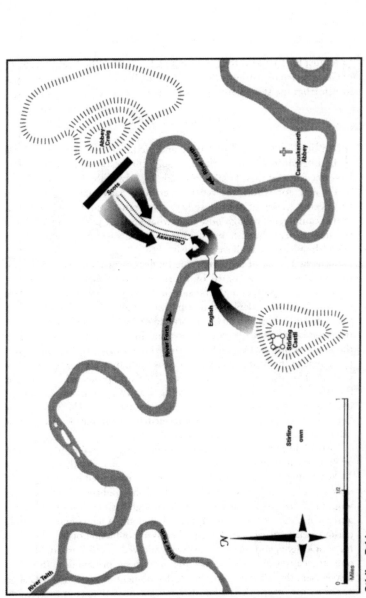

Stirling Bridge · *11 September 1297*

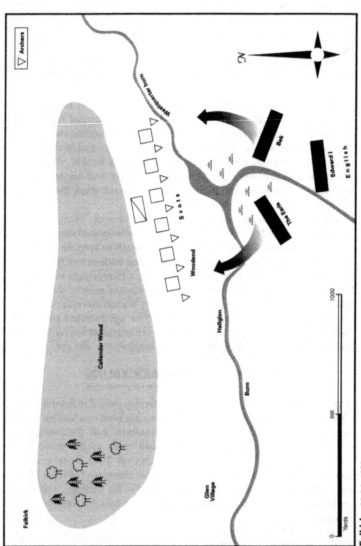

Falkirk - 22 July 1298

By July the host was plodding northward advancing up the east coast, an English fleet in close support. Bishop Bek took Dirleton and a brace of other garrisons but the logistical difficulties in feeding the army were considerable and supplies soon dwindled. Wallace and his power seemed to have disappeared and Edward was seriously thinking of retreat when Gilbert d'Umfraville and Patrick, earl of Dunbar, brought vital intelligence – the Scots were a bare 15 miles distant bivouacking in Callander Wood. That night, 21 July, the English themselves encamped east of Linlithgow, both sides knowing that the brief curtain of the short summer night would rise upon what must have appeared as the final act in the battle for liberty.[15]

Wallace has been criticised for deciding to fight at all, knowing his enemy to be superior in numbers and with a crushing advantage in terms of heavy cavalry. Simply to allow the English to continue would have been to lose the whole gain built up over the last year and the Guardian must have been aware of how his leadership depended on success in arms. He had chosen the ground with care: his troops disposed on the southern flank of Callander Wood, the foot covered by the fast-flowing burn which, where it met another stream running down from Glen village, spread wet and miry, a morass which, from their position, the English could not detect.[16]

The Scots force which now faced the might of the English cavalry on this feast of St Mary Magdalene was the product of Wallace's months in power. Lacking heavy cavalry and any form of standing army he had relied upon volunteers stiffened by a general levy of males between 16 and 60, most of whom came to the ranks with no training or experience. The foot thus formed up in bodies of spearmen, or schiltrons, a solid phalanx bristling with 12-foot iron-tipped spears. With the front rank kneeling and the second levelling over their shoulders the schiltron was a formidable obstacle to cavalry. As a further protection the men were encircled by a line of stakes, chained or roped together creating a makeshift palisade. At Falkirk Wallace disposed four schiltrons each comprising 1500–2000 spears. Aware of the vulnerability of static formations he had Scots bowmen from the forest of Selkirk, under Sir John Stewart, deployed between and a body of knights in reserve.[17]

The English began to deploy in battle order, the van commanded by the earls of Hereford and Norfolk, two of Edward's more quarrelsome barons. Bek led the centre and the king the rear. The steady advance of the van was jolted by the unexpected softness of the ground forcing the earls to echelon their men to the left whilst the bishop also led his men further to the left intending quite sensibly to launch a co-ordinated attack on the Scottish lines. A row erupted between the bishop and his lieutenant, Ralph Bassett, who bluntly told Bek what he might do with his caution and led the impatient knights forward. This was rashness indeed and on a luckier field could have given Wallace another victory; however, the Scots horse simply turned tail and abandoned their gallant bowmen, who were swiftly cut down, including Stewart, their leader.[18] None-the-less, the schiltrons held firm and the English could make little headway against them as they milled, gorgeous but impotent, around the squares.

Having given his impetuous knights their head and seen them get into difficulties, Edward now took control, sounding the recall, then bringing forward his Welsh and Gascon mercenaries, all masters of their chosen weapon and facing as perfect a target as they were ever likely to see. Men fell in droves as the arrow storm battered the massed ranks, gaps appeared, the lines wavered, the English charged, smashing through the depleted lines, hacking and trampling. The Scots resisted with the fury of despair, hundreds died beneath the drumming hooves. At last the Guardian was persuaded to flee whilst his army and his hopes died around him. 'They fell like blossoms in an orchard when the fruit has ripened,' an English chronicler exulted.[19]

Edward had won the battle but not yet the war. Though further resistance appeared pointless, Wallace never contemplated surrender and reverted to the life of bandit-cum-guerilla, enough to keep the tiny flame of defiance alive. The English, still hungry, fell back across the border, ravaging as they went. Life degenerated into a bloody saga of raid and counter-raid, terror and atrocity, the Lowlands and most of the Borders laid waste. Abandoned by the fickle nobility, Wallace never succeeded in rebuilding a viable powerbase, and in 1305 he was betrayed and taken. Defiant to the end, he was made to suffer the horror of lawful butchery and, though he died, his deeds – and his inspiration – did not.

The Road to Bannockburn

With Wallace dead, the mantle of leadership passed to Robert Bruce, though, in the early years, the future king lived – as had his predecessor – the life of an outlaw. Bruce, however, had the inestimable advantage of noble birth and a legitimate claim to the throne. On 10 February 1306 he met with his arch-rival John Comyn in the sacrosanct cloisters of Greyfriars' Church in Dumfries.[20] Harsh words passed between the two men, neither noted for his patience, and Bruce settled the argument with his dirk. Within five weeks, he was enthroned at Scone.

Experience had tempered the hot-blooded passion of the king's youth. He was dogged, single-minded, courageous, a superb warrior and natural leader who had the rare gift of being able to combine generalship with statesmanship; he would need both in abundance. He could be both violent and ruthless whilst capable of compassion; his conviction and charisma won over old enemies and promoted fierce loyalty.[21] He chose his subordinates well. The names of Edward Bruce, Douglas and Randolph became synonymous with valour.

Edward of England, though ageing, had not forgotten Scotland and he chose as his lieutenant his half-cousin Aymer de Valence, who also happened to be brother-in-law to the murdered Comyn. De Valence was given a free hand in his treatment of the Scottish rebels and set to work with a will. By June he had secured Perth and left a trail of gallows and grieving widows in his wake. Bruce rashly decided to take the offensive and on 18 June approached the town from the west but the English refused to be drawn and the Scots made camp in Methven Wood, an elevated position south of the Almond. Both discipline and intelligence were singularly lax. Men were scattered either in billets or foraging parties. Seizing the opportunity de Valence led his men out in a pre-dawn sortie and though Bruce and his partisans fought hard the Scots were utterly routed and many made captive.

The king's fortunes were now at their lowest, a fugitive, hunted, his family dead or in chains, his wife and sister held, like captive birds in iron cages hung suspended over the battlements of Berwick and Roxburgh. The very savagery of the repression guaranteed support for the rebels and, in the following year, the old tyrant died almost literally in the saddle as he prepared for yet another campaign. Though dead, his spirit seemed destined to live on – he left instructions for his son, now crowned Edward II, to continue the offensive and that the king's coffin, like some malevolent talisman, be carried before the army.[22] Edward II was not the man his father had been; indolent, pleasure-seeking, surrounded by favoured catamites, war did not hold the same allure.

As the pressure eased, Bruce rebuilt his army. By the autumn of 1308 he commanded a force numbering some 700. However, worn out by his efforts, he fell sick at Inverurie whilst in the north. It was a dangerous moment, for the earl of Buchan had raised forces from Buchan and the north-east and the invalid had to be carried to safety through the sparse Foudland hills to Slioch in Drumblade, the cold November wind biting as the tiny army huddled in bare woodland. A series of savage little skirmishes, with English shafts flicking through the trees, erupted as Buchan's men closed in, but the Scots broke contact, drawing off in good order towards Strathbogie and from there back to Inverurie.

On 23 December Buchan made camp at Old Meldrum. His skirmishers pushed forward and ambushed some of Bruce's pickets. Though still weak, the king rose from his sickbed, donned his mail and led out his men. The sight of the king, at the head of his troops, had the desired effect on morale and the rebels swept down upon Buchan's force like the wrath of God.

The victory, though relatively minor and largely bloodless, proved a turning point. Harrying the north, Bruce stamped his will on the region and then turned westward, never allowing the momentum to slacken; the key fortress of Dunstaffnage fell to him whilst Edward Bruce and Douglas, the son of the defender of Berwick in 1296, took control of Galloway. Raiding down the length of the Tweed, they freed young Randolph, a captive since the defeat at Methven. Linlithgow fell by deception in 1313 and early in the following year Douglas stormed Roxburgh, and Randolph, in a lightning attack, seized Edinburgh.[29]

Edward made no effort to stem the rot until 1310 when he came north in force. Declining battle, King Robert pursued a Fabian course until the English withdrew leaving Northumberland to bear the fury of Scottish vengeance. By 1314 Stirling Castle was the only major fortress that remained in English hands, her only significant claim to dominion. Soon Stirling was besieged and, according to custom, the castellan undertook to strike his colours if not relieved by 25 June. Stung into action by the peril attending this last remaining bastion, King Edward summoned a vast array of English arms including the flower of his chivalry. The army which mustered at Wark on 10 June may have numbered as many as 17,000 including a substantial Scots contingent: the Comyns, still unreconciled, MacDougalls and MacNabs. A train of 200 wagons was needed to equip and feed this great host. Though Edward himself commanded in name, he relied heavily on the advice of a council of war made up of such seasoned warriors as the earls of Hereford and Gloucester.[24]

Though King Robert was anxious to prevent the relief of Stirling, he could not hope to match the English numbers, relying, at best, on perhaps 5000 foot and 500 horse, pitifully few of whom were knights. Edward had longbowmen drawn from the breadth of his dominions, from Wales, Ireland, the northern shires. Bruce, by contrast, had but a few of those valiant bowmen from Ettrick, kin to those who had fallen at Falkirk and commanded now by Sir Alexander Keith. Behind the main Scots army came a motley of camp followers and barely armed militia, stiffened by clansmen from the west, mainly Robertsons under their chief Duncan Reamhair. This reserve, technically termed the 'small folk', were to remain concealed, some way to the rear of the main position in a valley behind Coxet Hill. In total they may have numbered 2000.[25]

The Scottish foot were deployed in four divisions; the first was commanded by Randolph, now Earl of Moray, and comprised the men of the north, from Ross, Moray, the citizenry of Inverness, Elgin, Nairn and Forres. Next came Edward Bruce who led the men of Buchan, Mar, Angus, the Mearns, Strathearn, Menteith and Lennox with a sprinkling of wild Galwegians. The third division was nominally under the command of Walter the High Steward, but as Walter was a mere boy the real power devolved on the redoubtable Douglas, whose followers were drawn from the untamed borderland and from Renfrew, Lanark and the west march.[26] The last, and most powerful, brigade was under the direct orders of the king, and beneath his standard fought the Highlanders led by Angus Og MacDonald of the Isles. Clans (if they may be so called at this early date) Cameron, Campbell, Fraser, Gordon, MacKintosh, MacLean, MacGregor, Ross and Sinclair were all represented – the pride and fury of the Gael allied to the cause of liberty.

On 17 June the English army marched from Wark, a dazzling array of the hot spring sun glancing from burnished plate and mail, a forest of pennons proclaiming the pride of English knighthood, the greatest host ever to cross the border. Edinburgh was reached without opposition and a halt was called to await revictualling by sea. On the 22nd the army marched on to Falkirk. The next morning the old Roman road echoed to the tramp of marching feet and the ring of hoofbeats as the English set out for Stirling. They had two days left before the deadline expired.

23 June 1314

One of the greatest failures of the English command which may be said to have led to all of the rest, and these were numerous, was their residual contempt for the Scots. Neither the defeat at Stirling Bridge, the dogged valour of Falkirk, nor Bruce's inexorable rise had managed to dent this condescension.

Keith's light horse operated as a screen, the king's division formed the rearguard whilst the rest laboured to improve the natural advantages of their position astride the road from Falkirk. The Bannock Burn, with its many feeders and uncertain ground between, created a strong base made stronger by lines of concealed pits and traps, sown with ghastly triangular spikes or calthrops designed specifically to maim horses.[27]

The Scots occupied an elevated position overlooking the low ground known as the Carse of Balquhiderock, whilst the line of the road itself lay inside the wooded area called New Park, the actual track passing between the Borestone and the Bannock Burn. The right front of the Scots was protected by scrubland and forest, the left followed the natural line of the escarpment swinging back towards St Ninian's Kirk. King Edward had come to relieve Stirling Castle but the despised battalions of the rebel king now effectively barred his further advance. To overrun them meant a frontal assault on a strongly posted position over ground disturbingly unfavourable, especially to heavy cavalry. If he sought to outflank the Scots the only viable line of march lay through the Carse where the ground appeared scarcely more encouraging.

The previous evening King Robert had pulled his own brigade out of their earlier position at Torwood and redeployed along the fringe of the trees crowding New Park. His brother's division was stationed on rising ground to the left, and to the left of him Randolph was drawn up by St Ninian's, overlooking the Carse. Douglas took the rear by the Borestone whilst the light horse patrolled and the lightly armed followers remained hidden in dead ground.[28]

Despite the difficulties posed by the terrain an English council of war determined upon a frontal assault combining both horse and foot, the latter mainly archers. A commanded party of between 500 and 800 strong under two proven knights, Clifford and De Bowmont, was to attempt a flanking manoeuvre by the margin of the Carse to interpose themselves between the Scots and the Castle. If the enemy were pushed back then they would be well placed to complete the rout.

As the English advanced one of their number, Sir Henry de Bohun, spotted King Robert, ambling in front of the Scots line, doubtless giving a word of encouragement to his men. Spurring forward, lance levelled, the fully armoured de Bohun charged towards Bruce, an ungallant act considering the King was without mail and mounted only upon a humble garron. He did, however, have his battleaxe and with matchless skill, turned, almost at the last moment, to avoid the Englishman's thrust and, rising in the stirrups, deal him a mighty blow cleaving helmet and skull.[29]

The incompetent de Bohun was not the only English knight to have miscalculated. The whole advance was soon in difficulties. Order began to dissolve as obstacles, both natural and manmade, took their toll. The Scottish horse darted like kingfishers and the attack foundered. The Earl of Gloucester, attempting to restore order, was unhorsed and obliged to retire, ignominiously, on foot.

Clifford and de Bowmont, trotting briskly by the fringe of the Carse, had somehow escaped notice and the king was obliged to send a sharp rejoinder to Randolph. Once awakened, Randolph strove to make amends leading his brigade, spears bristling, towards the lower ground. Clifford could not resist the urge to strike a blow at these despised rebels and gave the order to charge. In doing so he not only missed his objective but committed the cardinal folly of attacking whilst unsupported. English riders lapped around the solid phalanx, men and horses going down; at least one English knight, Sir Thomas Grey, was unhorsed, dragged unceremoniously beneath the Scottish spears and made captive. As the cavalry faltered the spearmen pushed forward, throwing the English back in disorder.[30]

At around three o'clock King Edward called a further council of war, undoubtedly a somewhat chastened gathering. Further offensive action was ruled out, the king preferring instead to concentrate upon his primary concern, the relief of Stirling. Sir Robert Mowbray, the castellan, had slipped out of the fortress, and, at least in theory, may have considered his position relieved. Edward ordered that the army move more circumspectly towards Stirling fording the middle reaches of the Bannock Burn. It is unlikely that any of the English commanders seriously considered the possibility the Scots might attack.

The Carse, towards which the English advanced was, at this time, an area of low-lying agricultural land, traversed by the Bannock Burn, the Pelstream and innumerable drainage ditches, some of which were effected by the ebb and flow of the tides. As the afternoon wore on the English struggled over the fords and ditches, the weight of men and horses jamming and slithering, chewing the soft ground into a quagmire. It is unlikely that any of the supply wagons were able to follow and the commissariat broke down altogether. As the light thickened it was a tired, hungry and dispirited army crammed into an area no more than half a mile square.[31]

Bruce was inclined to let them go; to chance all on a single throw would daunt any general. The younger men, Randolph and Douglas, were all for attacking and legend relates that it was the urging of a recently defected knight, Sir Alexander Seton, that completed the King's resolve: 'Now's the time.'[32] So be it.

24 June 1314

The northern nights are short at this time of the year and usually mild. Sunrise on Monday, 24 June, the feast of St John the Baptist, would be around 3.34 a.m. Swallowing down a hurried meal, those who had the stomach to eat, the Scots army heard Mass before 2.00 a.m. By 2.30 a.m. a pale light was already showing as the Scots began their advance, the forest of spears giving dreadful note of their intent. As there was insufficient room for the schiltrons to advance in line the attack was delivered with the brigades deployed in echelon. In front and on the right marched

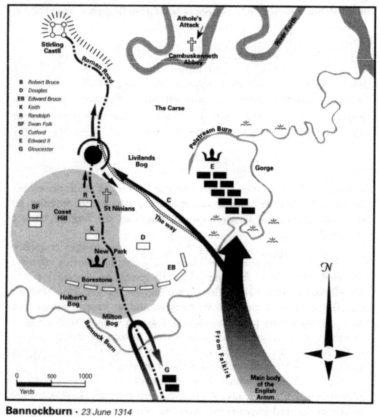

Bannockburn · 23 June 1314

Edward Bruce's brigade, then Randolph, and Douglas; the king followed, his own strong division forming the rear with Keith's horse as a reserve. Each division comprised eight files of 188 men, each warrior leaving one foot bare to ensure a sound grip. The 'small folk' were moved up from their previous position to the rim of the high ground, ready to exploit any opportunity.[33]

The night had been an unhappy experience for the English, few of whom had found either food or rest, though one of King Edward's Scottish allies, the earl of Atholl, had used the cover of darkness to 'beat up' Bruce's depot at Cambuskenneth Abbey, scoring a minor success and leaving Sir John Airth and his slender guard dead at their posts.[34] The English king was not quite the fool he has been portrayed and though the sight of the Scots advance may have been startling the outcome was far from certain. The right of the English position was protected by the Bannock Burn itself and the English army still enjoyed numerical superiority. What they lacked was space, and by attacking in echelon the Scots could exploit any area of weakness so that, if the invaders were forced to give ground, they would be pushed back towards the morass around the Pelstream.

Both sides threw out skirmishers, English longbowmen swapped missiles with Scottish slingers and archers. Though the longbow had the advantage of range the Scots were soon to close. Hungry for glory and having learnt nothing from the previous day's débâcle, Gloucester swept forward at the head of his knights, compounding this folly by riding out without full armour, a mistake that cost him his life.[35] The English crashed into Edward Bruce's brigade, making little headway until, taken in flank by Randolph's division, they precipitated a headlong flight scattering their own, already disordered, skirmishers.

Packed as tightly as they were, the solid mass of English foot utterly halted the advance and a savage mêlée ensued, English bills hacking Scottish spears with scarcely room for the dead and injured to fall. A body of King Edward's archers worked their way around to the left of the Scots and poured a deadly barrage into the massed ranks. The Scots' own bowmen failed to make any effective response, casualties mounted. Keith's mounted reserve smashed into the unprotected flank of the English archers, driving the survivors back behind the struggling mass of foot.

For an hour the ranks remained locked, like two battered heavyweights, neither giving ground, though the Scots, better fed and less heavily accoutred, tired less quickly. Douglas's brigade had been weakened by the flank attack from the English archers and the foot began to lap around his depleted files. For another twenty minutes or so the slaughter continued with undiminished fury, the Scots urged on by their officers chanting, 'Push, push, push . . .', as the relentless pressure was continued. Ominous gaps began to appear in the English ranks, the first cracks as the dam prepares to give way, dead and dying choked the Carse, defeat was near. Though he had fought bravely and well, King Edward had failed singularly to demonstrate any spark of generalship and was persuaded, guarded by 500 knights, to flee the stricken field.

Sir Giles D'Argentan, a renowned paladin, is said to have led the king towards the refuge of Stirling Castle, whereupon having seen his royal charge safe he returned unhesitatingly to the fight and spurring into the mass of Scots there met his death. As the Royal Standard vanished English morale foundered, at which point, with matchless timing, the final Scottish reserve, the 'small folk', appeared, sweeping jubilantly against the thinning ranks, picking up weapons from the fallen. This was too much. The English broke, though small groups continued to fight on with the fury of despair. Hundreds of fleeing men stumbled, fell and died in the churned waters of the Forth, Pelstream and Bannock Burn. The Carse became a butcher's yard. Before its confluence with the Pelstream the Bannock Burn flowed swiftly through a narrow passage and here the press of struggling men and horses became truly dreadful. Many an English knight who, the day before, had glanced contemptuously at the ragbag Scots, ended his life here. 'Bannock Burn betwixt the braes of horses and men so charged was that upon drowned horses and men, man might pass dry over it.'[36]

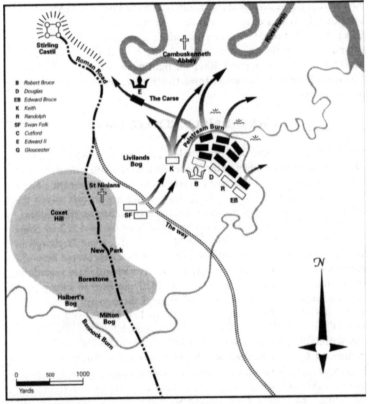

Bannockburn · *24 June 1314*

The Battle of Bannockburn was over and the English army lay in ruins; between 3000 and 4000 perished, 100 men of rank and all their magnificent equipage fell into Scottish hands. Casualties amongst Bruce's men were perhaps a tenth of those suffered by the English. De Mowbray, accepting the reality of defeat, handed over the keys to the Castle whilst Edward and his retainers spurred south in ignominious flight.[37] Bruce valued the Highlanders' contribution so much so that he awarded the MacDonalds the honour of holding the right flank of royal armies. (Over 400 years later they would need to remind a Jacobite Pretender of this proud tradition.)

Achievement of Robert Bruce

The memory of Bannockburn would haunt any king of England who dared to venture north of the border and never again would England reduce her northern neighbour to a mere dominion. The war left a bitter legacy. Scotland was now a nation in arms and her success meant the full fury would fall on Northumberland and the other northern shires.

King Edward had recovered his nerve sufficiently by 1322 to come north again, sacking Holyrood and Melrose and leaving Dryburgh in flames, but this bloodletting was brief. In 1318 Bruce recovered Berwick, the following year he overawed Edward at Mytton and three years later chased him from the field at Byland. In 1323 the English king agreed to a formal truce to last 13 years, and three years later, by the treaty of Corbeil, Bruce and Charles IV of France renewed the 'auld alliance'. In 1328 Bruce's excommunication, which Edward had secured, was withdrawn, while Edward, himself, was deposed in a *coup d'état* engineered by his estranged wife and her paramour Roger Mortimer. Imprisoned, the king was to suffer a hideous death whilst his son, a puppet of Mortimer and the Queen, was crowned as Edward III. In 1327 the young king made a foray against Scotland and was nearly captured by Douglas and Randolph. In March the following year a treaty was agreed by Queen Isabella in draft at Edinburgh and ratified by Edward at Northampton. Within two years he had taken Mortimer's head.

This was the crowning moment of Bruce's eventful career; he was recognised by his inveterate enemies as a free prince and, as his health failed, he bequeathed an orderly realm to his successor. After his death, his heart was taken by the faithful Douglas, now also ageing, on a journey to the Holy Land, an adventure the doughty Scot did not live to complete, dying a quixotic death in an insignificant Spanish skirmish. Randolph, the last of the paladins, died at Musselburgh in 1332, thus bringing a magnificent era to an end. With the death of Bruce, Scotland was left with two harbingers of dissent: a boy king, and a caste of exiles, Scottish nobles who had thrown in their lot with England and, as a direct consequence, suffered the forfeiture of their estates – the 'Disinherited'.[38]

The Disinherited

Despite having given his name to the Treaty of Northampton, Edward III was determined to avenge the humiliation of Bannockburn and to recover Berwick, upon which so much English treasure had been lavished and which remained, as always, the key to the eastern march. That class of redundant Scottish nobles led by Edward Baliol, son of the unlamented King John, provided a ready-made insurgency and the king was happy to provide a fleet of 88 ships, in which the adventures set sail from the Humber in the summer of 1332.

The Disinherited made an unopposed landing at Kinghorn and boldly marched inland to Dunfermline, preparatory to a descent on Perth. This manoeuvre was interrupted when they found their further advance blocked by a superior force under the regent Donald, earl of Mar. The royalists were deployed on the far banks of the Earn and though numbers for both sides are uncertain they considerably outnumbered the rebels. Mar certainly seems to have overestimated the force he was confronting and made no move during the rest of that hot summer day, 8 August, other than to put a strong contingent by the river crossing.

Whether it was his intention simply to block any attempt to force the bridge or whether he planned a more offensive move the next day is unknown. During the short hours of darkness Baliol seized the initiative, his men crossing by a ford to storm the regent's camp, putting to flight or killing anyone who opposed them. Though discomfited, Mar, by putting the bulk of his men by the bridge, had avoided catastrophe and in the morning he led his army, posted in one dense central column, flanked by two lesser formations in support, against the rebels.

Undismayed, Baliol fell back from the camp deploying on the slope behind and drew up in battle order, dismounted knights and men-at-arms forming the main battle, with skirmish lines of archers extended on the flanks and echeloned towards the centre. His only reserve was a troop of Continental mercenaries who remained mounted, no more than 40 riders in all.[39]

The proud banners of no less than 12 earls blazoned above the advancing host as the regent's strong central division crashed into the ranks of the Disinherited, and, by sheer weight of numbers, throwing them back. The fight became a gigantic scrum, the rebels turning to the side to push harder; though they lacked numbers the gradient was in their favour. As the flanking columns hurried on they were met by withering fire from Baliol's archers and recoiled onto their own main body. The press became so thick that many died of heatstroke or suffocation and the living had scarcely room to lift their weapons.

The attack halted, faltered and broke, the survivors streaming down the bloody slope already thick with their own dead. Leading the reserve and all who could mount, Henry de Beaumont swept after the fugitives hacking and stabbing at the mob in relentless pursuit. When the slaughter was finally done, Donald, earl of Mar; the earls of Menteith and Moray; Robert Bruce, lord of Liddesdale; Alexander Fraser, the High Chamberlain, 18 lesser nobles, nearly 60 knights and perhaps 2000 of the rank and file lay together in death.[40]

The Disinherited reported only thirty-odd knights and men-at-arms slain. Not one archer is said to have died. Baliol had won himself a kingdom and Dupplin Moor, as the battle is known, became a model for later English victories at Halidon Hill and Neville's Cross. (Baliol himself and Gilbert d'Umfraville fought again at Halidon Hill.) The lesson of Dupplin Moor was plain: lumbering spearmen would always be vulnerable to longbowmen and should not seek to engage unsupported – a lesson that went unheeded.

Baliol's flimsy grip on the throne proved as insecure as his father's and though crowned at Scone he failed to command any serious following. In December of that same year the new regent, Andrew Moray of Bothwell, passed the baton of command to Randolph's son, the earl of Moray, who surprised and scattered the Disinherited at Annan, driving Baliol 'half-naked' from the realm.

Halidon Hill

Short-lived as it had been, Baliol's incumbency had given him a taste for power and he remained game for another try. He sought, successfully, to solicit English support by promising to cede Berwick. Next summer Edward marched north with a formidable array and laid siege to the town. The king conducted his campaign with a professionalism and ruthless ferocity of which his grandfather would, doubtless, have heartily approved: the two young sons of the castellan, handed over as hostages, were hanged without compunction.

By 15 July the garrison was in desperate straits and the grieving governor conceded that he would strike his colours if not relieved by the 20th. A relief army, hastily assembled, was on its way, led by the new regent, Archibald, lord of Douglas – unfortunately a poor successor to his distinguished predecessor. Having feinted unsuccessfully against Bamburgh, seeking to divert Edward and failing completely, the Scots prepared to march directly to the aid of the beleaguered town and seek an encounter.

Leaving only sufficient men to deter a sally by the hungry defenders, the English withdrew from the trenches to deploy on the south-facing slope of Halidon Hill which rises some 600 feet above sea-level (now neatly bisected by the A6105), an ideal defensive site, the summit crowned by trees, a morass at the base. Edward formed his knights and men-at-arms into three divisions, or battles, drawn up in line with each battle flanked by a contingent of archers; the right was commanded by Thomas, earl of Norfolk, the king led the centre and Baliol took the left.[41]

Douglas, blundering onto the field, had the more numerous army, 1200 knights and men-at-arms with perhaps 13,500 spearmen formed into four dense schiltrons. The separate brigades were commanded first, by John, earl of Moray; the second nominally under the boy king but in reality commanded by Sir James Stewart; the third by Douglas with the earl of Carrick; and the last by Hugh, earl of Ross.

Attacking, apparently without pause for any tactical considerations, the Scots charged down a gentle slope but lost all momentum, stumbling and thrashing through the quagmire, barely having time to dress ranks and begin lumbering up the slope towards the English, when the archers first let fly. The English longbowman was a practised warrior accustomed since childhood to the strain of the bow. Calmly, methodically, volley after volley was loosed into the packed files, men dropping by the score, the tussocks soon slippery with blood. After the dreadful toil of that fatal climb the Scots never really came to grips, their momentum and valour spent. As the schiltrons wavered Edward gave the order to mount and the English knights swooped like falcons, lance and mace replacing clothyard shaft. The rout continued for five corpse-strewn miles.

Douglas paid for his blundering with his life, as did the earls of Ross, Sutherland and Carrick, many hundreds of men-at-arms and some thousand of the foot. King Edward had proved a master tactician, combining lance and bow to near perfection and keeping his horse in reserve, to follow and capitalise upon success. Berwick surrendered and the English balladeers finally had reason to be cheerful.

> Scottes out of Berwick and out of Aberdeen
> At the Burn of Bannock ye were far too keen.
> King Edward has avenged it now, and fully too I ween.[42]

Baliol now enjoyed a second spree, no more popular than the first. The Scots, though beaten, were not cowed and young King David was sent to safety in France. The puppet king danced to the same tune as his father, doing homage and ceding his acres on demand. Resistance continued and Edward was forced to administer some more of the same medicine three years after Halidon Hill, laying waste as far as Lochindorb in Moray. In 1338, in a spirited act of defiance, Randolph's daughter, the fiery Black Agnes, countess of March, defied English arms for five months from the walls of Dunbar. In time the English king began to lose interest, his attention focusing more upon his ambitions in France, where he would lead his armies to further victories.

Neville's Cross

In 1341 King David returned from France, a youth of 17 but apparently deemed fit to rule in his own right. His reign was destined to be long and far from happy. The promise of his youth was dissipated by middle age and the 11 years he had been held captive in England from 1346–57. King Edward's obsession with France seemed to have spared Scotland but David, unwisely, responded to a plea from the hard pressed King Philip to intervene on his behalf.

In the autumn of 1346, the head of his army, David descended upon Northumberland. Hexham and Lanercost were burnt and by 16 October the Scots had advanced as far south as Bearpark near Durham. King Philip naturally hoped that the harrying by the Scots would divert the king from his ambitions in France but Edward was fortunate in his northern barons, Neville and Percy, who were not intimidated by King David and his power.

Under the aegis of the archbishop of York the northern magnates were mustering at Bishop Auckland; by the morning of 17 October they were on the march and intercepted a raiding party under Sir William Douglas some three miles northwest of the town. The Scots were put to flight, clearly lacking intelligence that so purposeful a force was gathering. King David learnt of his imminent peril from the babblings of fugitives from Douglas's foray.

By this time the English, perhaps 15,000 strong, were deploying within sight of the Scots camp at Bearpark, along a low ridge running north to south, near to one of a series of ancient crosses that ringed the city of Durham renamed Neville's Cross in honour of their commander, Ralph Neville. The ground fell, quite gently towards the Scots position some 200 feet below. Drawn up in three battles with a mass of archers to the fore, Henry Percy led the right; Neville the centre; and Sir Thomas Rokeby, aided by the spiritual guidance of the archbishop, commanded on the left. Cannily Neville disposed a mounted reserve under the irrepressible Baliol, concealed by a fold in the ground behind the main position.

King David had the larger army, as many as 20,000, who advanced to the attack, deployed in three strong columns; Sir William Douglas, recovered from his discomfiture commanded on the right, the king led the centre and Robert, the High Steward, took the left. The ground was not suited to such cumbersome formations; Crossgate Moor, which the Scots were obliged to traverse, was split by a natural defile and bisected by a deeper cut which deflected Douglas from his line of march towards the English left, driving his men onto the king's division, the whole concentrated mass presenting a superb target for English longbows.[43]

The arrow storm struck hard, piling death on confusion. Already the Scots were in trouble and made little headway on the right. The left, under the Steward, fared better, driving hard against the English right, pushing back the screen of archers and crashing into the foot. The battle hung in the balance. On the embattled right of the English line sheer pressure of numbers began to tell. Edward Baliol, a doughty fighter whatever else, chose this moment and with superb tactical skill launched his horsemen in a flank attack on the Steward's division, neatly tipping the scales and driving the Scots back in confusion.

With the left flank gone and the right in disarray the king's brigade was horribly isolated, and the English, like wolves closing upon a wounded bear, hacked at the exposed flanks. King David, whose valour bettered his judgement, fought superbly, rallying his faltering ranks, now almost encircled, but mere valour was insufficient and the battle, passing from mêlée to rout and slaughter, was soon lost. Tired, wounded and dispirited, the king, now alone, was captured as he hid beneath the span of Aldin Grange Bridge.[44]

The loss of the king was a disaster for his country and he remained a prisoner in the Tower for the next 11 years whilst both sides haggled over his ransom. Edward Baliol enjoyed a final tenure as a vassal of England before Edward finally pensioned him off.[45] The Scots were neither cowed nor passive and won a skirmish at Nesbit Hill, briefly recovering the town of Berwick though the castle remained in English hands. King Edward retaliated with vigour, laying waste Haddington and Edinburgh. By the Treaty of Berwick, signed on 3 October 1357, the captive king of the Scots was returned to his throne, at a cost of 100,000 marks, payable over ten years.

King David resumed his interrupted rule and reigned until his death 14 years later. The realm was in a relatively prosperous state, despite being wasted by continuous war, and, after 1348, by the horrors of the black death. The king's popularity waned. In 1363, whilst visiting London and with the payments of his ransom hopelessly in arrears, he promised that, should he die childless, his crown would pass to England. The Scottish Estates refused to ratify so unpalatable an undertaking, preferring to seek yet a further rescheduling. David died in February 1371, though current appraisals of his reign have tended to rehabilitate his reputation and suggest he was more astute than previous writers have allowed.[46]

'A Douglas, a Douglas'

It was inevitable that so warlike a family as the Douglases, frequently active on the marches, should clash with the leading family of Northumberland, the Percies, who though they only acquired the manor of Alnwick from Bishop Bek in 1313, soon became pre-eminent, their property interests colliding with those of the Douglases. Both families claimed ownership of Jedburgh, with title stemming from the Scottish occupation after 1314 and the English possession after 1333. The martial vigour of the Percies equalled that of their Scottish rivals and the most famous scion was the son of the first earl, called Henry, but known to history and legend as 'Hotspur'.

In the autumn of 1388 the Scots were resolved upon a major incursion into northern England. James, second earl of Douglas, and the Earl of March were nominated to command a diversionary force, which was to strike down the east coast route whilst another far larger stormed through the west. In the event Douglas's army, perhaps 3000 strong, proved the only effective contingent to take the field that year.[1]

Sweeping through Northumberland the Scots harried as far as Durham before falling back as swiftly as they had come, leaving a trail of burning thatch and empty byres behind. Legend would have it that Douglas and Hotspur swapped strokes outside Newcastle's walls and that the Scot, having the better of the encounter, made off with the Northumbrian's banner or 'guidon'. Torching and looting as they withdrew, the raiders levelled Ponteland and briefly laid siege to the Umfraville hold of Otterburn. Whilst the Scots battered the defences Percy mustered a fighting contingent at Newcastle and marched off in pursuit. Hotspur came upon the Scots at twilight on 19 August, St Oswin's Eve, and, with an impetuosity of which any Douglas would have been proud, determined upon an immediate engagement – he had perhaps 6000–7000 men, easily twice as many as Douglas. The traditional site of the battle is marked by a battle stone and, as shown on the Ordnance Survey map, lies a mile or so north of the present township, with the waters of Rede on the left and rising ground to the right. More recent research, however, has placed the Scots camp well south of Otterburn, nearer Elsdon at the appropriately named 'Battle Hill',[2] so the exact position must remain open to speculation.

Percy, coming from the south, with the light thickening, deployed for the attack, detaching, it is said, a portion of his army under Umfraville to sweep northward around the Scots flank, an unlikely tactic given the gathering dusk. Indeed, there is some question as to whether Umfraville was ever present and the best he may have achieved is a rampage through the largely deserted Scots camp.[3]

Though taken by surprise, and coming to the fray only partly armoured, March split his force into two divisions, the first of which advanced to engage the English, whilst the second, led by Douglas, prepared to strike at the flanks. The mêlée was long and hard, hand-to-hand through the gloaming. Darkness deprived the English army of any chance of using the longbow and as the fight wore on the long day's march began to take its toll. When Douglas's attack smashed home the Northumbrians faltered, though the earl himself, leading the charge with berserker fury, was brought down with a catalogue of wounds, from which he presently expired. As his army disintegrated the wounded Hotspur was taken, together with his brother Ralph.

Despite the loss of one of their leading captains, the Scots won a resounding triumph: over 1000 English fell either on the field or in the rout whilst the invaders lost under 100. Though another English force under the bishop of Durham came up the next day, battle was not resumed and the Scots, bearing the corpse

of the earl, retired unmolested. Though not a major fight, the
very intensity of Otterburn, and the balladry which this inspired,
guaranteed its fame. Froissart, whose pen chronicled an abundance of bloodletting, was sufficiently inspired to write:

> Of all the battles and encounterings that I have made mention
> of heretofore in all this history, great or small, this battle that
> I treat of now was one of the sorest and best foughten without
> cowardice or faint hearts.[4]

In June 1402 another Douglas[5] led a *chevauchée* into
Northumberland carrying fire and sword virtually to the walls of
Newcastle. As his host, perhaps 10,000 strong, sought to with-
draw, Hotspur, issuing from Alnwick, blocked his escape near
Homildon (now Humbleton), near Wooler in Glendale.

The Scots drew up on the lower slopes of Homildon Hill
which rises sharply from the natural plain, their backs covered
by the encroaching slope. Hotspur commanded a strong contingent of Welsh longbowmen, mercenaries brought back from his
campaigning against Glendower. Persuaded against precipitate
attack by the older and wiser counsel of the earl of March, he
allowed his Welshmen to advance, unsupported and let loose.
Disconcerted, Douglas could summon no response as his lightly
armoured spearmen began to drop. The arrow storm was unrelenting every time the Scots charged, the bowmen steadily fell
back, the speed and fury of their volleys never slackening. Men
fell in droves, Douglas displayed not the slightest degree of leadership, his force wavered, foundered and broke, the river claiming as many lives as the Welshmen when stampeding survivors
succumbed to the current.[5]

It is said that as many as 500 drowned and as many again lay
dead on the field, including Sir John Livingstone, Sir Alexander
Ramsey, Sir Walter Scott and Sir Walter Sinclair.[6] Douglas, who
had lost an eye, besides sustaining a further five wounds, was
made prisoner along with most of the surviving men of rank.
The ransom haul included a further two earls, two barons and
80 knights. Hotspur marred his triumph by the cold-blooded

execution of one of the captives, Sir William Stewart of the Forest, who he swore had wronged him. This bloody-minded act bore bitter fruit for it was a pernicious dispute over the distribution of ransom monies that led to the final schism with Henry IV which set Hotspur on the irrevocable path to death and dishonour at Shrewsbury.

A later earl of Northumberland, fated to die at the hands of his fellow countrymen in the opening encounter of the Wars of the Roses, led a wardens' raid into Scotland in 1435. His 4000 riders were intercepted by the Douglas, earl of Angus, warden of the Middle March some two miles south of Wark at Piper Dene. In a swirling border mêlée the Northumbrians were put to flight and a great number made captive. In 1448 the same lord mounted another raid across the Sark, crossing near Gretna only to be met by a Douglas leading an array of border levies, who, once again, trounced the English, taking many prisoners and leaving as many as 500 slaughtered or drowned in the waters of Sark.

Castle Building

As the fifteenth century wore on the old feudal practices virtually died out. Barons preferred to commute their tenants' dues in return for a cash consideration, which could be spent on hiring professional retainers, mercenaries, whose employment was often very much a double-edged sword. A lord needed quarters for these liveried bands and felt more secure if his own quarters were not adjoining, better too if he could keep the main gate under his direct control. Tantallon Castle in East Lothian, with its dramatic coastal location opposite the natural grandeur of Bass Rock, dates originally from the last quarter of the fourteenth century. Its principal feature is a massive curtain wall, effectively closing off the landward site of the promontory, flanked by impressive towers and with a substantive central gateway incorporating the castellan's dwellings.[7]

By the mid fifteenth century the development of artillery reached a level where the whole art of defensive building had to be reconsidered. Big guns were fatal to castle walls and, properly sited, could reduce the defenders' finest creation to rubble; the stout bastion of Norham, 'Queen of Border Fortresses', successfully resisted virtually two years' continuous siege in the fourteenth century but fell to a mere five days' bombardment during James IV's ill-starred campaign of 1513.[8]

This was bad enough; worse from the view of any petty lordling or overmighty subject was the ruinous cost of the new technology, which was beyond the pockets of all but the wealthiest magnates and princes. The use of hand-held firearms, which appeared towards the end of the century, added further problems but also created new opportunities.

Throughout the preceding centuries the emphasis in castle building had favoured the vertical, giving the defenders their advantage through extra height. The advent of cannon, which could tumble masonry with such contemptuous ease, led to a rethinking, now placing emphasis on the horizontal and aimed at maximising the defenders' own fire. Projecting jambs were shifting from right angles to the diagonal, the L-plan opening out so that more of the main block could be covered by gunloops in the wing. To increase the value of available firepower, it made sense to add a matching wing echeloned at an opposing angle, thus creating a Z-plan structure. Examples dating from the late fifteenth century and through the sixteenth century abound particularly in the north and the east: Claypotts, Angus; Glenbuchat, Aberdeenshire; Noltland, Westray, in Orkney. Walls became studded with distinctive bell-mouthed openings, complementing the earlier arrow slits – grim-visaged Hermitage in Liddesdale exhibits some fine examples.[9]

Artillery

In Edinburgh Castle, amongst many fine relics of the nation's warlike history proudly stands the great gun, 'Mons Meg', still a mightily impressive piece of ordnance that could project a stone ball weighing nearly 550 lb for a good two miles. Legend asserts that the gun was cast by Molise McKim, the hereditary smith of Threave in the mid fifteenth century. As a reward for his industry and skill McKim was granted the estate of Mouance (pronounced 'Mowans') – and named his masterpiece after his shrewish wife. In reality, the gun was most certainly cast in Flanders.[10]

In fact, the piece is more likely named after the town of its manufacture and of First World War fame, in present-day Belgium, and may have been a gift from the duke of Burgundy, delivered in 1457; 13ft 4in. long with a 20 in. bore, Meg saw active service through several generations. The pace of technological advance moved at a more gentlemanly speed in the fifteenth and sixteenth centuries. When its campaigning days were done it was retained for ceremonial and royal salutes. Whilst delivering a cannonade in honour of James VII and II whilst duke of York, in 1680 the gun burst, and whether the duke destined to reign as James II took this as an omen is not recorded, but thereafter it was left to rot.

Redemption came with the Romantic revival early in the nineteenth century. Scott himself petitioned on its behalf and, in 1829, George IV ordered its reinstatement. With the pipes of the 73rd Foot skirling bravely and the regiment on parade supported by three troops of horse, the old gun returned to Edinburgh in style, where it has remained since and few who have stood next to Meg can have failed to be impressed by its functional beauty and a still potent hint of its awesome power.[11]

A Franciscan friar, one Roger Bacon, working in the 1260s, has been accredited with the invention of gunpowder, said to have been inspired by readings in Arabic – the secret having been known for some time in the Near and Far East. An early fourteenth-century recipe recommended four parts saltpetre, one part carbon, one part sulphur, all ground fine in a pestle and mixed. From such uncertain beginnings the science of gunnery developed, references from later in that same century refer to early cannon, some capable of hurling a 200-lb ball.[12]

These early guns were not cast, but made up of iron loops, not unlike a beer barrel – strips of metal were bent around a timber

core and secured by bands made to fit snugly; these were heated
to slip over the core which they gripped securely on cooling. The
bands were then welded and the core burnt out.

The smith now had a metal tube, open at both ends, and the
breech was formed by the addition of an iron chamber. The
smaller bores had a removable chamber which was filled with
powder and wedged behind the ball; heavier pieces, supported
on crude formwork and loaded at the muzzle, were fired virtually at ground level. Despite the risks and despite a vulnerability
to damp, these cumbersome bombards were soon in demand.[13]

By the dawn of the following century big guns had become the
dominant factor in siege warfare rendering the earlier engines
obsolete. Quite when they appeared in Scotland is uncertain,
though we know that James II, to his cost, had a fatal fascination with the new weaponry and we also know he used artillery
against the Douglases when reducing Threave in 1455. The king
was able to experience the unreliability of early cannon at first
hand, dying when a gun burst at the siege of Roxburgh.

Though proving to be the nemesis of castles, the logistical
problems involved in providing an efficient siege train were
immense. The guns were very heavy and the miry tracks of the
period ill prepared for such massive loads. At least a dozen or
more oxen were needed to move the cumbersome ordnance
and it was not until the later years of the fifteenth century that
wheeled carriages were introduced. Still fired prone, the heavier guns were fitted with a moveable timber screen or shutter
designed to afford the gunners some cover, whilst smaller pieces
were often mounted several to a carriage. Breech-loaders were
surprisingly common, the block shaped something like an over-
sized beer tankard complete with handle, which, when filled
with powder, was wedged in place.[13]

As the science of artillery developed guns were increasingly
defined by category, usually determined by weight of shot:
falcons; sakers ('sparrow hawks'); culverins ('snakes'); basiliskes.
By the final quarter of the century barrels were being cast, often
in brass or bronze. James III established a foundry in Edinburgh

Castle from 1474 and employed masons to cut stones for shot – rock being lighter and cheaper than iron.[15]

Loading and firing these monsters demanded care. Once fired the matross (gunner's assistant) thrust a wet mop down the hot barrel to extinguish any trace of powder, fresh powder was ladled in the barrel, rolled down and rammed. In the sixteenth century a remedy was discovered that inhibited the tendency of early powder to separate – 'corned' powder[16] involved mixing in a solution of alcohol and water, which, when dried, formed a block. Mashed into a loose compound, this proved more reliable and more powerful, so much so that only a gun of cast manufacture was strong enough.

Following behind the cannon's thunderous roar came the more commonplace handgun. Though less demonstrative than their larger brethren, individual firearms had an almost equal impact. For most of the medieval period the knight had dominated the battlefield. True, his hegemony had been rudely challenged by the longbow and interrupted by the phalanx of spearmen, but archery was a highly specialised art requiring years of constant practice at the butts.

The English Royal Accounts for the year 1386 first make mention of handguns, crude implements, comprising short barrels of cast brass supported on a rudimentary wooden stock, designed to be held two-handed and steadied by either jamming the stock under the arm or looping it over the shoulder. The piece was discharged by lowering a slow match into a touch-hole and, presumably, hoping for the best. As a missile weapon the handgun was markedly inferior to the longbow, less accurate and posing a not inconsiderable risk to the firer.[17]

As the fifteenth century progressed, barrel lengths increased and the stock became more curved so that it could repose more comfortably on the chest of the musketeer. The firing mechanism also became more refined with the match being held in the upper arm of a lever or serpentine which was fixed to the side of the stock and pivoted downward towards a side-drilled touch-hole when the arm beneath was depressed. The slow match itself was merely a length of cord which had been soaked in saltpetre. Fine priming powder was held in a pan adjacent to the touch-hole to guarantee ignition of the main charge. Handguns soon became fixtures in castles and towers and often the weapon was secured by a lug slotted into a hole in the masonry which compensated for the savage recoil of these early muskets or 'hackbuts'.[18]

Arms and Armour

By the fifteenth century the armourer's craft was approaching its zenith and complete harnesses of plate were being produced. Donning the armour was a complicated and time-consuming business, with the knight requiring the assistance of his squire. First, the arming doublet, padded and reinforced by mail with laces to tie on sections of plate. The leg harness came next, secured by means of straps. The articulated shoe-pieces, or *sabatons*, were sometimes attached to the leg harness. The breastplate and backplate, known as the *cuirass*, and with a skirt section attached, were put on and secured by straps. It was common-place to wear a short mail kilt beneath the plate protecting those vital parts which might be the target of an ungentlemanly thrust. The complete arm defence known as the *vambrace* and comprising sections for the upper and lower arm, *couters* for the elbow and *pauldron* for the shoulder followed, secured by straps, laces or catches. The gauntlets and helmet were last.[19]

We know of several armourers who were working in Scotland at this time: John Moncur of Dundee, active in the mid fifteenth century, was one of a family of craftsmen; another was John Tait who may have been based in Leith and was retained by James III.[20]

A number of fifteenth-century swords survive, long-bladed with rather distinctive downswept quillons ending lobe-shaped or spatulate terminals; a fine example can be seen in the National Museum of Antiquities in Edinburgh.[21] Generally, thrusting was now more important than slashing; searching out the weak spot or joints in an enemy's armour was more profitable than blindly hacking away. Daggers, usually of foreign manufacture, began to proliferate, but by the early sixteenth century a particular Scottish variant was developed: slim, graceful, single-edged and deadly at close quarters, wooden hilted with rounded lugs or ballocks – the ballock dagger, an early example of which was found by Coldingham, near Eyemouth.[22]

As armies became more professional they became more organised. In addition to specialised artillery trains, armourers, smiths, sutlers and surgeons marched behind. Full use now was made of light field-guns, often sited behind earthworks and palisades.

When James III fell from his horse at Sauchieburn and met his inglorious end his passing, barely noticed and scarcely lamented, marked the end of an era: the passing of the Middle Ages.

The Rough Wooing

The three pillars of state in medieval society were God, the Pope and the King, but the modern or Renaissance prince became a subtly different character from his forebears. He should be cunning and ruthless, yet learned and cultured, his passion for war and intrigue matched by a genuine interest in the arts, his schooling owing far more to Machiavelli than the Scriptures. To rule was an end in itself, to preserve order he had *carte blanche*, enemies for the block, morality for when he had nothing more pressing. James III had some of these qualities; he was cultured and patronised the arts but he lacked the essential single-mindedness; his son did not.[1]

James IV (1488–1513) was eclectic in his interests: ships, artillery, the tournament, the arts, even surgery. He was a passionate believer in the concept of chivalry and nursed the ambition of leading a crusade against the infidel Turk whose advances had been sending shudders through Europe since Constantinople had been breached in 1453. Rather than rely on the ponderous advice of his nobles, he preferred a smaller council, often staffed by 'new' men of the bourgeoisie. As a king he was resolute and conscientious: he overhauled the machinery of state, utilised the administrative skills of the clergy, sought to create a standing army and developed the infant navy.[2]

Battles at Sea

The late fifteenth and early sixteenth centuries were a period of profound change in naval engineering, which had begun to transform from the cumbersome 'round' ship of the medieval era into the sleek warships of the Elizabethan age. Galleys, the Hebridean type apart, had never been as popular in wild northern waters as in the more tranquil reaches of the Mediterranean (exemplified, most notably, by the Knights of St John). The merchantman, only twice as long as it was broad, fat bellied, slow to steer with square fixed mainsail, was the jack-of-all-trades; for conversion to warship timber castles were built fore and aft. Tactics were restricted to grappling and boarding, missile power being provided by archers. Even ramming was nearly impossible and as likely to damage the aggressor.

On sea, as on land, guns made the difference. There is a reference dating from the early 1400s to ordnance aboard ship, but naval gunnery was not really a factor much before the end of that century. Initially, light pieces were mounted in the twin castles intended mainly to kill opposing personnel; the idea of actually sinking the enemy came later. To carry the weight of the guns, superstructures were enlarged and strengthened, soon rising to several storeys and extending way over the prow and stern, bristling with ordnance – the internal elevation of both castles likewise armed so that the 'tween decks could be swept by fire.

Warships were essentially armed merchantmen and the masters of the day doubled as privateers, hiring their ships and their swords to the crown. Though Robert Bruce had attempted the beginnings of a navy, it was left to James IV to instigate a serious programme of shipbuilding, spurred by the development of the English fleet under Henry VIII and the new horizons opened up by the voyages of discovery. He was also able to profit from the enterprise of some of his bolder skippers, particularly Andrew Wood of Largs and the redoubtable Bartons: John, the father, and his three able sons, Andrew, Robert and John.

Wood had begun his career as a pilot serving James III but by 1489 he owned two vessels each of 300 tons and well provided with ordnance; the *Flower* and the *Yellow Carvel*. In that year a handspan of English buccaneers raided along the Firth of Forth, a truce notwithstanding, but Wood caught up with them off Dunbar and captured the lot. Henry, despite the fact his subjects had been engaged in blatant piracy, was mighty put out and commissioned a tough mariner, Stephen Bull, who commanded three keels, to exact retribution.

Bull's squadron made for the mouth of the Forth, having received intelligence that this quarry was sailing from Flanders. Keeping out of sight in the lee of the Isle of May, the English privateers blocked Wood's two vessels as they sought to beat up the Firth. Undismayed, the Scotsman closed to grapple amidst a furious cannonade. A vicious mêlée ensued as vessels locked together. The battle lasted all day. At sunset the battered craft cut lines and parted. At dawn the proceedings were continued, the ships drifting as far north as the Tay. Villagers lined the coast to cheer the home team and in the end the English conceded defeat.[3]

Wood survived into a comfortable retirement. From his house at Largs he had a canal dug to the parish church so that, on Sundays, the old seadog might be conveyed to his prayers in a manner befitting.

The Bartons were active both as traders and privateers. The family declared war on Portugal after the patriarch was plundered and possibly slain by natives of that country. Andrew, the best and fiercest of the sons, commanding the *Lion*, took ample compensation from the Portuguese with a score of prizes. Having chastised one nation, he fell out with another, slaughtering a shipload of Dutch buccaneers and pickling their severed heads in their own salt-beef casks. If the Portuguese and the Hollanders were not sufficient, he next made war on England. Henry VIII's wrath was easily aroused and he commissioned his aristocratic captains Lord Thomas and Sir Edward Howard to rid English waters of this mettlesome Scot. In the Downs the brothers in the two English ships encountered the *Lion* and a small pinnace, the *Jenny Pirwen*, returning from yet another fray against the unfortunate Portuguese.

Battle was joined as the guns thundered and the grappling irons flew. One of Barton's particular specialities involved tying a heavy weight to the yard-arm which, when released at an appropriate moment, holed the enemy. Sir Edward was aware of the risk and detailed his most expert bowman to let fly at any who sought to untie the weight. Two sailors crashed to the deck writhing in mortal agony and Barton, trusting in his armour, shinned up the rigging himself. The first shaft glanced from the metal, but the second found the vulnerable spot beneath the arm and Barton tumbled. The dying Scot called on his men to strive to the last but, as he expired, so did their will to fight and both vessels struck their colours.[4] The death of Andrew did not quench the spirit of the Bartons, who continued to war with their many enemies.

In 1511 James watched the *Great Michael* slide into the water, the mightiest ship afloat, 240 ft long, a beam of 56 ft, planking 10 ft thick, built of native and Norwegian timber. She carried 36 great guns and 300 lesser pieces. The ordnance was served by 120 gunners, the ship crewed by 300 sailors, a force of 1000 marines. After James's ruin and death at Flodden his fleet was sold as a job lot to France and his proud young navy died with him.[5]

War on Land

In the sixteenth century artillery came of age, though size and bore were still far from uniform: the larger guns, bombards, threw a ball of 260 lb, a curtauld, a ball of 60 lb, a culverin 18 lb, a lizard 12 lb and a minion 8 lb; there were also bastard cannon and demi-cannon (30–36 lb), cannon periers, demi-culverins (9 lb), bastard culverins, sakers, falconets and robinets.

As the century progressed, so did the science of gunnery. By the middle decades the culverin was the usual field-piece; with a bore of 5½ in. it could hurl shot some 2500 paces. The lesser demi-culverin was preferred for war at sea – a lighter ball of 9 lb from a 4½-in. bore carried the same distance. For siege work cannon and demi-cannon were hauled up, the former sending a 50-lb shot up to 2000 paces and the latter a 32-lb ball a somewhat lesser distance. Smaller pieces mounted on ramparts or onboard ship could be used to spray a burst of small-shot, like a large shotgun, wreaking messy havoc at close quarters. Most guns of the period were cast with two large and distinctive loops located at the point of balance and intended to facilitate raising and lowering from the carriage.[6]

Larger guns could be discharged 50 times or more in a hot day's service, two gunners and ten matrosses sweating to feed the iron monsters. So profound was the impact of the new technology upon the design of fortifications that the sixteenth century saw the eclipse of the traditional castle in favour of the artillery fort. Although finally in English hands the impressive ramparts constructed at Berwick-upon-Tweed in the reign of Elizabeth remain the finest example of the period.

Handguns remained largely unchanged in design, the matchlock doing good service throughout the period, although the mechanism remained particularly vulnerable to damp. A prudent musketeer would usually remove the glowing match from the serpentine whilst seeking to reload and keep it held in the left hand, though this did not make for a swifter or easier load. A technique gleaned from Germanic mercenaries was to carry a series of measured charges in small wooden flasks held on a bandolier; as these were traditionally 12 in number the rig became known as 'apostles'. Calibres varied wildly and each man carried his own mould. The length of both barrel and stock now increased so that the piece more closely resembled the accepted profile. Towards the end of the sixteenth century a newer and far more sophisticated firing mechanism, the wheel-lock, was invented. Considered too expensive for common foot-soldiers, the elegant wheel-lock proved far more suitable for use on horseback and by 1600 the horseman's pistol had arrived.[7]

Full harness remained *de rigueur* for knights and gentlemen who usually formed the heavy horse, armed with lance and sword, whilst their inferiors mounted on garrons made up the light. Both English and Scots made full use of their own

Borderers, the famous, or rather notorious, 'steel bonnets'. Superb horsemen, they eschewed leg armour, preferring thigh-length boots and wielding lances using their carbines,[8] advancing at the trot, discharging a volley, virtually point-blank, then wheeling around to reload.

The horse were marshalled in companies like the foot and in addition to the unkempt Border reivers it was usual to employ mercenary cavalry, frequently of Germanic origin, called *reiters*, who tended to rely upon firepower rather than shock impact.[9]

The foot were divided into pikes and billmen and the shot, who generally went unarmoured, save for a helmet and jack. At the outset pikemen wore breast and back, usually of the rounded German pattern with tassets to cover the thighs and a hinged neckpiece, or *gorget*, to protect the throat. By mid-century breastplate design favoured a prominent vertical rib or keel which bellied out below the navel, thus providing greater deflection. The burgonet was replaced by the distinctive morion, an elongated kettle-hat, the brim swept fore and aft and rising to a point, as in the Spanish style, or fitted with a raised flange or comb, after the Italian.

Armies of the period were still divided into three 'battles' – the van, main body and rear – though these divisions were increasingly referred to as regiments, each of which was subdivided into companies of 100 men, commanded by a captain, a junior officer and sergeant whose responsibility extended to include drill. The company had its own colours borne by an ensign and marched to the accompaniment of fife and drum.[10]

On the march the divisions were ranged in lines astern, each with a central core of pikemen, a body of shot front and rear, flanked immediately by archers, the guns pulled alongside and an extended screen of horse on the further flank, a long motley train of camp followers – wives, whores and sutlers – straggling behind. The colours were retained in a body in the midst of the block guarded by halbardiers. Dress was still optional though efforts at uniform were being made and regiments might adopt a single colour for doublets and breeches.

Duelling

Military swords of the sixteenth century featured a heavy double-edged blade with simple guards and could be used single-handed or as a 'hand and a half'. These weapons were natural descendants of the medieval patterns though latterly, under the influence of civilian fashion, additional guards could be fitted. Gentlemen of the medieval period could settle their differences by foot combat in the lists. Fought out in full armour, these combats could last for hours and exhaustion finished more fights than effusion of blood. Such affairs were frequently enacted at the Hie Gate in Edinburgh.

By 1530 a pattern of civilian sword, intended to be worn as part of everyday dress, had become commonplace – essentially a thrusting weapon with slender yard-long blade and comple-mented by matching or *main gauche* dagger, with the swords-man's hand protected by an elaborate cage of slender bars or a semi-spherical 'cup'. The art of fencing replaced slash and parry. Though the broadsword and buckler remained generally popu-lar, rapier, the name possibly derived from the Spanish *espada robera* – sword of the robe – and dagger became the preferred weapons of a gentleman. Italian fencing masters set up shop in the major cities, their essential philosophy being that the point is always deadlier than the edge.[11]

Duelling was rife, often sanguinary and not infrequently fatal. In France during the reigns of Henry III and Henry IV as many men of noble blood fell in private quarrels as died in the civil wars. A man mortally wounded by a thrust from his opponent's rapier might yet have sufficient strength to reciprocate with a dagger.

The celebrated duel between Sir George Wharton and Sir James Stuart sparked by a quarrel at cards also ended in double fatality. Yet more bizarre was the case of Lord Sanquhar who suffered a disfiguring wound in a friendly bout with his fen-cing master. The noble gentleman thought nothing of the scar as the hurt was pure mischance. At the court of Henry IV it was

enquired how he came by such an injury and whether the offend-
ing party yet survived. Sanquhar now construed this disfigure-
ment as a slight upon his honour and went so far as to hire
a gang of cut-throats to waylay the unfortunate and innocent
Italian – a point of honour which led the Scot to the gallows.[12]

The Road to Flodden

There was, within James's character, a fatal fascination with the
art of war. Though he had subdued his rebellious Highlanders,
quelled the troublesome Borderers and dreamt of the great
crusade, he was no general. His interest in the navy was mirrored
by his interest in the science of gunnery and by 1508 he was
casting his own guns in Edinburgh Castle. He attempted, but
was never successful in, establishing a standing army along
Continental lines, though by 1502, he was none-the-less able to
send a force of 2000 men to Denmark.

A portion of his inheritance was the 'auld alliance', which
he had renewed in 1491–2.[13] In England the victorious Henry
Tudor still did not sit easy upon his throne and the early years
of his reign were beset by a series of pretenders. He could not,
therefore, afford to fall out with his powerful Scottish neighbour
and as early as 1493 the English king hinted at a marriage alliance. In September 1497, at Ayton, James and Henry came to
terms and a seven-year truce was agreed. By a further treaty,
signed in 1502, the English king pledged his eldest daughter in
marriage to James and the nuptial agreement was supported by a
further treaty for 'perpetual peace', the first such mutual undertaking since 1328. On 8 August 1503 the 14-year-old princess
married King James in the Abbey Church of Holyrood, and for
the rest of Henry's reign the two countries existed in amity.[14]

His son and successor, Henry VIII, was a man of a very different stamp, outwardly jovial and good-humoured but essentially
bombastic and aggressive. At a very early stage he headed for a
collision with France by allying himself to the wily Ferdinand
of Spain. France was obviously anxious to avoid English

interference in the seemingly endless Italian wars and James was effectively employed as a diplomat to find an understanding between the warring parties. None-the-less, in November 1511, Henry joined the Pope, King Ferdinand and the Venetians in a Holy League against France.

James was now in a difficult position: he was bound to France by the 'auld alliance' and yet was bound to England by the accord of 1502, though these agreements now appeared mutually exclusive. A more unscrupulous and more cynical man than James could have exploited this situation to his considerable advantage. He certainly used his best endeavours to remain above the struggle in Europe but the French were naturally anxious that their old ally should support them against England. Henry had determined upon his hour of glory and accordingly prepared to invade France, which he did in the summer of 1513. Prior to this he had taken good care to ensure that the northern shires were in a state of defence and had appointed the ageing but competent earl of Surrey as Commander-in-Chief.

James felt bound by his relations with the French to intercede on their behalf and on 24 July he began to summon the shire levies. On 12 August he made a last-ditch attempt to negotiate with Henry and sent his chief herald Lyon, King-of-Arms, to deliver an ultimatum. This was curtly dismissed and on 22 August the Scottish host crossed the border.[15] Lord Home, with 5000 east march riders, led the first foray into Northumberland. Having wasted the valley of the Till he was ambushed, whilst returning, by 1000 English foot under Sir William Bulmer of Brancepeth.[16] In the ensuing mêlée the Scots were worsted leaving several hundred dead – not an auspicious start. Undeterred, James pressed on. His mighty host is said to have numbered 30,000. His artillery train included a number of heavy siege guns, two culverins, four sakers and six demi-culverins.

The first English hold to feel the punch of the Scottish cannon was Norham, after which came the turn of Etal and then of Ford which, once taken, the Scottish king made his headquarters. There is a romantic legend associated with James's stay at Ford whereby his rather lethargic conduct of the war owed not a little to the abundant charms of Lady Heron, her unfortunate husband having previously been incarcerated as a hostage in Fast Castle as a surety for his equally wild half-brother, the bastard Heron. This is likely romantic fiction as the king torched Ford without compunction. Before the age of artillery Norham, 'Queen of Border Fortresses', had resisted a conventional siege for nigh on two years, but such was the firepower of James's train that the castle was reduced in five days.

The very size of the Scottish host began to pose problems as small groups, now replete with loot, began to drift off homeward. This trickle of desertions was exacerbated by an outbreak of disease which further thinned the ranks. By the early part of September James had probably lost the best part of a third of his force.[17]

Surrey, despite the weight of his 70 years, displayed considerable energy. By 1 September he had reached Newcastle and the shire levies of Lancashire, Cheshire, Yorkshire, Wensleydale and Swaledale began to filter in. The quality of these often unwilling recruits was at best indifferent and the only regular force upon which Surrey could rely were the 1200 marines from the fleet under the command of his eldest son, the Lord Admiral. Surrey, who understood the vainglorious nature of his opponent's character, began a careful campaign of taunts and insults delivered through heralds. This daily barrage of gentlemanly abuse was carried by the English herald Rouge-Croix who found the Scottish king and his army drawn up in a strong position on the north-eastern slopes of Flodden Hill. James, alone amongst his nobles, having no objection to giving battle, at least had the good sense to detain Rouge-Croix and avoid making Surrey aware of his dispositions.[18] Surrey now marched his army to Wooler, where he arranged an exchange of hostages to recover his herald. The intelligence delivered by Rouge-Croix can hardly have been encouraging. The Scots were deployed in a position of considerable strength, the guns had been dug into the hillside effectively covering the passage between the east end of Flodden

Hill and the line of the Till. A low-lying, waterlogged track was the only approach to the Scots position and any attempt to advance would be subject to galling fire from above.[19]

It is uncertain who of Surrey's council of war suggested the idea of a flanking march to the north. It may have been the bastard Heron himself, whose useful bandits had swelled the English ranks. The next day the English army broke camp, splashed across the Till and headed north, marched past Doddington up towards the heather-clad moors and then out of sight of the watching Scots. Next evening the English camped on Watch Law, invisible to the enemy who appeared baffled by the manoeuvre. From the top of the hill Surrey and his officers were able to get a far better view of the Scottish lines.

The enemy position now lay to the south and a line of advance from the north, though equally precipitous, would be free from artillery fire. Local historian John Ferguson has now located the probable site of the English camp, shown on a hitherto unconsidered survey map from 1786.

Early on 9 September, the army was again on the march, abandoning all heavy baggage and gear and advancing in battle order. To advance necessitated a further crossing of the Till. This proved difficult in that the narrow bridge at Twizel could not accommodate the great array of men, horses and guns. Whilst the van and the Lord Admiral crossed by this route Surrey led the main body across the shallows at Mill-Ford.[20]

By about 1.00 p.m. the English deployment became all too visible and the alarm was raised. The Scottish lords were all for caution, urging James to withdraw though he, throwing a violent tantrum, determined upon giving battle. In this rather unhappy resolve the Scots began the cumbersome task of moving their position by almost a mile to the north and redeploying along the ridge of Branxton Hill, heaving only the lighter pieces, which could be more easily shifted, with them. Although their new position was less strong it still gave them a substantial advantage in height.[21]

On the left stood Home and Huntly's division, then that of Errol, Crawford and Montrose. In the centre the king and on the left the Highlanders, Lennox and Argyll. Bothwell's division remained in reserve. In the Lowland divisions there were a number of French officers and the whole army had been re-equipped at French expense. As the Scots decamped the followers began burning the abandoned gear and refuse so that a great cloud of greasy smoke hung over the ridge effectively obscuring each side from the other.[22]

Though clear of the Till the English were not clear of difficulties. The soft and marshy ground by the Pallinsburn was churned into a quagmire by marching feet. The van, under the Lord Admiral, was the first to clear the morass and in fact advanced too far, outstripping the main body. Had the Scots swooped down from the heights, the van would have been isolated and the army defeated in detail.[23]

Realising his error, but not losing his nerve, the Lord Admiral marched boldly on, along the southern bank of the Pallinsburn. Despite his appearance of confidence he was sending repeated messages back to his father urging the main body forward. When finally deployed the English right was under the command of Edward Howard, Surrey's third son. The Lord Admiral stood left of him with Surrey himself taking the centre. On the English left the line was held by the experienced Edward Stanley. In front of Surrey's position, in the centre, there was a moderate decline falling into a mire. This was to prove of considerable importance, for the Scots, in order to attack, would have to cross the mire and advance up their incline, thus losing most of the downhill momentum. James had schooled his spearmen in the latest Swiss pike tactics with the aid of his French advisers. The successful deployment of the pike phalanxes depended upon long and hard training, strict discipline and determined ferocity. All three were lacking in the Scots and the choice of ground was disastrous.

Surrey was concerned about the position on his right. Apart from Howard, a handful of retainers and hard core of Cheshire knights such as Bryan Tunstall, this division was made up of raw levies from Lancashire and Cheshire.[24] This scratchbuilt brigade was facing Home's tough Borderers bred to endemic warfare.

Moreover, as these were Stanley retainers they expected to fight under their own Eagles' Claw standard.

The English guns were sited between the bodies of foot and very soon began to make their presence felt. Coolly directed by Sir Nicholas Appleyard and William Blakenall, the English gunners methodically raked the Scottish line and a furious artillery duel developed. It was now that the relative inexperience of the Scottish gunners began to tell and one by one they were silenced. With his guns disabled and his gunners dead, James's line was exposed to the full fury of the English cannonade.[25]

The king, whatever the shortcomings of his leadership, had detected the weakness of the English right and he launched Home and Huntly's division upon them. The tough Scottish Borderers cannoned into the English ranks and quite literally swept them from the field. The men of Lancashire and Cheshire dissolved in rout, leaving Howard and a few diehards to sell their lives as dearly as possible. The heroic Tunstall flung himself upon the Scots, cutting down Sir Malcolm McKeen and several others before he himself was killed.

Despite this opportune beginning James now proceeded to commit what appears to have been a masterpiece of reckless folly. Seeing his advantage on the right and thinking the battle won, he placed himself at the head of his own division and led them down towards the English centre. In so doing he effectively deprived the Scottish army of any vestige of leadership. For a king to abandon his position as Commander-in-Chief and to elect to fight as a common knight was an act of gross negligence and was to cost both king and country dear. In James's defence his tactics were entirely consitent with the Swiss precedent, which asserted that commanders should lead by example. Besides, once the pike columns were committed there was little a commander-in-chief could do to determine the outcome.

The men of the king's division were exposed to the aim of the English longbowmen as they raced downhill. The Scots had, however, finally devised a tactic to resist the clothyard storm, the front ranks being equipped with heavy wooden shields or pavises which could be raised by the holders as a protective screen and then discarded.[27]

What did disconcert the Scottish host was the mire into which they descended at the base of the hill. Their momentum was checked and lost, so that it was they who now had to lumber uphill towards the English ranks. The two sides met with a terrific shock – Scottish pikes levelled against English bills. Momentum and mass, critical to the success of Swiss tactics, were irretrievably lost.

The bill – a basic but effective weapon – was a hybrid of the battlefield, born of a useful union between the agricultural implement, the billhook and the military spear. Originally the peasants of the feudal levy had simply mounted their billhooks upon longer shafts until, around 1300, the weapon was developed with a hefty blade, a long spearlike head and a shorter, narrower cutting edge at the back. The bill now proved lighter and more versatile than the cumbersome pike and Surrey's men were able to lop off the heads of the enemy's weapons and then hack down the pikemen.

Both sides fought with undiluted fury, casualties began to mount, the muddy ground puddled with gore. Errol, Crawford and Montrose all fell at the head of their division and their levies could make no headway against Howard's élite marines. Increasingly the king's division became isolated as Howard's lapped around the flanks. From one of difficulty the king's position deteriorated to one of desperation and, though the fight was to rage bloodily for a further two hours, there was little doubt as to the outcome.

The Scottish right wing and reserve had been scattered by a bold and timely charge from Stanley's division. The Englishmen had cannily infiltrated the north-eastern slope of the hill from whence they were invisible to the Scots until they descended upon them. The English longbowmen made short work of the lightly equipped Highlanders who, ill suited to this form of defensive warfare, took to their heels. Both Argyll and Lennox, in the company of several clan chiefs, died in an attempt to rally their men.[27]

King James, though defeated, remained undaunted and legend relates that, with his few surviving retainers, he launched one last Homeric charge against the banners of Surrey himself. Cut and slashed by bills, James fell dying, almost unnoticed by his men.[28]

Dawn revealed the scale of the English victory. Surrey claimed that some 10,000 Scots lay dead upon that terrible field and the toll amongst the nobility had been frightful: one archbishop, one bishop, ten earls, 19 barons and 300 knights had joined their king in oblivion. Whole counties and towns were stripped of the cream of their manhood. All of the Scottish artillery, arms and baggage fell to the English. The English themselves had lost some 1700 men.[29]

The morning after the battle a half-naked corpse was dragged from the pile of Scottish dead. Transported to Berwick, it was formally recognised as the mortal remains of James IV of Scotland; the body was disembowelled, embalmed and sent, first to Newcastle and then, in a lead casket, to London. Catherine of Aragon debated sending the grisly trophy to her husband in France but finally sent the dead king's bloody surcoat instead. The body remained in the Monastery of Sheen and was thrown into a lumber room after the dissolution. Years later workmen in the house found the remains, cut off the head and used it for a macabre plaything. Thereafter it apparently came into the possession of one Lancelot Young, Elizabeth I's master glazier, who kept it as a curio at his home, until finally it was buried in an anonymous grave.

A contemporary chronicle offered this epitaph for the dead king: 'How could the matter be, hitherto we want, quhen we want him, a stout, just and devote King, who won great honour both in peace and war when other princes of his day contracted ignominie.'[30]

James V (1513–42)

Despite the violent demise of the ruling monarch and the loss of so many nobles, the machinery of government in Scotland did not collapse and this is perhaps a fitting memorial for James whose zeal and industry as a reformer outlived his folly on the battlefield. The realm braced itself for a Tudor storm, but this never came. Flodden was Henry's only victory and he soon lost faith in his ally, the cunning Spaniard. By the following year he was ready to patch up his quarrel with France, and Scotland was spared.

Spirited, indeed passionate, James was a man of strong emotions. He had charisma but lacked his father's depth of character, and resentful of the overmighty Douglases, pursued a savage vendetta, laying siege to Tantallon Castle and causing Lady Glamis, a relative of Angus, to be burnt at the stake for alleged witchcraft. Like his father, he also had troubles in the Highlands and his efforts to win over Clan Donald came to nothing, the irrepressible renegade Donald Dubh escaping from confinement and raising the standard of rebellion by nailing his colours to England's mast; only a timely death in Ireland put paid to his mischief.[31]

In concluding peace with England in 1533–4, James was able to secure some useful concessions, but it was a Gallic bride he sought, the French king's youthful third daughter Madeleine. Her father was reluctant to give the child away, fearing for her health. These fears proved well grounded for the bride lived but a few months and James had to choose a second consort, the altogether more robust Mary of Guise.

Henry was not best pleased, but hid his ill temper behind a façade of goodwill; he had urgent need of allies for there was talk of a Catholic crusade against heretic England. James was pressed to parley and reluctantly agreed to meet Henry at York in September 1541. Persuaded by his attendant clerics that he might be kidnapped, James elected not to appear, leaving Henry enraged and frustrated.

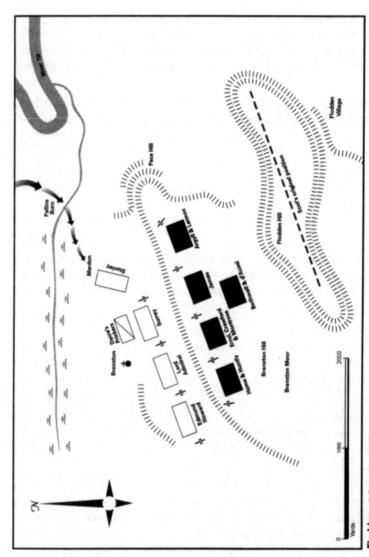

Flodden · 9 September 1513

Solway Moss

Tension and trouble mounted an English incursion was routed at Haddon Rigg but a subsequent *chevauchée* led by the earl of Norfolk saw Roxburgh, Kelso and a score of lesser townships reduced to ashes. James was determined to retaliate, though – despite his earlier exhortations, the victors of Haddon Rigg had declined to push their luck across the border. Lord Maxwell, warden of the west marches, succeeded in raising a force of some 10,000 levies for a retaliatory strike.[32]

From the start the expedition was dogged by suspicion and ill fortune. The king proposed to lead in person but fell sick, going no further than Lochmaben, and command devolved on Maxwell, undoubtedly the best suited to exercise it, but James could not bring himself to trust the warden and gave secret orders to his favourite, Oliver Sinclair, that he was to assume the generalship once the army had crossed into England. These intrigues had a distinct and damaging effect on morale, never high, and it was already into November when the invaders broke camp. In part the king's overall strategy had been successful in that he had convinced Norfolk that the blow would fall upon the east, which left the back door through the western marches seemingly undefended.

In the early hours of 24 November 1542 the Scots were on the march advancing from Langholm and Marston Kirk. In the chill of a late autumn dawn they splashed over the Esk, beyond which lay the barren waste of Solway Moss. Lord Wharton, warden of the English west march, was a veteran of countless border forays and not given to panicking. A less resolute captain might have been content to shelter behind the formidable walls of Carlisle which had habitually defied the Scots but Wharton was determined to fight, having some 3000 lances at his call.

Shadowing the invaders, Wharton commanded Musgrove, his deputy, to harass the Scottish van. With perhaps 500 riders Musgrove swooped to the attack, struck like lightning, and wheeled to re-form. Wharton knew how to best use his men, to keep pricking and avoid a general engagement. In this he received inestimable assistance from the Scots themselves. Sinclair had chosen to announce his previously undisclosed commission. Maxwell was understandably perturbed and an unseemly wrangle ensued. No orders were given, no dispositions made, the army remained inert whilst the Cumbrians hacked and harried the flanks.[33]

Wharton, to his amazement, witnessed the rapid disintegration of the Scottish host. As the warden dryly noted, 'Our prickers ... gatt them all in a shake all the waye.'[34] James had dreamed of avenging the catastrophe at Flodden but his own débâcle – though the loss of life was trifling by comparison – was an even greater humiliation. The army simply fell apart. Over a thousand Scots surrendered. Some hundreds died for the loss, according to Wharton, of only seven of his own marchmen.

James's brittle personality, enfeebled by sickness, simply could not endure such an outcome and he died at Falkland Palace on 14 December, not yet 31. Both of his infant sons had preceded him to the grave and his only heir was a baby daughter. Worse, the child's nearest male relative was her great-uncle, Henry VIII. The grim spectre that had harried Scotland after 1286 had returned.

The Rough Wooing

A significant event in James's reign had been the first stirrings of religious discontent. New ideas and new thinking did not sit easily with the pomp and religiosity of the established church, where worldliness, nepotism, carnality and corruption were rife.

After the débâcle of Solway Moss and James's death, Henry appeared in an unassailable position. Wharton's victory won prestige and valuable prisoners; the queen was a minor and a strong anglophile party existed. Arran, the regent, was undistinguished. The English king had, at last, had a son and a marriage proposal was soon on the table. This was anathema to the spirited royal widow, French by birth and staunchly Catholic. Aided by Cardinal Beaton, she attempted a coup but failed miserably and Beaton was obliged to endure incarceration. The Treaty of Greenwich, signed in August 1543, formalised the betrothal and the throne of Scotland appeared within England's grasp.[35]

In this, his moment of near triumph, Henry proved his own worst enemy; his arrogance and condescension alienated many Scots and the pendulum of opinion swung back towards France. By December of that year Beaton was free and Mary of Guise in control. Henry responded with his usual brutal vigour and the Lowlands suffered attack in 1544 and again the following year. Though Angus won a notable victory at Ancrum Moor and the French sent reinforcements, the Borderers, as usual, bore the brunt.

Henry plotted to remove Beaton from the scene by having the mettlesome prelate murdered using the radical George Wishart as his tool. Having studied at Cambridge and in Germany Wishart was a prophet of the new religion, fervent and ruthless, but he proved less successful as an assassin and ended at the stake. In May 1546, however, a gang of ruffians finally managed his design and Beaton was savagely killed.[36]

After the burning of his mentor, the banner of Reformation was passed to John Knox. Born near Haddington in 1514 he had trained as a priest before being assailed by doubts and converting to the Protestant cause. The murder of Beaton did the anglophile party little good and the queen mother harried the rebels behind the walls of St Andrew's Castle, where they continued to hold out for a period. The death of Henry VIII and the accession of a sickly boy put paid to any hope from England and encouraged France in more overt support for the royalists. St Andrews was reduced by naval gunnery and the 'Castilians' obliged to submit. Knox was sent to the galleys, where he languished till released through English influence. He remained a pensioner at the court of Edward VI until his return to Scotland in 1559.[37]

The Battle of Pinkie

Edward Seymour, duke of Somerset, was, as Jane Seymour's brother, the young king's uncle and Lord Protector. His patience exhausted by what he saw as the intransigence of the Scots, he mustered his forces at Newcastle throughout August and by 1 September was on the road north. His army comprised some 16,000 men, the bulk footsore pike and shot, but also a fair array of horse captained by Lord Grey of Wilton, 2000 lances under Sir Francis Bryan, 500 brought by Grey from Boulogne, 200 mounted harquebusiers led by the mercenary Pedro de Gamboa, Italians under Malatesta and the Gentlemen Pensioners of the royal bodyguard.[38]

Four days later the host approached Cockburnspath, some 16 miles over the line. A brief alarum flared when it was feared the Scots were lying in wait where the outriders of the Lammermuirs drift towards the coast. High cliffs along the ragged coastline would have sheltered defenders from naval gunfire, for the English fleet under Clinton shadowed the army but the regent Arran refused battle allowing Somerset to harry at his leisure. That evening the invaders approached Tantallon Castle whose formidable defences seem to have deterred the Lord Protector despite his train of 15 heavy guns, sixty-odd lighter pieces and 1400 artisans and sappers.[39]

The following dawn the English marched westward again through East Linton, making camp at Longniddry. On the 8th the march was resumed over ground since consumed by Prestongrange Golf Course, behind which the land shears away from the coastal plain and rises to form Fa'side and Carberry Hills. Always a prudent man, Somerset pulled his troops back to draw up in good defensive order along the lower reaches undisturbed by the hostile garrison in Fa'side Castle. He had reason to be concerned, for arrayed against him were the 25,000 men that Arran had mustered, resolute and strongly posted. Though the numbers and *élan* of the Scots were impressive, their army lacked anything like their opponent's hefty firepower and remained lamentably short of cavalry.

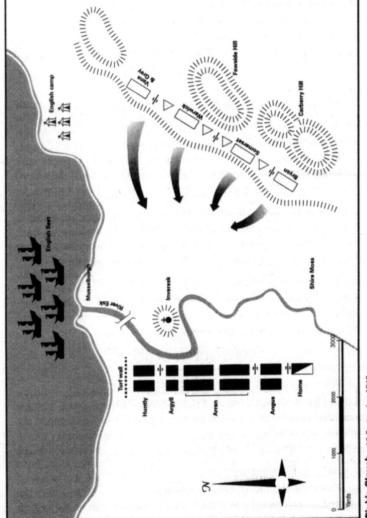

Pinkie Cleuch · *10 September 1547*

Arran had shown a shrewd eye for ground, his line fronted by the sweep of the Esk bellying out towards the sea with steep banks on the defenders' side. Huntly, on the left of the line, had thrown up an earthen parapet to shield his men from Clinton's great guns and his division, with Argyll's 3000 clansmen, commanded the only bridge. Arran took the centre, strongly posted on Edmonstone Edge, and Angus took the right, his flank covered by Home's 1500 lances and shielded by a morass to the south.[40]

Perplexed but undismayed, Somerset knew his hand was stronger than it seemed and summoned his advisers for a council of war. Clinton's seaborne vantage gave him a perfect view of the whole Scottish line and one doubts he left the Commander-in-Chief with any illusions as to its strength. The Englishman knew he had to draw the Scots from their inexpugnable position and tempt them to attack, allowing his guns to exert their fearful superiority. In the meantime he had not failed to appreciate the tactical significance of the slight rise which fronted the Scottish right. Control of this vantage would allow Somerset to pound the left of Arran's line, with a complementary naval barrage, and thus expose a weak spot which the dominant English cavalry could exploit.

On the 9th, Home's Borderers splashed across the Esk, trusting in their swift and sure-footed Border garrons and seeking some sport with their enemies. Grey was all for the charge but Somerset preferred caution, the English line remaining inert whilst the Scots capered. Grey insisted, Somerset relented, the trumpets blared and the cavalry advanced. Caught completely by surprise, the Borderers fled, some fell, and many including Home himself were taken. This minor catastrophe robbed Arran of what effective horse he possessed and the harsh professionalism of the English gave dire warning.[41]

A little after 8.00 a.m. on Sunday, 10 September, the Lord Protector ordered the advance, his immediate goal the hillock, sweating and cursing his gunners and matrosses manoeuvred the great guns. By concentrating against Arran's left he was exposing his right, but the Scots were unable to derive any advantage, having squandered their cavalry arm the day before. The English gambit succeeded beyond Somerset's wildest expectations. Whether the Scots were overcome with martial fury at the sight of their foe on the move or whether, and more likely, Arran suddenly perceived the importance of that fatal hill, he gave the order to abandon the defensive and assume the offensive and, in so doing, blundered mightily.[42]

Argyll's lightly armed kerns, supported by Huntly, swarmed over the river, but in so doing offered themselves to the full weight of Clinton's guns and were broken long before they could come to grips. The Scots advance became one dense phalanx, a bristling hedgehog of steel, hugely formidable as long as momentum was maintained. Angus, who always tended to do things in his own way, saw the folly of this rash manoeuvre and declined to commit his own division.

Somerset was not slow to appreciate the gift he had been offered and slewed his own line around to exploit the advantage, frantically dragging up the guns. Dense as the ranks were, the Scots came on at an impressive pace. To curb the rush of pikes Somerset used his cavalry, charging, turning and re-forming, dead horses and men piling up before the Scots, who, as described by Somerset's secretary, Patten:

> Stood at defence, shoulders nigh together, the fore-rank stooping low before their fellows behind them holding their pikes in both hands, the one end of the pike against the right foot, the other against the enemy's breast, so nigh as place and space might suffer. So thick were they that a bare finger should as easily pierce through the bristles of a hedgehog as any man encounter the front of the pikes.[43]

Though undeterred, the pikes were dramatically slowed and constantly galled by the continuing fire from the ships and from the shot. The advance ground to a halt, hemmed by the press of dead, many of the cavalry paying the ultimate price including the commander of the Boulogne horse or 'Bulleners', Edward

Shelley, but their sacrifice was not in vain.

From a range of 200 yards or less the English guns raked the massed files, arrows and bullets peppered the ranks. Swooping like vultures, De Gamboa's harquebusiers nibbled at the flanks. As they could not advance and simply to stand was to invite destruction, the Scots attempted to withdraw, a difficult manoeuvre for pikemen. The phalanx shivered, stumbled and then, like a torrent, broke, pursued by the jubilant cavalry. The loss on the Scottish side was dreadful, perhaps as many as 10,000 failing to reach the north bank of the Esk. Amongst the rank and file lay many of the nobility, but wily Angus evaded both death and capture and slipped away with the mass of fugitives streaming towards Dalkeith. English losses barely exceeded 250, mostly, as noted, from amongst the horse – the foot were barely engaged.[44]

Mary, Queen of Scots

In December 1560 the young and chronically unstable King of France died and his Scottish consort, Mary, found herself unpopular with her formidable mother-in-law, Catherine de Medici. The following year she returned to her native land, cold and impoverished. It was a poor substitute for cosmopolitan France. Mary had at least sufficient sense to ignore Huntly's dangerous overtures and make herself amenable to the Protestant clique, the Lords of the Congregation. She would not, however, agree to ratify the Treaty of Leith which had ended hostilities with her adopted country as a clause in the draft excluded Mary from the English succession, a potential prize which she would not willingly relinquish.[45]

Her position was difficult, a Catholic queen in a now virtually Protestant country. In the early years of her reign she made no move to interfere with the Reformation but remained demonstrably wedded to the old order, despite frequent and unsolicited advice from John Knox.

The young queen, attractive and vivacious, did not lack for suitors but her choice fell disastrously on Henry, Lord Darnley,

a son of Lennox, whose handsome exterior hid a shallow, disso-
lute and mercurial character. The love match soon turned sour
and the queen threw prudence to the wind, embarking on a series
of rash adventures that included support for the rabid Shane
O'Neill in Ulster and dangerous conspiracies with papal agents.
Her estranged nobles made a bid for the throne though she
successfully drove them southward across the border, an episode
that became known as the 'Chase About Raid'. One of those
who fled was James Stewart, Mary's protestant half-brother,
an accomplished intriguer, who had been elevated, firstly to the
earldom of Mar in 1562 and then to the earldom of Moray the
following year.

Meanwhile Darnley, increasingly petulant, allowed himself to
be used as a tool of the swelling opposition and his murderous
jealousy fastened onto the Queen's Italian servant David Riccio
whose rise in the royal household had caused mutterings. On the
evening of 9 March 1566 the terrified Riccio was dragged, wail-
ing, from the queen's apartments and bloodily butchered. Lord
Darnley was one of the assassins.[47] The exiled James Stewart had
also enmeshed Darnley in his manipulative coils and procured
his own return and reinstatement.

Despite her revulsion, Mary, who never lacked courage, bided
her time. Increasingly she was coming under the powerful and
unstable influence of James Hepburn, fourth earl of Bothwell,
a thug in courtier's clothing. Isolated and sick, Lord Darnley
enjoyed a spectacular exit when his house at Kirk o' Field
exploded in fine style on 10 February 1567. Darnley's corpse –
he had been strangled – was discovered beside the lifeless body
of his manservant in the garden. The garish style of the murder,
clearly seen as the work of Bothwell, was sufficient to cause
outrage, which clamoured anew when the lovers were wed on
15 May – Hepburn having speedily divorced his first wife.

A wave of popular revulsion sparked rebellion and an army
cornered the pair at Carberry Hill near Musselburgh. Bothwell's
ruffians declined to fight and Mary was made captive. On 17
June the queen was imprisoned in Loch Leven Castle and the

following month was compelled to abdicate in favour of her infant son James who was speedily crowned at Stirling on 29 July. Moray slid neatly into the role of regent.[48]

The queen, however, was not about to accept her redundancy with equanimity and she still did not lack for friends, including the earl of Arran, who, prior to the birth of the young king, had a direct claim on the throne. In May 1568 Mary made her much romanticised escape from Loch Leven and was escorted by Arran's kinsman, Lord Claude Hamilton, to Cadzow Castle, where more than a thousand of her supporters were mustering.

The Battle of Langside

The regent was in Glasgow when he received the news and acted with commendable speed, summoning such troops as he had to hand. Further intelligence intimated that Mary's army was marching westward along the south bank of the Clyde, quite clearly heading for the important fortress of Dumbarton, held by Lord Fleming. This prize Moray could not afford to lose; if Mary could secure a key bastion such as Dumbarton her position would be immensely strengthened. Seeking to avoid an encounter, the queen's troops were proposing to swing wide around Glasgow, marching through Langside, Crookston and Paisley.[49]

The village of Langside has long since disappeared within the urban sprawl, but in the sixteenth century was a gaggle of cottages lining a low ridge bisected by the road which had been worn into a sunken way lined with hedges, the inhabitants' gardens straggling the southward slope. Displaying an admirable eye for ground, Moray dispatched his horse to secure the hamlet, each rider, it is said, carrying a musketeer as pillion. Behind this commanded party trudged the van, led by Morton, and after them the main body, under Moray himself. The foot were divided conventionally into pike and shot with a detachment of Highlanders.

The flying column, led by Kirkcaldy of Grange, was easily able to dismount and deploy before the enemy were sighted and their commander did not overlook the tactical value of the thick hedgerows lining the road, behind which he posted the shot, who with comparative immunity could pour concentrated volleys onto the line of the narrow way.[50]

Moray yet had time to consolidate his position before it could be attacked. He deployed his right along the line of the ridge, turning the village into a strongpoint and extending his centre and left nearly as far as Pathhead Farm along a line of high ground near what is now Queen's Park. His guns he unlimbered before the centre – altogether a strong position.

From Rutherglen Mary had marched by Blackhouse and the Hanging-shaw to Clincart Hill (now Mount Florida). This eminence was a shallow ridge from whence the ground sloped gently to rise again towards Langside, a mere 400 yards, and there could have been no mistaking the businesslike ranks drawn up opposite. For a commander Mary relied upon the earl of Argyll, notwithstanding his lack of qualifications and who, for want of more inspired thinking, resolved upon a frontal attack. The queen showed every intention of remaining with her troops and sharing their peril but was constrained to remove to the relative sanctuary of Cathcart Castle, where she could enjoy an unrivalled view of her own nemesis.

The battle started with a thundering, if largely ineffectual, cannonade, neither side taking any serious casualties. To break the deadlock Argyll sent the gallant Lord Hamilton at the head of a commanded body of foot to force a passage by the road. Grange's shot held their fire till the last, raking the exposed column to deadly effect. Hamilton's party reeled back in disorder, were re-formed and led on again, but the massed fire was too much and they fled, the lane choked with dead and dying.

Argyll next attempted a cavalry charge, his horse crashing against Moray's left, but the levelled pikes did not waver and the horse fared no better than the foot. In the village itself and in the sloping gardens a hard-fought mêlée developed as pike and shot hotly contested the ground. Throughout, however, the regent's men had the advantage of height, steadily driving their opponents down the shallow slope. A timely and spirited charge from the MacFarlanes decided the issue, and the queen's army dissolved in rout, all her hopes fleeing with them from the stricken field. To his credit, Moray would not allow the usual murderous pursuit. He had already achieved his objective and saw no reason for the further effusion of his countrymen's blood.[51]

On 13 May, Mary despairingly sailed south from Abbeyburnfoot in Galloway to throw herself upon the mercy of her English cousin and so began a life of imprisonment and intrigue that led her inexorably to the last and tragic act of her life at Fotheringhay Castle, Northamptonshire, nearly 20 years later.

James VI

The opening years of the new reign were not auspicious. Power resided in a series of regents, none of whom enjoyed popularity and most of whom died violently. Moray held on until January 1570, when an assassin's bullet found him. His successor, Darnley's father, Lennox, lasted until September the following year when he was ignominiously killed in a fracas with partisans of Mary at Stirling. His ineffective successor, Mar, was replaced in November 1572, by the altogether more formidable James, fourth earl of Morton.

This, the fourth regent, dealt ruthlessly with Mary's surviving adherents, defeating both Gordons and Hamiltons. He reduced Edinburgh Castle with the aid of English guns and hanged its commander, his erstwhile comrade, Kirkcaldy of Grange. Though effective, he had few friends and was deposed by a cabal of nobles in 1578. The following year he enjoyed a brief revival but two years after that he ended his career by an appointment with the 'Maiden', a prototype form of guillotine which, by supreme irony, Morton had himself invented.[52]

James by now had had enough of regents, though he continued to be influenced by both Lennox and Arran. His mother remained a problem, a captive queen who was still prepared to assert her authority and a constant focus for plots against

England. Though physically unimpressive and reduced to terror by the sight of a drawn sword, James was a skilful ruler who managed well in an almost unmanageable situation. Constantly hamstrung by the growing power of the Kirk and always with an eye on the English crown, he nevertheless steered a navigable course through the numerous factions which surrounded him. Like his predecessors, he had problems with disaffected nobility and in August 1582 was taken and held as a virtual captive of the earls of Mar and Gowrie at Huntingtower in the Ruthven raid. The following year, however, he successfully turned the tables and drove out his oppressors.[53]

He was always aware of the need for an English alliance and Elizabeth, too, needed allies in her rising conflict with her brother-in-law of Spain. In 1586 the two monarchs came to an accord and James's slender resources were boosted by a pension of £4000 a year.

Mary's execution did not sour relations, indeed his mother's death served to concentrate the king's mind on the dazzling prize of the English succession. This was by no means guaranteed – the English despised their poorer neighbours but a Protestant succession was essential and in 1589 James married Anne of Denmark. When Queen Elizabeth's long reign finally ended, James succeeded the vacant throne in 1603 without opposition and a King of Scots would henceforth rule England. The long battle for supremacy was over.

Raids and Reivers

William Armstrong of Kinmont, known to history and to legend as 'Kinmont Willie', was a stalwart ruffian with a record of lawlessness. From his tower at Morton Rigg on the fringe of the Debateable Lands, the wildest tract in the west march, he led regular forays across the Border, lifting sheep, beasts and anything else that took his fancy.

In the spring of 1596 he attended a truce at Kershopefoot on the Scottish side. After the formal business he rode, seemingly alone, along the north and Scots bank of the Liddel. On the far bank rode a squadron of English horse. Safe in the knowledge that he was inviolate till sunrise the next day when the truce expired, Will felt free to indulge in some less than genial banter with his less than friendly neighbours over the narrow waters.

Exactly what transpired next remains unclear. In all probability, the English, stung by this arrogant posturing, and seeing their inveterate enemy so close, found the moment too tempting and spurred across the Liddel Water to make the astonished reiver captive. What is certain is that he was borne beneath the fortress walls of Carlisle and there incarcerated. Such an act, occurring as it did on a truce day, was considered an outrage, notwithstanding the nature and misdemeanours of the alleged victim. It is possible that the English warden, Lord Scrope, was embarrassed by his subordinates' act but his own subsequent intransigence would lead to his undying shame.[1]

The Border reivers, mosstroopers and cattle thieves, drawn and descended from those clans whose lands lay within the marches, owed their pedigree to the wars of Edward I of England

and the nationalist struggle which followed. From then until the Union of the Crowns in 1603 a state of lawlessness, internecine feuding and frequent raiding prevailed. The Scottish Border, like its English counterpart, was divided into three administrative districts or marches, each with its own governor or warden.

The warden's duties were to maintain law and order and liaise with his opposite number, most usually on truce days when both sides met at an appointed spot in a quasi-judicial atmosphere, hopefully without recourse to arms. It is fair to say that many wardens were as rapacious and predatory as the outlaws and broken men who skulked on their marches. Some, such as Ker of Cessford, were models of brigandry whose power was built on connivance and corruption. Others on the English side, such as the wily Sir John Forster, whose turbulent career spanned the whole of the sixteenth century, were little better.[2]

Liddesdale in the middle march was generally reputed, outside the Debateable Lands, to be the true home of total lawlessness. Its hard-riding inhabitants – Armstrongs, Elliots, Bells and Crosers – wreaked ample havoc over the line, so much so that Liddesdale was regarded as a sufficiently tough patch to warrant a junior warden, or keeper, of its own.[3] Tynedale men – Charltons, Robsons, Dodds and others – were perfectly happy to make common cause with the Liddesdale thieves and wreak havoc on their own countrymen!

The powerful Homes dominated the Merse to the east. Kers and Scotts vied for power in the middle whilst the Maxwells and Johnstones were frequently at each other's throats in the west. Further west still the Douglases and Crichtons inhabited Nithsdale. The Debateable Lands – an unclaimed waste inland from the Solway Firth between the waters of Sark and Liddel, where sovereignty was disputed by both crowns and exercised by neither – provided a base for the troublesome Grahams and a motley host of assorted renegades.

The almost constant strife, which reached its nadir in the sixteenth century, was exacerbated by the feud which pitted family against family and left whole generations locked in a murderous circle of slaughter and reprisal. Not surprisingly, perhaps, the landscape took on an embattled appearance. No thought was given to comfort or pleasure, and buildings were constructed for defence and the 'long view' that was an essential ingredient to survival. The Scottish tower-house, as distinguished from the peels of Northumberland, is a four-square stone keep, perhaps three or four storeys high with crowstepped gables flanking a pitched stone-slated roof and parapet walk. The entrance, usually a single narrow portal at ground level, leads to a barrel-vaulted basement with hall and apartments above. The whole is surrounded by a palisade or barmkin, often studded with loopholes for firelock or cannon.[4] Many examples still survive, such as picturesque Smailholm, near Melrose, or Newark, whose barmkin bears the imprint of gunfire, a legacy of the slaughter of Montrose's men after defeat at Philiphaugh. Gilnockie or Hollows, near Canonbie, is reputed to have been the hold of the infamous Johnnie Armstrong of Gilnockie, whose colourful career was cut short by James V, who also did not baulk at violating a truce day to string up the unfortunate reiver and his followers.[5]

The more powerful marchers built themselves castles, such as Home Castle in the Merse, distinctive three-sided Caerlaverock by the Solway and grim Hermitage in Liddesdale. This last-named gaunt and forbidding fortress has a history that matches its appearance. A medieval incumbent, Lord Soulis, who was reputed to practise the black arts, was carried off by his disgruntled tenants, rolled in a sheet of lead and melted at the Ninestanerig, an ancient stone circle. Mary, Queen of Scots, nearly died of influenza contracted when she struggled through appalling weather to tend her wounded lover Bothwell, who, as keeper of Liddesdale, resided at Hermitage and had been cut up pursuing a notorious reiver.[6]

Hadden Rigg

In addition to the innumerable minor raids and forays the inhabitants could also expect the odd 'big raid' – a major incursion, usually led by a warden of the opposite side and mounted with the tacit consent or even positive encouragement of government. One such scourge descended on Teviotdale in the summer of 1542 when the English east march warden, Sir Robert Bowes, was aided by the renegade Angus and his Douglas kin, currently out of favour at Holyrood. The raid was no mean affair; some 3000 riders gathered to beat up Teviotdale, whose own people, it has to be said, excelled in the reivers' art.[7]

Following the pattern for such affairs Bowes stationed his main body at Hadden and despatched two flying columns, one under Heron and comprising the rough riders of Redesdale and Tynedale, and the other, more sedate, the regular complement stripped from the defences of Berwick and Norham. The Scots, however, refused to submit meekly to such organised brigandry and a local force under Huntly interposed itself between the two vanguard detachments and the main body. Random skirmishing in the Border mould developed as the riders clashed. Angus, a doughty fighter, and not one given to panic, blamed men from the English dales for thinking more of their loot than their honour. The Scots continued to apply pressure and the English force, now totally disorganised, dissolved into rout, leaving both Heron and Bowes as captives. Angus, himself, succeeded in hacking a way clear but was chased back across the Border in ignominious flight. Some seventy-odd of the English riders were killed and Hadden Rigg, though a small affair in national terms, ranks as a resounding victory for the Scottish Borderers.

Ancrum Moor

On 27 February 1545 Angus and his Douglas kin were in action beneath the cross of St Andrew. The débâcle at Solway Moss and the early death of James V had plunged the country into the deep uncertainty of an unstable regency – the recurring nightmare of Scottish politics. England, pushing her territorial ambitions through a proposed marriage alliance, was sharply rebuffed, and resorted to that more aggressive policy known as the 'rough wooing'. In May 1544 a force under Hertford landed at Newhaven on the Firth of Forth and wasted Leith and the capital. With the Scots demoralised, English inroads became bolder, fostering dreams of conquest and many Border holds bristled with English arms. The riders of Liddesdale and Teviotdale, as pragmatic as ever, simply changed sides and joined the oppressors, swapping their blue crosses for red.

Distinguished, even in so rapacious an era, by his ruthless greed, was the English middle march warden, Sir Ralph Eure. Together with Wharton and Dacre, who were active in the west, he mounted a campaign of terror, targeting the Merse, Teviotdale and Lauderdale. So effective was he that a royal warrant was reputedly issued ceding him all the territory he could conquer. Angus, whose martial temperament was never more sorely needed, had been appointed Lieutenant of the Border and declared his intentions by putting pressure on Eure's Scots allies, particularly the Nixons and the Crosers, and it was their appeals for aid that led to his decision to act swiftly. Finding an able subordinate in another tough adventurer, Sir Brian Laiton, he assembled a motley force of about 3000 whose ranks were bolstered by an influx of foreign mercenaries: Germans, Italians, French, Spanish, Irish and Greeks, the dregs of Continental armies. Crossing the Border he picked up a few hundred Scottish riders who soon seem to have fallen out with the rest of the hired help.[8]

The English ploughed through the marches like a whirlwind leaving Melrose in ashes, the abbey, with its Douglas tombs, wantonly desecrated. Such horror could only stiffen Angus's resolve but he did not have the men to offer battle and had to be content with nibbling at the enemy flanks.

Angus was joined by Arran but, even reinforced, his numbers barely exceeded 300. Some time later he was bolstered by another force led by the Master of Rothes. By this time the English were encamped, replete with plunder on Ancrum Moor, hard by the banks of the Teviot, and a bare five miles from Jedburgh. With the arrival of the Leslies and Lindsays, Angus's force now numbered some 1200 and more were on their way, led by the redoubtable Scott of Buccleuch. Though he had initially drawn up his forces on a slight rise overlooking the moorland rim, Angus was persuaded, probably by Buccleuch, to withdraw and deploy out of sight of the English with riders dismounting and horses led to the rear. Possibly the English mistook this move for a general retreat and in consequence hurried forward to secure their advantage. If so, their confidence was ill founded.

Prior to the battle and whilst 'taking up' the march, the invaders were said to have fired a tower at Broomhouse incinerating the elderly châtelaine and her people immured within. At any event the cry of 'Remember Broomhouse' would ring the death knell for many who had watched the flames.[9]

Laiton hurrying on with the van topped the rise and ran headlong on to the levelled pikes and lances. Blinded by the rays of the setting sun, the attackers floundered. Behind, Eure advanced with the main body, mounted men at arms in the centre flanked on one side by archers and on the other by harquebusiers. The Scots fought hard, emptying saddles and sending the van crashing back upon the centre.

Seizing the moment, Angus ordered the advance and the dogged files surged forward, hewing through the rapidly disintegrating ranks of the invaders. Eure and Laiton struggled to rally their polyglot army, knowing they themselves could scarcely expect quarter. The slaughter was prodigious. Of the English force who took the field some 800 fell, a further 1000 were made prisoner. To add to the general discomfort, the marchers riding beneath the English banner selected the most judicious moment to revert to their national allegiance, swapping their crosses of St George for the Saltire. Neither Eure nor Laiton survived.[10]

Border Arms and Armour

The 'steel bonnet' of the Border rider was a close-fitting, peaked helmet of the type described as a burgonet, which covered the cheeks but left the face exposed, thus protecting the rider against a blow delivered to the rear or sides. The foot soldiers of this period frequently wore the morion which, in profile, offered a semi-oval outline with raised comb and flatter rim.[11]

Body armour comprised, for those of rank, a simple breast and back; lesser mortals had to rely on a leather or canvas jack padded for comfort and reinforced with iron plates sewn on. A more sophisticated version was the brigandine – defensive plates and chains were sometimes stitched onto doublets or breeches to provide rudimentary protection. Leg harness was rare, most riders preferring thigh-high leather boots. The Borderer was essentially businesslike in his appearance – after all, he rode for plunder not for glory. Forms of ostentation were shunned and in war the combatants were distinguished by the device sewn on or worn as an armband. This lack of display had a disadvantage in battle; many a Border laird was slain alongside his tenantry, as at Pinkie where the dead of the Scottish armies proved difficult to distinguish by rank.[12]

The horseman's chosen weapon was the lance mounted on an ash shaft some 13 ft in length, used couched for thrusting or hurled overarm like a javelin. Swords, axes and daggers were in regular use, as was a handy form of crossbow known as a latch.[13]

A particularly fearsome weapon was the Jedburgh axe or *Jedhart staff*, which receives its first mention early in the sixteenth century. Craftsmen, working in the ancient burgh, produced these formidable arms whose heavy elliptical blades averaged 4 ft in length, set upon an oak handle, the head socketed and secured by long flanges extending down the shaft. These served to prevent the head from being lopped off in close combat and the fighter's hands were protected with iron stops or *vamplates*, similar to those featured on lances for the tourney.[14]

The cumbersome matchlock received little favour as it was essentially unsuited to the cavalry arm. Wheel-locks, when introduced, proved more practical though expensive and a gentleman might carry a brace of pistols secured in holsters worn each side of the saddle, in addition to sporting a carbine or caliver which, as the sixteenth century wore on, replaced the latch as a missile weapon.[15]

In military terms the Borderers operated as light cavalry, incomparable scouts in their own marches though far less reliable for any other role. Throughout the Border wars the marchers showed a distinct reluctance to see blood shed, particularly their own, in the cause of national honour. It limits the incentives when there is a good chance a victorious king will deploy his power equally against his own subjects and the complexities of clan loyalties, marriage alliances and sheer pragmatism combined to limit or defeat any show of patriotism. Lord Home's celebrated reluctance to commit his own, largely unscathed division, to the final carnage at Flodden smacks of hard-headed reality. Defeat by the English would see the Scottish Border ablaze and a prudent man husbanded his resources to defend his own.

To a Borderer his mount was everything and the shaggy little garrons or 'hobblers' were prized for their surefooted stamina. The raiding season got under way in the autumn as the nights drew in but the mosses remained dry from the summer sun. The reivers' paths across the trackless wastes were numerous and devious. A raid could cover formidable distances, far in excess of those to which conventional cavalry might aspire. As good mounts were so valued, horsebreeding became a local and national pastime. The Stewart kings imported stock from as far afield as Hungary, Poland and Spain. Racing was equally popular, especially amongst the Borderers, and race meets – like truce days – were an escape from the relentless grind.[16]

The Raid of the Reidswire

One truce degenerated into the fracas that became known as the Raid of the Reidswire, in the summer of 1575. The Reidswire lies on the line of the Border, some three miles from Carter Bar, with the whole magnificent sweep of the Border hills as a backdrop, the 'swire' being a narrow neck of land linking two hunched and rolling crests. The English were represented by the middle march warden, Sir John Forster. In his mid-seventies and destined to hold sway until his tenth decade Sir John was a man who thoroughly understood the full wickedness of Border ways, having practised most of them in earnest since his youth. Sir John Carmichael, Keeper of Liddesdale, appeared for the Scots.

For three hours the meeting continued amicably, though there was little love lost between the two or between Liddesdale Crosers and the Tynedale men. An argument over a particular bill or matter degenerated into a slanging match between the wardens. Their respective compatriots, fuelled by drink, followed suit, insults quickly followed by blows. A chance arrow slew Fenwick of Wallington and first blood seems to have persuaded Forster and Carmichael to calm themselves and their followers. A precarious peace was almost restored when the Scots suddenly fell upon the English warden and his party, capturing the outraged Forster and leaving his deputy, Sir George Heron, dead upon the turf.[17]

Now the Tynedale men surged forward, their longbows creating havoc amongst the Scots, who wavered but, at the last, rallied and charged again, bolstered by a timely contingent from Jedburgh. It was the turn of the English to flee and they dissolved in rout, hotly pursued by the victors.[18] The Scots were left to celebrate their win but the matter was most embarrassing to the government who were seeking to foster good relations with England, and Forster, old rogue that he was, soon gained his freedom and regained his wardenship.

No more bitter rivalry existed between any of the riding families than the enmity between the Maxwells and Johnstones. In 1528 Dacre was able to report that the state of open warfare which existed between the two kindreds had resulted in the devastation of the Debateable Lands and much of the west march.

The prize most sought was the march wardenship itself and the office passed like a bauble between the factions with almost bewildering speed. In the 1580s each kindred possessed an active and aggressive chieftain, Johnnie Johnstone clashing frequently with John, eighth Lord Maxwell. Maxwell had two spells in office around 1580, being dismissed once and latterly imprisoned, an experience he came to understand well. When Johnstone was outlawed in 1581 Maxwell entered upon a third term of office. The following year he was once again removed and Johnstone reinstated. Maxwell was not the man to submit lightly, however, and he rebelled against his detested rival.[19]

The Chancellor, Arran, was kin to Johnstone and purported to punish Maxwell for his impertinence by stripping him of the office of Provost of Dumfries, a lucrative sinecure. Enraged, Maxwell raised the stakes by importing English Grahams to harry and burn. By the spring of 1585 administration of the march had degenerated into anarchy; 80 Johnstone towers had been sacked or razed but far from being intimidated Johnstone allowed the tide of violence to increase by laying waste the Maxwell village of Duncow, and they naturally responded in kind. The body count continued to rise steadily.[20]

By the summer Maxwell's star was firmly in the ascendant and he had taken the march by storm; by August Johnstone was captive. At this point King James, bowing to what appeared inevitable, acquiesced to Maxwell's reinstatement. Unable to keep clear of mischief, Maxwell's political adventures, linked to his unfashionably ardent Catholicism, landed him back in gaol the following year. Johnstone was swift to make capital from his enemy's discomfort and he laid waste Maxwell territories. For this he was in turn incarcerated. Though he was subsequently freed, the years of strife had taken a heavy toll and Johnstone died in 1587, a broken man.

Maxwell, as ever, proved more resilient. In exile now he busied himself in Spain abetting plots against England and in the year of the Armada was stirring up resentment in the Catholic cause. Not unsurprisingly, he was once again imprisoned. Somehow he managed to talk his way out again and by 1592 he was re-appointed as warden, this time for life.

Fully in control, he arranged for the young Johnstone chieftain to marry a Maxwell girl and the feud seemed, if certainly not forgotten, at least under control. Matters might have rested thus, at least for a while, but a petty feud led to a violent clash between the Johnstones and the Crichtons, which left 15 of the latter dead. Maxwell, for once, appears to have been reluctant to become involved but his promises of succour to the offended Crichtons and their Douglas allies came to the ears of the Johnstones who yet again entered the fray.[21]

With the Johnstones once more antagonistic, Maxwell decided upon a draconian solution to the problem of his quarrelsome neighbours. Formally summoning Johnstone to surrender the warden moved towards Lochwood with a force amounting to some 2000 men. Desperate for allies to bolster his thinner ranks Johnstone was joined by Elliots, Scotts, Irvines and the English Grahams, who were always available for mayhem. Despite these reinforcements he could barely muster 400 riders.[22]

On 6 December 1593, as Maxwell's force lumbered past Lockerbie, Johnstone appeared at the head of forty-odd riders. Maxwell countered by unleashing twice as many of his 'skur-rouris' or scouts, who gave chase to the now retiring Johnstones. This apparently precipitate retreat was no more than a ruse, for Johnstone had concealed his whole force, 'Lyland Darnit', in a wood and the warden's vanguard was thrown into wild disorder as the main body swept from the fringe of trees and fell upon them with a vengeance. It was the Maxwells' turn to flee and the ensuing rout threw the centre into confusion.[23]

A hacking, sprawling mêlée spread over the plain, known as Dryfe Sands, and knots of fighters spilled into the streets of Lockerbie. So many fearsome wounds were dealt by the axes and staffs wielded by the Johnstones, fighting with the fury of utter desperation, that such injuries were thereafter referred to as 'Lockerbie licks'. The Maxwells were cut to pieces and the warden, himself, was counted among the fallen, who numbered over 1000.[24]

Dryfe Sands was the bloodiest 'clan' fight in Scotland's history. Johnstone was outlawed for his victory and though the warden-ship continued to change hands he gained a pardon and the appointment, thus becoming the last warden of the west march.

In 1608 a formal truce was arranged and Johnstone met with the new Lord Maxwell, son of the formidable father killed at Lockerbie. Though the meeting was intended finally to heal the rift Maxwell proceeded to empty a brace of pistols into the warden's back, a crime for which, on 21 March 1613, he went to the block, the last of four chiefs to die in the vendetta.

The Paladin

Background to the Civil War

James VI of Scotland and I of England has generally not enjoyed a good press: slack-jawed and unprepossessing, learned yet often foolish, his achievements have been largely overlooked. A proficient linguist who rode and hunted well, he managed to prevail against both the rampant anarchy of the nobility and the arrogant intolerance of the Kirk whilst successfully merging the crowns, no mean task in itself. He is regarded as a highly successful king of Scots. None-the-less, his English subjects were disappointed: he appeared a poor successor to Elizabeth and his son Charles even worse. Whilst James, a wily tactician, readily exploited the differences between his opponents, Charles very early mastered the knack of uniting the opposition against him.

Charles had many virtues – he was tolerant in an age of creeping intolerance, cultured, pious and brave – yet he showed little interest in his northern kingdom and less understanding. His policy, such as it was, encouraged Laudian-style episcopacy, an anathema to many Scots. He excluded the Lords of Session from the Privy Council and then terrified the nobles by threatening to seek recovery of all property taken over since the accession of his grandmother, Mary, in 1542.[1]

These concerns were rendered trivial when Charles thought to introduce the Book of Canons (incorrectly labelled as 'Laud's Liturgy', and generally considered more popish than the English prayer book). Riots ensued and an outraged populace flocked to sign the National Covenant in 1638. As opposition swelled, protestors demanded the withdrawal of the liturgy and the expulsion of the bishops from the Privy Council. Anti-episcopalian sentiment began to mount and the Covenanters, as the signatories to the Deed were known, sought a free Parliament, the General Assembly of the following year openly defying the king and purporting to abolish episcopacy.[2]

Charles was persuaded to use force against his Scottish subjects, but his attempts to raise a viable army foundered. The rabble he managed to gather drank and pillaged their way north but never amounted to a military expedition. The following year saw Charles once again trying to recruit adequate forces to constitute an army and, to no one's surprise, other than perhaps his own, meeting with scant success. The Scots fared better, their regiments swelled and drilled whilst the tide of change gathered momentum. The clerical estate was abolished. The Covenant became an obligation rather than a choice. The executive power rested in a Committee of the Three Estates and the Kirk, ably championed by Argyll, took effective control.[3]

At the head of 20,000 foot with 2500 horse, Alexander Leslie, who had won renown as the defender of Stralsund in the Thirty Years' War, splashed across the Tweed on 20 August 1640. A scratch royalist force at Newburn on the Tyne, under Lord Conway, sought to bar his passage south. The English could field no more than 3500 foot, mainly musketeers and perhaps a couple of thousand horse. A brace of earthwork redoubts commanded the ford (on ground now occupied by Stella Power Station). At dusk on 27 August the two armies faced each other over the placid waters. Leslie made good use of the short summer night causing his guns to be dragged down to the riverbank where they opened the morning's hostilities with a brisk fire. Under cover of the cannons' roar a commanded body of Life Guards forced the crossing, precipitating a hasty withdrawal by the English which swiftly dissolved into rout. Even a spirited charge by the cavaliers could not stem the rot and the 'rout of Newburn Ford' was quickly ended.[4]

Charles now faced the humiliation of seeing virtually the whole of Northumberland and Durham, including Newcastle, under Scots occupation. He was forced to negotiate from a position of weakness, a stance which further dented his crumbling prestige. The concord agreed at Ripon was formally ratified by the King's Commissioners in 1641 and the Scots marched home having earned their country some £200,000.

Armies and Tactics of the Civil Wars

The Civil War took Britain almost by surprise – these islands had thus far been spared the carnage of the Thirty Years' War that ravaged Germany. None-the-less, as previously mentioned, many Scots had fought as mercenaries and learned their trade under such Continental masters as Gustavus Adolphus.

By the middle of the seventeenth century the use of the musket was growing in importance, the heavy matchlock weapons were cumbersome to carry, slow to fire and at best unreliable. Few could manage more than one round per minute. Some units, particularly dragoons, were equipped with the more manageable doglock, precursor to the venerable flintlock that was to dominate battlefields for so long.

The file of musketeers or 'shot' was drawn up in a body for five or six ranks deep and fired by 'extraduction', each rank retiring to the rear to reload after discharging a volley or 'giving fire'. This process should, in theory, produce an almost continual roll of gunfire and the manuals of the day showed an almost balletic sense of movement, extremely hard to practise in the field with raw troops.[5]

On average, most foot regiments still included about 40 per cent of pikemen – stout lads with morion helmets, breast and back with steel guards, or tassets, for the thighs. The puissant pike could range from 12 to 15 ft, the head protected by steel bars or languets which stretched down to the ash wood shaft. The principal function of the pike was to protect the shot from cavalry and opposing formations frequently came to 'push of pike', in some ways a kind of particularly vicious scrum with much heaving and relatively few casualties. The pikemen usually carried short swords or hangers in addition to their body armour. The shot, on the other hand, went unarmoured, being sufficiently encumbered by the weight of the weapon itself and the forked rest used to steady the long barrel. Twelve 'apostles' hung from a bandolier, a flask of fine grain powder being carried for priming the piece.[6] To load, a measure of powder was poured down the pan followed by a ball, an experienced man having three or four ready in his mouth. The charge was wadded and rammed and the piece primed. The firing mechanism or cock was operated by pressure on the trigger, which lowered the lighted match over the pan. The maximum range was generally little more than 60 yards, though wind and rain frequently frustrated the musketeers' efforts.[7]

Ranking officers were distinguished by the use of armoured neckpieces or gorgets and carried rapiers and pole-arms such as the partisan. Sergeants carried halberds. Dragoons were essentially mounted infantry whose role encompassed scouting and guard duties, providing harassing fire against cavalry and skirmishing.

Cavalry regiments were generally considered an élite; on the royalist side most troopers were gentlemen or sons of gentlemen, schooled on the hunting field and with the means to mount and equip themselves. The Swede Gustavus had done away with the stately but largely ineffective manoeuvre known as the caracole and reintroduced the idea of shock tactics, troopers thundering into the charge and riding knee to knee, heavy wheel-lock pistols discharging and not infrequently used as missiles, broadswords flashing.[8]

Full armour was largely obsolescent and the traditional breast and back went out of fashion as the war progressed displaced by the ubiquitous buff coat, the bridle arm perhaps protected by a steel gauntlet.

The wheel-lock was a far more sophisticated mechanism than match, though vastly more expensive, and thus became a gentleman's weapon. The cavalry man would carry a brace of pistols holstered either side of the saddle. The mechanism comprised a serrated steel wheel which sparked when struck by a piece of pyrites held in the cock. The wheel itself was wound up like clockwork using a key. Pressure on the trigger released the spring, showering sparks into the touch-hole.[9] Most troopers carried swords – graceful, swept or cup-hilted rapiers, more businesslike than broadswords or the purposeful 'Walloon' hanger.

A typical regiment of foot was divided into ten companies, each of 100 men save the colonel's company which was at double strength. These companies were commanded by field officers and the rest by captains; a ratio of two-thirds shot to one-third pike was the norm. In battle the regiment deployed the pikes in the centre with the shot drawn up on the flanks. A field army would form up in three or four lines with the foot in the centre and the horse commanding the flanks, dragoons being used as skirmishers. Behind this screen the first line would move forward and deliver a series of volleys before both sides came to 'push of pike'. If assailed by horse the pikes would form a defensive hedge sheltering the shot.

The regiment was also the typical tactical unit for cavalry, though no set standards existed. The horse might be divided into six troops, commanded by field officers and the rest by captains. A fighting formation of three ranks was usual, though for full shock effect the horse would advance six ranks deep.[10]

Medical care was rudimentary; regimental surgeons existed but many wounded succumbed to shock, loss of blood or disease. Contemporary accounts stress the horrors of the battlefield with heaps of dead and wounded left unattended, exposed to the savage mercies of climate and scavengers. The fallen were ruthlessly stripped of all they possessed and local people were often less than sympathetic to men who had hitherto looted and pillaged at will.

The science of artillery was growing in scope and importance; lighter field-pieces were stationed on the flanks of foot battalions and heavier pieces were sited to fire over the heads of the soldiery. Redoubts, sconces and bastions were thrown up to accommodate the heavy guns and the Swedish practice of assigning two light field guns to each foot regiment was almost universally adopted. Round shot was the customary missile, supplemented by case shot (a canister of musket balls which could scythe down whole files at close range). Each piece was serviced by a gunner, his mate and one or more labourers or matrosses.[11]

An army was commanded by a captain-general, assisted by a staff and a lieutenant-general or field-marshal. The foot were similarly commanded, a general, his lieutenant, and a major-general, customarily a professional soldier, often a rarity in Civil War armies. Command of the horse was similarly structured and the general of ordnance commanded the artillery.[12]

A Prelude to War

James Graham, fifth earl and later first marquis of Montrose, was born in 1612 and succeeded to his inheritance at the early age of 14. His academic career as a student at St Andrews was distinguished more by sporting than scholastic achievement. Chivalrous and quixotic, destined for glory, yet doomed to failure, he remains an oddly enigmatic individual despite a welter of biographical detail.

As early as November 1637 he was identified with opposition to the king's policies and was one of the four representatives of the nobility on the 'Tables', the *ad hoc* forerunner to the Committee of Estates. He was one of the very first to sign the Covenant.[13]

In 1639, the Estates became concerned at the apparent intransigence of the marquis of Huntly, whose fief encompassed wide and prosperous lands in the north-east. Fearful of invasion from the south, a potential enemy in the rear seemed too great a threat, thus Montrose received a colonel's commission and was soon raising levies in Forfar and Perthshire. By mid February he was marching north with 200 recruits.[14]

In the capital, on 26 March, Leslie with considerable *élan* surprised the royalist garrison holding the castle in a bloodless coup. This success was followed by the taking of Dumbarton, thus closing the back door from Ireland. Covenanting families in the north rushed to join the earls of Montrose and Kinghorn, effectively isolating Huntly and his numerous Gordons. Earlier, on 14 February, the opposing forces had met at Turriff where the arrival of the marquis and his royalist clansmen precipitated a hurried, though, as it transpired, untested defence. Bolstered by fresh supplies, Huntly waxed enthusiastic for his royal master's cause, though his native caution soon prevailed and prevarication followed. By 20 March Covenanting forces occupied Aberdeen and on 4 April at Inverurie the vacillating Huntly met with and was arrested by Montrose.

The royalists had some 800 foot mustering as the Strathbogie regiment, six full companies armed by Huntly and led by an experienced professional officer in the person of Colonel Johnson. They were out-numbered by the Covenanting lairds some 1200 strong and assembled at Turriff.

Determined to 'beat up' their opponents' quarters, the royalists on 14 May marched 15 miles through the mild spring evening, led, at least in name, by Ogilvy of Banff and Gordon of Haddo, but in practice by the redoubtable Johnson. The Covenanters were taken completely by surprise and though they may have been able to draw up before the town they were soon forced back into the streets. Here their hastily erected barricades were flung aside by the ardour of the Strathbogie men and some well-directed roundshot precipitated a rout, subsequently christened the 'Trot of Turriff'.[15]

The royalists failed to exploit this early success and, though they marched on Aberdeen, achieved nothing and failed to stand when Montrose, at the head of 4000 soldiers, approached. The marquis judged the situation sufficiently under control to return to his recruiting in Forfarshire – too soon, perhaps, for the king's men, bolstered by recruits of their own, moved to reoccupy the city, political command being bestowed upon the absent Huntly's son, Lord Aboyne.

On 14 June Aboyne took the initiative, his drums and lances heading south, seeking an encounter with the Earl Marischal then at Dunnottar. The Covenanter sent word to Montrose and drew up behind barricades at Stonehaven. With him he had some 1200 foot and 14 guns. At dawn on the 15th the royalists hove into view, 2500 horse and foot with 500 Highlanders soon deployed to the north of the town on Megray Hill.

Skirmishers swapped shots and Aboyne felt secure enough to concentrate upon finding a decent breakfast. His horse, however, pressing too close, were worsted by fire from the defenders and the continuing cannonade raked his assembled foot. The Highlanders, who had not joined up to be wasted as cannon-fodder, promptly dispersed, demoralising their Lowland comrades, who soon followed suit. Fortunately for Aboyne, the Covenanters failed to appear and thus follow up their success, and he managed to rally his Lowland levies but not his Highland allies whose enthusiasm did not survive this baptism of fire.[16]

Montrose was quickly in pursuit but found his way to Aberdeen barred by a contingent of Strathbogie men led by Nat Gordon, who had fortified the only viable river crossing at the Bridge of Dee some two miles away above the town. With the Dee still swollen from the spring thaw, they would have to be dislodged.

The marquis commanded some 2000 foot, drawn from the Earl Marischal's regiment and bolstered by newly raised companies from Angus and Tayside, some squadrons of horse and a brace of the 20-lb guns which had done so well at Megray Hill.

Now their fire was less effective and the royalist reply no more so. Gordon was steadily reinforced by contingents of horse and foot, including the Aberdeen militia, who were posted to the bridge itself crouching in the lee of the stone parapet and flanking bays.

Montrose had by now resited his ordnance and their renewed fire blew in the gatehouse and flayed the span of the bridge with a storm of roundshot and grape. With dead and wounded lining the bridge, royalist morale began to waver. Sensing the moment Montrose bade Lt-Colonel Middleton prepare a commanded party to storm the crumbling defences. A final crashing cannon-ade broke the spirit of the militia and wounded the gallant Johnson; the way to Aberdeen was open and the war in the north and east was over.[17]

The Battle of Marston Moor

Events in England were now moving with a dread momentum of their own and the civil war began in earnest when the king raised his standard at Nottingham. Neither side was prepared for war and each believed naïvely that the issue could be resolved by a single trial of arms. Edgehill was as inconclusive as it was bloody and the realisation began to dawn that the struggle between Charles and Parliament would be prolonged.

In Scotland there was disunity; many, including Montrose, felt that loyalty to the crown would always remain a paramount concern and there was a swelling opposition to some of the constitutional changes which Argyll and the majority were bent upon. Montrose and those who had entered into the Bond of Cumbernauld feared that Argyll sought the crown for himself, an assertion that led to the marquis's temporary incarceration. Charles's efforts at interference did little good and rumours of a plot to kidnap Argyll caused his stock to plunge even further.[18] The king's efforts to win over his Scottish subjects were soon overshadowed by the crisis in Ulster and his worsening work-ing relations with Parliament. The bungled attempt to arrest five Members in January 1642 led inexorably to the raising of the royal standard on 22 August.

As the pace of the war intensified both sides sought to seduce the Scots. In this the dying Pym with his Presbyterian colleagues was more successful and in August 1643 the General Assembly accepted the Parliamentary overtures. Popery and prelacy were to be extirpated throughout England and Ireland, the Presbyterian faith was to be enforced, a move perhaps accept-able to Parliament but far less so to England as a whole where the Puritans tended to comprise the majority.

In mid January the following year Alexander Leslie, now raised to the earldom of Leven, crossed the swollen waters of the Tweed at the head of 18,000 foot and 3000 horse. The first of the Articles of War, which enjoined discipline and strict morality, provided that every man was to give his oath 'according to the heads sworn by me in the Solomne League and Covenant of the three Kingdoms'.[19]

The Northumberland into which the Scottish host was advancing had given its steadfast support to the king, and his loyal lieutenant in the north, the marquis of Newcastle, had earlier defeated the Fairfaxes, father and son, at Adwalton Moor.[20] Now the royalists were driven southward and bottled up in York, a city entrenched and now massively fortified. Leven was joined before the walls by a parliamentary army under Fairfax and Manchester.

The *beau sabreur* of the royalist cause, Prince Rupert, with an army of 12,000, was marching to the marquis's relief. By 23 June he arrived at Preston, then immediately moved out toward Skipton, causing the parliamentary commanders to break off the siege and concentrate their combined forces to the east of the city and onto a barren heath between Tockwith and Long Marston. Rupert, moving fast, stole a march on his adversaries and reached the suburbs of York where he joined forces with Newcastle. Determined to force a battle, the headstrong prince and the unenthusiastic marquis marched out the next day, 2 July. Leven, who, as senior officer, commanded the whole parliamentary army, had ordered his foot south to hold the bridge at Tadcaster. He was thus much discomfited when royalist banners were seen to flutter above Long Marston.[21]

Though both sides were in position by four o'clock, the battle proper did not begin until three hours later – Newcastle, thinking it now too late for serious fighting, had withdrawn to his coach to smoke a pipe. Leven's nephew, David Leslie, was in the second line of parliamentary horse on the left flank commanded by Cromwell, whilst Fairfax commanded the cavalry on the right. The foot in the centre comprised a mix of six regiments from all three contingents and the allied host swept down the slope to their front at a sharp pace, as the heavens opened and nature added its fury to man's folly.[22]

Cromwell was wounded in the first charge. On the right Fairfax fared badly, pushed back by Goring, and many of his squadrons were routed. The infantry battle raged in the centre and the crisis came when a spirited charge by royalist horse broke several regiments; at that moment it seemed Rupert might win the day. The Scots foot fell back. Leven, believing the battle lost, prepared to quit the stricken field. Cromwell, however, by now had had his wound dressed and returned to the field, his leadership proved decisive and royalist hopes in the north died that day on Marston Moor, the slaughter on the heath followed by a merciless pursuit. Newcastle's own regiment, the Whitecoats, was decimated, and the marquis, humiliated by his defeat, fled to the Continent.[23]

After the battle Leven retired northward and in the autumn became bogged down at the siege of Newcastle. Eventually the city fell by storm and the earl settled into winter quarters there, increasingly perturbed by news from the north and by the widening gulf with his English allies. Tidings from over the Border concerned Montrose, now the king's lieutenant-general in Scotland and fast becoming his most potent champion.[24]

Year of Miracles

In 1643 Montrose, now thoroughly out of step with Argyll and the Covenanters, offered his sword to the king, who, true to his nature, responded with indecision. Montrose, in these early days, does not seem to have impressed his English counterpart, Prince Rupert. In the following year he resumed his commission as the king's lieutenant-general in Scotland and in May was made a marquis. Slipping past Covenanting forces, he entered Perth at the head of a delegation comprising himself and two companions. Whilst there, however, he heard that Alistair MacColla had landed in the west on the long finger of Kintyre and was waging war against Clan Campbell in Ardnamurchan.[25] The Irish brigade amounted to some 1600 men, with their women, children and a gaggle of followers, divided into three regiments, one of which was commanded by Manus O'Cahan. MacColla, himself, was an experienced fighter whose warrior prowess had already assumed legendary proportions.

A veteran at 21, MacColla had hacked his way through a score of bloody scrimmages in Ireland. His reputation for reckless valour perhaps fails to do him full credit and he was undoubtedly a more skilled commander than his brute image would indicate. He is credited as the originator of the highland charge, turning the wild rush into a formidable tactic. He and Montrose were to form an exceptional partnership, each respecting the skills of the other and each delighting in war. The Year of Miracles would be the high point in both their lives.[26]

Montrose deserves to rank as one of the great commanders, though he is certainly not without his critics. His use of irregular troops, mainly Highlanders, stiffened by his veteran Irish, was remarkable; he out-thought, out-fought and out-manoeuvred all of his Covenanting opponents and convincingly smashed every army they sent against him. He has been castigated for his often reckless daring and impatience – for a guerilla commander he often suffered from a lack of proper intelligence and a neglect of thorough reconnaissance, failings which often landed him in difficulties as at Fyvie, Dundee and Auldearn.[27] Finally, at Philiphaugh, away from the sheltering Highlands, these weaknesses ruined him and cost many of his brave Irish their lives.

His greatest failing was political naïvety. He could win Scotland by his sword but he could not hold it. He could shake Argyll, MacCailean Mor and decimate his Campbell kin, but he could not topple him.

Though often defeated, the government forces always rallied and yet Montrose, once beaten, found he had few friends. The Year of Miracles was an impossible adventure sustained by a heady tide of success; failure brought reality and reality meant defeat.

Montrose, at Perth, needed to link speedily with MacColla, who had blundered into Lochaber in Campbell country, with Argyll already moving against him. The fateful union occurred at Blair, where Montrose's timely arrival served to prevent a fracas between the Irish and his own Athollmen. MacColla by now had no more than 1100 men and the whole brigade barely numbered 2000. In August, whilst beginning the march south, Montrose was reinforced by 500 'bowmen' under the command of his brother-in-law, Drummond of Madderty. The epithet 'bowmen' may have been anachronistic and it appears likely that Drummond's men were, in fact, musketeers.

Tippermuir, 1 September 1644

On 1 September 1644 the marquis and his diminutive army were on the road to Perth. Whilst they were still some two hours distant, Lord Elcho, commanding the garrison, was preparing to stand and fight. His men, mostly raw levies from Angus, Fife and Tayside, were mustered at first light, reveille calling the untrained and wholly inexperienced foot to death or glory. Three miles west of the city, just short of the village of Tippermuir, Elcho made his dispositions: the foot, 3000 strong, stood with two bodies of horse, perhaps 800 troopers in all, guarding the flanks; his seven light field-pieces were unlimbered before the foot who stood six deep. Elcho himself commanded on the right, Murray of Gask the centre and Scott of Rossie the left. Fortified by further exhortations from the attendant hordes of ministers, the Covenanters waited.[28]

Heavily outnumbered, but otherwise undaunted, Montrose likewise divided his forces into three, stretching his line out to match the Covenanters' own front of, say, 1000 yards. Though his men stood only three ranks deep, he could not afford to be outflanked. On the right he placed his bowmen; MacColla took the centre and Montrose the left. Kilpont's 'bowmen', who were certainly Lowlanders and not Highlanders, may not, like Drummond's men, even have actually carried bows – more likely they were conventionally armed with musket and pike. Lord Kilpont's loyalty was open to question, which may explain his subsequent murder by a disgruntled subordinate. Montrose's own command on the right were mainly Athollmen, Robertsons and Stewarts.[29]

As was frequently the custom, an initial parley was attempted but the Covenanters contemptuously seized the royalist emissary with the promise of a hanging. The formalities dispensed with, the slaughter could now begin. Lord Drummond, on Elcho's left wing, led a commanded party of horse and foot, probably intended as skirmishers, to attack the royalist centre. MacColla sent forward a 'forlorn hope' of musketeers, who, experienced as they were, held their fire until it would have most effect. Drummond's troops pelted back to their own lines, much discomfited.[30]

Seizing the moment, Montrose ordered a general advance, the Irish discharging their single volley at virtually point-blank range and then advancing to the mêleé with pikes levelled and muskets clubbed. Accounts do differ and it may be that their superior fire had a decisive effect. A cavalry charge against Montrose's poorly armed Highlanders was met by a volley of stones, sufficient response to discourage the horse who were soon in full flight as the Covenanting army began to disintegrate.[31] Perth surrendered. The city's abundant clergy, amazed that the forces of righteousness should perform so poorly, deemed that the catastrophe must have been occasioned by 'the pleasure of God', punishing the faithful for their sins so that they could be worsted by 'a company of the worst men in the earth'.[32]

Aberdeen, 13 Sept 1664/Fyvie, 28 Oct 1664

The fate of Perth served to put the Committee of Aberdeen on their mettle; on 6 September they ordered the fencibles from Mearns, Aberdeenshire and Banffshire, together with the men of Moray, to assemble. Despite this comprehensive summons, the overall response was poor. Poorer still was the Committee's choice of Lord Balfour of Burleigh as commander; they would have been better served by Lord Gordon but mistrust blocked his appointment and denied the Covenanters his valuable support.

Meanwhile the royalists were moving northward from Dundee and, finding the Bridge of Dee, scene of the marquis's earlier triumph, once more barricaded, they moved up river to cross at Mills of Drum. On 11 September the army bivouacked on ground recently vacated by the Covenanting forces, who had withdrawn into the city.[33]

Montrose drew up his men on Willow Bank, lying a little to the south of How Burn and to the east of Hardgate. The royalist left was commanded by Colonel Hay, leading Nat Gordon's thirty horse and a hundred shot under a Captain Mortimer of O'Cahan's. The right was led by Sir William Rollo, who had with him a party of horse under Sir Thomas Ogilvy and a further commanded party of musketeers. Montrose himself had the centre with the three redoubtable Irish regiments, Laghtnan's flanked on the right by O'Cahan's and MacDonnell's on the left.

There is no surviving order of battle for the Covenanters, but their right seems to have been flanked by two troops of horse, the foot in the centre with the men of Fife on the left, hemmed by two further squadrons of horse. Lord Forbes's regiment was held in reserve.[34]

Hay began the fight when he stormed the sprawl of buildings at Justice Mills driving out the defenders but he, himself, was attacked in turn by lancers. His shot discouraged the Covenanters' horse who withdrew in some disorder. Forbes's regiment, masking their approach, were deployed for a potent counter-attack, which, if fully exploited, could have outflanked the whole royalist position. The stroke, when it came, was half-hearted and Hay, reinforced by a further commanded party of shot, held his ground.[35]

Montrose, apparently oblivious to the drama on his flank, ordered a general advance: a steady movement, regular volleys from the shot till it came to push of pike and swinging musket butt. For the Covenanters Forbes of Craigievar led a spirited

charge against O'Cahan's but the Irish opened ranks to let the
horse through and then loosed a volley at their backs. Men
and horses crashed to the ground and the gallant Forbes was
captured.[36]

The infantry fight lasted for well over an hour but O'Cahan
routed some of the Aberdeenshire militia and the royalists simply
rolled up the defenders' line; only the Fife men managed to withdraw in good order, the rest simply ran. No quarter was the order
and the victors carpeted the bloodied streets with dead. Though
the Covenanters had probably lost a mere handful in the fight,
the total dead numbered 500 or more whilst the royalists admitted to no more than seven fatalities, almost certainly an understatement, given the length of the battle and the Covenanters'
more effective use of artillery.

The sack of Aberdeen proved a short-lived diversion for
MacCailean Mor was already marching, thirsting for vengeance. With him he had at least two experienced regiments
under the earl of Lothian and Sir Mungo Campbell of Lawers,
together with several battalions from his native Argyll, mostly
Highlanders and Dalhousie's regiment of horse, his numbers
probably amounting to 4000 foot and just under 1000 horse.
He, therefore, enjoyed a significant advantage as Montrose was
soon short of MacColla and 500 Irish who departed to relieve
their comrades manning garrisons in the far west.[37]

On 27 October the marquis led his depleted force on a 15-mile
march from Huntly to the Castle of Fyvie, but his scouting and
reconnaissance were poor. Montrose had perhaps 1500 men in
all: 800–900 Irish, perhaps 200 Athollmen and the rest uncertain
recruits, mainly Gordons. The following morning, his picquets
woke him with the unpleasant news that Argyll was a bare two
hours' march away. The royalists' position, though not desperate, was scarcely favourable. They were so short of ammunition
that they had been obliged to melt down all the pewter they
could find in Dunfermline.[38]

Argyll was approaching along the line of the present A947,
having marched from Inverurie by Old Meldrum. Montrose

dismissed the idea of defending the castle itself, too canny to bottle himself up in the illusory safety of its walls. Instead he disposed his meagre forces to take best advantage of the available ground. The position was ideal for a defensive fight; the royalists had the River Ythan on their right and a patch of woodland on their left, deployed across high ground, while, facing west over the valley, their foot was protected by a brook which meandered over low ground before flowing into the river. Moreover the ascent was broken up by a series of stone dykes and natural outcrops, improved by frantic digging. Lying to the west of the stream, enclosed by castle and hill, was an area of dead ground rising to a low mound bisected by further dykes and earthen walls.[39]

Practically before a shot had been fired Montrose's small force was further reduced by the desertion of the Strathbogie men, which precipitated an early crisis when one of Argyll's regiments, probably Lothian's, battered their way into the lower enclosures, causing a number of royalist casualties. Montrose immediately ordered a counter-attack, led by O'Cahan's deputy, Lt-Colonel Donoghue O'Cahan; this appears to have been entirely successful, as the Covenanters withdrew.[40]

Argyll now had recourse to his cavalry, who were sent in largely unsupported. The royalists again fell back but this was now a mere ruse intended to draw the horse into an ambush. Montrose hoped to lure the Covenanters across the burn where the main body of the royalist foot were ready to pounce from the dead ground beyond. The scheme was spoilt when the Athollmen fired too soon, alerting Argyll's troopers to their peril. As the horse withdrew they were charged by the royalists, precipitating a rout.[41]

Increasingly frustrated, Argyll now launched a third attack involving both horse and foot, again to no avail, the royalist position being too strong. The affair spluttered on for another couple of days with both sides sniping at each other, but eventually on 30 October, having achieved very little, Argyll, by now short of provisions, deemed it expedient to withdraw.

Montrose, who though he could scarcely claim a victory, had at least avoided a defeat, was glad to let him go and slipped away northward towards Turriff.

As the royalists withdrew Argyll once again set off in pursuit and by virtue of dogged persistence began to get the upper hand. Short of supplies and short of recruits, Montrose was hunted from Gordon country, most of the Gordons preferring to make a separate peace with Argyll. The royalists, though unbeaten, were effectively on the run and desperately short of everything.

Any self-congratulation was to prove premature; at Blair Atholl, Montrose with his tired and hungry survivors was rejoined by MacColla, whose recruiting amongst the restless clan of the west had been fruitful. In addition to his own tried and tested regiment he brought in a further 5000, MacDonalds from Keppoch, Glengarry, Clanranald and the Isles, MacLeans from Morven and Mull, Stewarts of Appin and Farquharsons from Braemar. It was a roll call sufficient to depress any member of Clan Campbell and it was upon the hitherto inviolate and private domain of MacCailean Mor that the next blow was to fall.[42]

The Day of Clan Donald, Inverlochy, 2 Feb 1645

The royalists swept towards the Campbell heartland, down the length of Loch Tay past Crianlarich, driving through Glen Orchy and on by Loch Awe. Everywhere their progress was marked by burning thatch and the cries of men and beasts. The swiftness and savagery of the raid took the Campbells unawares and Argyll appeared utterly impotent. Inverary was sacked and torched.

Argyll felt it wise to slip quietly down Loch Fyne in his comfortable galley rather than share the degradation of his clan. He would not, however, forget.

Never had Clan Donald enjoyed themselves so heartily; the living symbol of Gaelic independence, they had watched as the Campbells eroded their ancient power and liberties.

Increasingly they looked backward rather than forward remembering the great days of the Lordship of the Isles when they acknowledged no power and justice save their own. Vengeance so long awaited was sweet and the wealth of Clan Campbell ample recompense.

Replete with loot, many Highlanders saw little need to continue in arms and began to drift homeward. Soon Montrose was down to fewer than 2000 men. Reaching Kilcumin, the royalists were preparing to march the length of the Great Glen and fall on Seaforth's levies mustering at Inverness. It was here that Montrose received disturbing intelligence. Argyll, having recovered his nerve and a degree of initiative, was at Inverlochy, an army at his back. It would be a safe assumption that his intentions towards the royalists were hostile to a degree.[43]

It was at this stage, while the Convenanting forces believed they had Montrose safe within a trap of his own making, that he determined on a spectacular gamble, a forced march over mountainous Highland terrain in the very depths of winter. The route took the royalists past Culachy and through Glen Roy, stumbling over the stone-girt lower reaches of Ben Nevis, enduring agonies of cold and fatigue. After passing a freezing night huddled on the slopes they emerged from the mist on the morning of 2 February 1645. Below them, unsuspecting, lay Argyll's forces.[44]

The Convenanters were, perhaps not unsurprisingly, confused by their opponents' manoeuvres. No one would expect Montrose's force to have been able to march 30 miles in 36 hours over some of the most inhospitable terrain in the British Isles and in the dead of winter. There was some ineffectual skirmishing between picquets, but at dawn on Candlemas Day, Sir Duncan Campbell of Auchinbreck rose, uncertain of his enemy's strength. Argyll, prudent as ever, remained on his galley but doubtless shared his commanders' dismay when the royal standard rose out of the mist and the pipers, coaxing frozen fingers, began the Cameron rant 'Sons of Dogs, come and we will give you flesh'.[45]

Montrose divided his trusted Irish into two divisions, MacColla taking the right, O'Cahan the left. With them marched

Highlanders from Glengarry, Glencoe, Atholl, Appin and Lochaber. Ogilvy's few threadbare horsemen clustered beneath the standard. Priests marched before the host, giving absolution to those who must fight and fall this day.[46]

Auchinbreck, with 3000 men, outnumbered the royalists by two to one and drew up his line facing their advance. His Lowland companies, seconded from Baillie's command, were assigned to the flanks. His Argyll militia and Campbells he placed in the centre with a screen of skirmishers before. Beneath the stout ramparts of Inverlochy Castle he hid a commanded party of shot, ready to enfilade the royalist charge.[47]

O'Cahan drove the Campbell skirmishers, commanded by Gillespie of Bingingead, back onto their main body. MacColla fell upon the left. The Lowland companies managed to loose off several wild volleys, but the advancing Irish again held their nerve to the last, blasting by salvée and closing with levelled pikes.[48]

The Lowland levies simply disintegrated; a single company made a desperate dash for the refuge of the castle but Ogilvy's horse fell upon them, Ogilvy himself receiving a mortal wound when a stray bullet smashed into his thigh. The Campbells were made of sterner stuff and, though soon surrounded, died fighting, Auchinbreck and a score of lairds falling around the standard. Swift and merciless as wolves, the Highlanders fell upon the fugitives, strewing the banks of Loch Linnhe and Loch Eil with dead. Argyll discreetly put out to sea whilst the shot, who had remained relatively secure behind the castle walls, laid down their arms.[49]

The royalists, as usual, admitted to few casualties but boasted the deaths of 1500 Covenanters, many of whom were Campbells. For the MacDonalds Inverlochy was a victory over their traditional foes. Montrose had been successful because he was able to exploit and divert a flood of Gaelic fury to the service of the king. But this did not create an army – Montrose and the clansmen were allies of convenience rather than conviction and such a flimsy alliance could never secure control of Scotland.

Auldearn, 9 May 1645

Having dealt with Argyll, Montrose marched his triumphant army back up the length of the Great Glen, past Inverness to Elgin. Whilst there he was reinforced by the arrival of 300 Grants and perhaps 200 horse led by Lord Gordon, who now seems to have felt it opportune to reassert his support for the king. The royalists then moved down the east coast once more and Aberdeen again enjoyed the pleasure of playing host. Brechin was torched, Dundee taken and pillaged. Whilst the army was thus pleasantly engaged they were very nearly trapped by Covenanting forces led by Hurry and Baillie, who between them commanded 3000 foot and 800 horse.[50]

Montrose had again demonstrated a lamentable failure of intelligence and reconnaissance in allowing himself to be so surprised. Undaunted, he now showed a superb grasp of tactics in extricating his disorganised forces, drawing Baillie towards Brechin and then slipping away into the hills, winning salvation from near disaster.[51]

By May the royalists were highly concerned about Hurry, who was proving far more energetic than previous Covenanting officers. Montrose knew that he needed to give battle before the enemy grew too strong and the two forces were soon skirmishing in the north-east as Hurry sought to regain Inverness and pick up further troops before assuming the offensive. Montrose again seems to have lacked sound intelligence. On the evening of 8 May the royalist army was encamped around the village of Auldearn some two miles from Nairn, their general proposing to push westward the following day towards Inverness, a bare 17 miles away.

On that same day, however, Hurry had himself picked up his awaited reinforcements outside the Highland capital; he could now field five regiments of foot: Loudon's, Lothian's, Lawer's, Findlater's and Buchanan's. These regulars, many of whom had fought at Marston Moor, were stiffened by local levies led by the Highland gentry. When fully mustered, his force comprised

3000 foot and about 300 horse. Hungry now for battle and for the glory attendant upon victory over the undefeated royalists, Hurry force-marched his troops eastward to Nairn, the columns plodding through the short spring night. His intentions, based upon sound intelligence, were to fall upon Montrose's army at Auldearn in a dawn attack.[52]

He very nearly succeeded. It is said that some of the shot, whilst cleaning their pieces, alerted the royalist vedettes who tumbled back to acquaint the marquis with the unwelcome report that his enemies were very nearly at his door. The village of Auldearn, soon to be dragged so savagely from rural obscurity, was little more than a ribbon of cottages running in a line southward from St Colm's Church; west of the village proper lay the remains of an old motte-and-bailey castle. The village was not, as some accounts suggest, located at the crest of a ridge, but on the westward incline.[53]

Montrose now deployed McColla's Irish along the flanks of a low rise lying west of the village, the Auldearn Burn meandering around its foot. Hurry drew up for battle at Kinneachie and, undaunted by the fact that his quarry now knew of his approach, sent Lawer's veteran foot regiment to test the Irish. He cannot have believed that MacColla's detachment represented the whole royalist force and held the bulk of his own men in check. Lawer's foot surged forward, exchanging volleys with the Irish, who appear, in this first clash, to have come off rather the worse. With Lawer's and Seaforth's men pushing hard, the royalists fell back in good order, taking up a secondary position amongst the straggling gardens and broken ground to the rear of the village. Though the Covenanters were held MacColla's own counter-attack foundered, his men stumbling and falling amidst the reeds and mosses. Though this abortive charge has been hailed as an example of MacColla's fatal recklessness it was probably prompted by necessity, his musketeers having run dangerously short of, or completely out of, ammunition. Reckless or not, Alistair fought as the paladins of old, his weighted broadsword doing fearful execution, and the fight raged on.[54]

By now Montrose was ready to commit the remainder of his forces and ease the pressure on MacColla. It is possible that he now deployed his reserves in a line running south from the village, the royalists now having taken the initiative with Aboyne's horse mounting a flank attack against Lawer's regiment. It may be that the foot were able to form up to meet the attack but more likely they were relying on a troop of Covenanting horse led by an officer named Drummond. Exactly what befell this unfortunate is uncertain, but his squadron, in complete disarray, blundered into the mass of foot still struggling with the tenacious Irish. Though Aboyne thundered amongst the now disordered ranks and certainly relieved the pressure on MacColla, neither Lawer's nor Seaforth's men were broken – they gave ground and withdrew but did not rout.[55]

However, as the Strathbogie men, forming Montrose's division, and having recovered their allegiance, swung into line, Lord Gordon's cavalry mounted their own spirited charge on Lawer's brigade. The Covenanting horse were chased off and the foot soon followed. The initiative had now passed to the royalists, who strove forward to attack the rump of Hurry's forces who, thus far, had not fired a shot. The Covenanters seem to have been taken by surprise with the remaining and unbloodied regiments not fully deployed. Lothian's and Loudon's foot clashed savagely with the Strathbogie men, a murderous exchange of fire before the pikes and clubbed muskets collided. The crescendo of battle rose to its savage climax, the royalists attacking with an almost demonic fury, which even veteran regiments could not withstand.[56]

The line broke in a great torrent of despair, the foot scrambling for safety, the royalists at their heels. Hurry, his dreams of glory rent in bloody tatters, succeeded in extricating the bulk of his horse and fled the field.

The butcher's bill was appallingly high: some 2000 Covenanters are said to have died either on the field or in the rout. Lawer's regiment alone lost its colonel, most of the officers and as many as 200 rank and file. Lothian's and Loudon's were likewise decimated.[57]

The unfortunate Major Drummond, who provided an ideal scapegoat for the disaster, was shot out of hand before the survivors stumbled into Inverness.[58] Meanwhile the royalists, whose casualties numbered possibly 200 or under, enjoyed the spoils of victory, a rich haul of abandoned muskets, pikes, ammunition, powder and provisions. Despite their success, Inverness was still too strong and the defenders, though doubtless dreadfully shaken, remained resolute and Montrose had to turn his battered victors eastward to meet a new threat in the shape of General Baillie.

Alford, 2 July 1645

Baillie's tenure as commander of the Covenanting forces was not a happy experience. The Committee of Estates interfered relentlessly in his decisions and hamstrung him at every move, whilst he was not sufficiently forceful to withstand their generally ill-advised intervention.

Montrose played cat-and-mouse with Baillie throughout June. The latter's army was weakened when he was obliged to trade 1200 of his regulars for a mere 400 of Lord Lindsay's raw levies. On 24 June at Keith, the marquis had caught up with his quarry but Baillie, advised of the royalist approach, drew up in an excellent defensive position, deterring any attack. On 1 July the royalists splashed across the Don and made camp at a place known, perhaps appropriately, as Gallows Hill, near the hamlet of Alford. Baillie was less negligent than his many critics have surmised and did not cross the Don at the Boat of Forbes, as has been suggested, but almost certainly downstream at Mountgarrie, some little distance from Alford.[59]

There has been some disagreement as to the sequence of events on that day, an uncertainty which appears to hinge on the exact location of the village of Alford in the mid seventeenth century, Alford itself being confused with Muir of Alford, which lies west of Gallows Hill.[60]

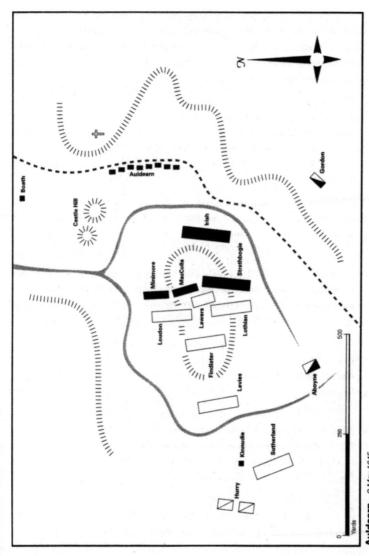

Auldearn · *9 May 1645*

Montrose guessed the Covenanting General was endeavouring to outflank him, though, in this, he probably overrated Baillie's initiative. At Mountgarrie Baillie could at least deploy in relative safety. With him he had six regiments of foot – those of Cassilis, Elcho, Lanark, Moray, Glencairn and Callendar – a probable total of some 1800 foot, some of whom, especially Cassilis's, were veterans, having done good service at Marston Moor and the rest, if less experienced, were certainly not raw recruits. For cavalry he had Balcarres's and Hackett's horse, with some Aberdeenshire levies, perhaps 300 in all. For once the royalists enjoyed superior numbers and, fearful of being outflanked, Baíllie stood his men in ranks three deep, the foot drawing up in the centre, Hackett's horse on the right flank, Balcarres's to the left.[61]

Montrose commanded a total of some 2000 foot and 200 horse, mainly Gordons, whom he divided on the flanks, Lord Gordon leading the right and Aboyne the left. In the centre stood the Strathbogie men together with a motley of Highlanders, referred to as 'Huntly's men' but including some Farquharsons and Badenoch men as well as Gordons and a MacDonald contingent. Laghtnan's bolstered the horse on the left, O'Cahan's and MacDonnell's their mounted comrades on the right. The redoubtable MacColla was again absent on a further recruiting mission.[62]

Baillie may well have wished to avoid battle. He knew the royalists were strong but the bulk of their army was concealed on the reverse slope. Balcarres's horse pushing forward may have precipitated the fight, and the general, seeing no alternative, committed the rest of his command.

It is said that Lord Gordon was so stung by the sight of a herd of cattle looted from Gordon territory and penned behind the Covenanting forces that he immediately charged upon Balcarres. This almost quicksilver onslaught discomfited Balcarres but his second and third squadrons, on coming up, were able to exert considerable pressure on the royalists and the fight raged fiercely till Laghtnan's foot weighed in, hamstringing horses and dirking fallen riders. This was too much for Balcarres's men, who fled. Whether

Left. Pictish stone, Aberlemno, depicting a battle scene (National Museums Scotland)

Below left. Bannockburn (Historic Scotland)

Below right. Reginaldus of Islay (National Museums Scotland)

Siege battery in action (Le Blond 1746) (Historic Scotland)

Building a bastion salient (Rüsensteen 1668) (Historic Scotland)

Above. Threave Castle
(Historic Scotland)

Left. Smailholm Tower
(Historic Scotland)

Greenlaw Stone, Kinkell Kirk, depicting an armoured Gilbert de Greenlaw, who fell at the Battle of Harlaw in 1411 – 'the only authentic contemporary memorial of the Battle of Harlaw' (W.D. Simpson). (Ian Shepherd)

James Graham, 1st Marquess of Montrose, attributed to William Dobson
(National Galleries of Scotland)

Bonnie Dundee (c.1649–1689) by David Paton (National Galleries of Scotland)

John Campbell, 2nd Duke of Argyll and Greenwich by William Aikman
(National Galleries of Scotland)

John, 6th Earl of Mar (1675–1732) by Godfrey Kneller
(National Galleries of Scotland)

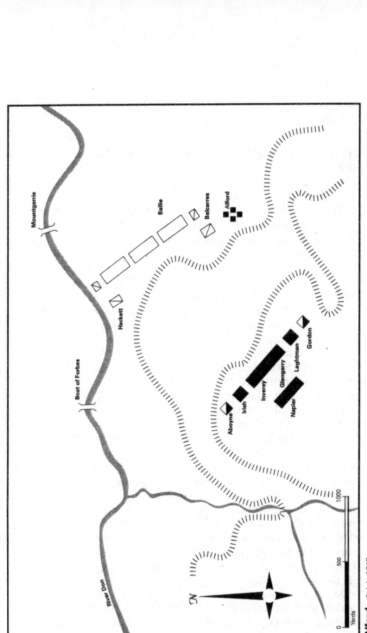

Alford · 2 July 1645

dismayed by the flight of their comrades or themselves disordered by a charge from Aboyne's horse, Hackett's men on the right were soon routed, leaving the foot horribly exposed on both flanks.[63]

The infantry battle had, until then, been undecided with Baillie's experienced foot contesting every foot of ground at push of pike, but now, assailed on both flanks and in the rear, they simply gave way. As always the rout and pursuit were terrible with little or no quarter being given. Cassilis's and Glencairn's regiments were reduced to no more than 100 men apiece and the rest badly mauled. In all nearly 1000 fell and Baillie's army, as a tactical formation, ceased to exist. For Montrose, Alford was another victory, though undoubtedly more dearly won than the royalists were prepared to admit.[64]

The most noted casualty on the royalist side was Lord Gordon, shot down as he led his victorious cavalry against Baillie's rear. His death was a great sadness to Montrose and vastly damaging to his cause. He would never enjoy such an affinity with Aboyne and his hold over the often fickle but vital Gordons was diminished.[65]

The Road to Kilsyth, 15 August 1645

However optimistic they might feel, it was by now impossible for the Committee to deny the seriousness of Montrose's rebellion. The royalists had broken out of the north-east, laid waste the loyal towns by Tayside and the east coast, decimated Clan Campbell and roundly thrashed every army sent against them.

With Baillie defeated the road to the Lowlands lay open. Montrose was rejoined by MacColla who had raised 1400 Highlanders and Athollmen. Aboyne was left to recruit in Gordon country while the marquis feinted against Hurry who, dispirited by his recent defeat and wearied by the Committee's ceaseless interference, sought to resign. Aboyne managed to raise some 800 foot and 400 horse, enabling Montrose to muster 4500 infantry and 500 cavalry, the largest force he was destined to command. In the course of the alarums and skirmishing of this period, a group of royalist camp followers, left foraging in Methven wood, were attacked by a party of Hurry's horse and casually butchered, an atrocity that would not be forgotten.[66]

One of Montrose's great talents was the ability to weld his disparate forces into an army, to reconcile the many prickly honours of his subordinates and their followers. Such charismatic leadership contrasted sadly with the opposing forces where Baillie was obeyed to 'work out his notice' whilst a replacement was sought from Ireland.

The Covenanting army marched from Stirling to Denny and then to Hollandbush Farm, a bare couple of miles from the royalists' position at Kilsyth. It cannot have been a happy march for the rank and file must have been aware of their officers' squabbling. Baillie, through awkwardness or caution, shied away from a confrontation, but Argyll, who now had many scores to settle, was spoiling for a fight. Baillie, doubtless, would have preferred to wait for the earl of Lanark who was bringing another 1500 men.

The classic account of the events which followed has the Covenanters deploying in a strong position overlooking the royalists. Baillie, at his most eloquent when seeking to divert the blame for the ensuing débâcle from himself, insisted that he wished to wait for Lanark but, once again, was overruled by Argyll and the other members, who insisted on a general movement to the right, purporting to outflank the royalists. In so doing they would expose their own flank to the enemy and thus invite an attack, virtually gifting the victory to Montrose.[67]

The reality is undoubtedly less simple for neither Baillie nor Argyll were complete fools, though they may have been completely at loggerheads. The army was indeed in a strong position, deployed on the reverse slope to the east of the high country lying between the present-day village of Banton and the A803 at Kelvinhead and though the position was inexpugnable it was equally impossible to advance directly, the ground being extremely rough and broken.[68]

Given this difficulty, Argyll's suggestion that the army should re-form on the hill to the right was not unreasonable. Baillie, inevitably, had reservations which he expressed as a fear that, should it come to a race for this eminence, the royalists might reach there first. One can hardly blame Argyll and the Committee men for being short of patience. Their unwilling Hector was being cautious in the extreme and was clearly seeking to avoid an encounter, at least until Lanark, whose whereabouts was uncertain, came up.

In the circumstances, the move to the right, bearing north-west to the hill crowned by the hamlets of Easter and Wester Auchinrivoch was a highly sensible option. It allowed the army to at least maintain contact with the royalists, block any move to the north or, if it came to a fight, at least engage on ground which was not entirely unfavourable.

Now committed, Baillie sent a commanded body of shot to race ahead and secure the summit, the general himself with Balcarres and the horse trotted behind. This manoeuvre involved the entire army in an echelon to the right, thus converting line into column, a movement invisible to the royalists as the bulk of the Covenanting army remained concealed by the angle of the slope.[69]

Montrose was not the man to stand idly by whilst the foe were at hand and the decision to stand and fight had already been made. Initially the royalists, judging their enemies' line of march, may have drawn up facing to the south or south-east. Baillie's manoeuvring, undetected though probably guessed at, necessitated a sharp 90-degree turn to face north-east.[70]

Baillie's disunited command probably comprised 3000–3500 foot in five regiments – Argyll's depleted since the carnage at Inverlochy, the earl of Crawford's, Lindsay's, Colonel Robert Home's and the earl of Lauderdale's – together with a motley of survivors from regiments too badly mauled to muster under their own colours. The horse were even more depleted; Balcarres's and Hackett's – both savaged at Alford, could barely scrape together 300 troopers between them – divided on the day into two squadrons, one of pistoleers, another of lancers. Trudging behind the horse came Lauderdale's then Argyll's, Crawford's, Lindsay's and the reformadoes – the latter two, in all probability, flanking Baillie's three raw battalions of Fife levies, intended as a reserve.[71]

Facing them Montrose had his magnificent, but much depleted, Irish – Laghtnan's, O'Cahan's and MacDonnell's – his hardy clansmen may have numbered 1400 with a further 200 Athollmen and the Strathbogie regiment, perhaps 3000 foot in total. With the addition of the Gordons he undoubtedly had a distinct superiority in cavalry, some 500–600 riders. The exact deployment of the royalists remains uncertain. Baillie indicates that the Highlanders, led by MacColla, stood to the fore with the Irish and Gordons behind.[72]

Almost from the start Baillie's plan, such as it was, began progressively to come unstuck. Haldane and his commanded musketeers turned aside from their immediate objective to engage a body of Highlanders slipping into the enclosures around Auchinvalley. Haldane may have felt obliged to respond to this threat but the exchange drew in, first the Glengarry men and then MacColla and the rest of the clansmen. Baillie, as usual, was quick to heap blame on Haldane for exercising a surfeit of initiative, though it may well be that Baillie's officers, judging their commander's sour mood, no longer reposed any degree of confidence in his ability and were prepared to react according to their own judgement.

Baillie, undoubtedly, was incensed by what he regarded as Haldane's flagrant disobedience. He was equally frustrated in that most of his regiments plodding up the reverse slope were not in a position to attack. Worse was to come: Home's regiment, the strongest of the Covenanters' battalions and veterans of the Irish war, now launched a precipitate attack of their own, surging forward to relieve Haldane's outnumbered shot.[73]

The Covenanters had now split into three bodies, the first, comprising some 1600 foot, were by now hotly engaged with MacColla's clansmen amongst the confusion of the Auchinvalley enclosures and more or less under Baillie's direct command. Behind them were the remainder of the regular infantry, together with Baillie's horse, whilst behind them, probably to the left, stood the Fife levies. The situation was by no means critical, however, for MacColla's swift-footed Highlanders were rebuked by the narrow enclosures and galled by the musketeers' fire.[74]

Balcarres, in the meantime, was in some difficulties. Strung out on the march, he was struck by a spirited charge from a body of Gordon horse and forced back upon his own foot battalions, who, however, held firm and the small body of royalists were soon in considerable difficulties. Aboyne, seeing his comrade's plight, galloped to the rescue. Despite enfilading fire from Home's regiment, the Gordons fought hard, yet Balcarres still managed to hold his own. The decisive moment arrived when Nat Gordon and the earl of Airlie led the bulk of the royalist cavalry into the fight.[75] The refreshed Gordons proved invincible. Balcarres was swept from the field, his reeling horsemen colliding with their own infantry, spreading panic.

At the same moment as the royalist horse charged to victory MacColla steeled his clansmen for a renewed assault, the Highlanders leaping the dykes and coming to grips with Baillie's regiment. Quite suddenly it was over. The Covenanters, unnerved by the determined resolution of the Highlanders, gave way, their rout completed as Airlie's victorious horse joined in the assault.[76]

Kilsyth was a disaster, with Baillie's army utterly defeated. The usual slaughter of fugitives did not take place as several regiments probably succeeded in retiring, more or less in good order and took final refuge behind Stirling's unassailable walls.

The battle made Montrose military master of Scotland. His seemingly quixotic adventure had become a reality, at least in terms of armed conflict. The victory, none-the-less, exposed the political weakness of the royalist cause. By supreme irony, Montrose in his hour of triumph was more isolated than ever. And the king needed him. Charles's Oxford army, the flower of his hopes, had been crushed at Naseby – Fairfax, Cromwell and the 'New Noddle' as the Cavaliers derided Parliament's 'New

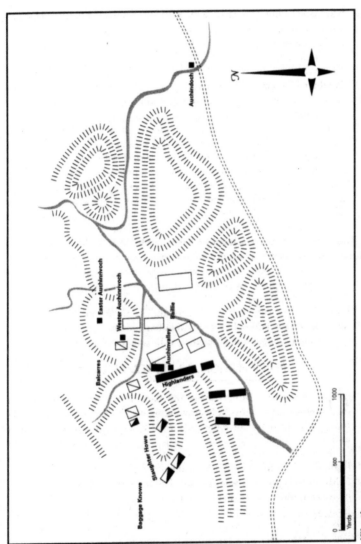

Kilsyth · 15 August 1645

Model' army, had won a massive victory. Retreating more and more into the twilight world of pious hopes the king placed increasing reliance on Montrose and on the great army he was to bring from north of the border.

Replete with loot and glory, with their dead to mourn, the clansmen once again slipped away. New recruits were slow to come in and Montrose, separated from MacColla who had returned to the west, now looked to the Scottish Borders and its turbulent gentry to swell his diminishing ranks. In these unfamiliar hills his intelligence system, always faulty, failed him altogether, with fatal results.

Philiphaugh, 13 September 1645

On 7 September Montrose met the marquis of Douglas at Galashiels and was greeted by the heartening sight of 1000 Border horse ready to accept his orders. These men, descendants of the tough mosstroopers and reivers of Elizabeth's reign, were desperately needed as the royalists could barely muster 500 foot and 100 horse. Despite this auspicious beginning the remaining Border magnates proved less enthusiastic.

Montrose's position was delicate. Though ruler of Scotland in name, he was painfully aware that David Leslie commanded a veteran army in England and that his political support in the vital Lowlands was minimal. Should Leslie return, Montrose could be in severe difficulties. Leslie was a commander of a far different stamp from those Montrose had previously encountered and, without exception, defeated. A hard-bitten professional, he had crossed the Border on 6 September with four regiments of foot and six of horse. He was undeterred by Montrose's string of victories and anxious to come to grips. Unlike the royalists he seems to have benefited from a more than adequate intelligence system and, upon hearing that Montrose was across the Border, turned to seek a confrontation, spurring ahead with his cavalry.[77]

By 12 September, the royalists had reached Selkirk and encamped on the banks of the Ettrick Water at Philiphaugh.

Whether seduced by their previous successes or grossly negligent, few picquets were posted – the combination of complacency and inefficiency ensured that this time there would be no reprieve.

Leslie's force consisted almost entirely of cavalry; three of his regiments – the earl of Leven's, David Leslie's and John Middleton's – were well up to strength and all of them together with Lord Kirkcudbright's and Lord Montgomery's regiments were veterans of the war in England. In Scotland he had received drafts from two other units bringing his strength up to a shade under 3000 horse, his command being further swelled by some dragoons and around 700 foot.[78]

Montrose's intelligence was lamentable, his patrols failed to discover so large a body of the enemy even as they advanced down the valley of the Ettrick. A few miles north of Selkirk an advance guard under a certain Charteris of Amisfield was surprised and either taken or routed. The battle began to splutter into life at dawn on the 13th but did not really begin before 10.00 a.m. By this time the marquis was finally alerted to his imminent peril by the breathless arrival of a Captain Blackadder.[79]

Although the odds were unfortunate, the royalists at least had the advantage of a strong position. Flanked on the left by a deep and miry ditch, they were deployed in a series of enclosures whilst, between the infantry and the river, Montrose's few remaining horsemen were drawn up under Lord Ogilvy and Nat Gordon. Leslie, advancing inexorably down the valley, sent a strong contingent splashing through the Ettrick to beat up the town, whilst he himself led the remaining squadron around the base of Lingle Hill, contemptuously driving in the royalist skirmishers.

For a while the royalist horse managed to hold their ground, beating back two initial charges. In so doing, however, they became hopelessly over-extended, crossing the Philiphaugh Burn and being unable to return. Spurring on with the courage of desperation, Ogilvy, Gordon and a few survivors hacked a path through the Covenanters and galloped clear. Their loss was fatal to Montrose as the whole of his left flank between the enclosures and the river now lay open.[80]

Leslie charged at the head of his men, smashing against the royalist foot who, as always, fought doggedly, but the issue was never really in doubt. The body of horse under Colonel Agnew which had been ransacking Selkirk, sweeping clear of the town, cannoned into the flank and rear of the few remaining royalist cavalry, who were simply overwhelmed.[81]

The foot were still fighting for their lives but breaking up under the fury of the onslaught and sheer weight of numbers. Colonel Stewart, the Adjutant-General, managed briefly to rally a few diehards at Philiphaugh Farm but, under renewed assault, surrendered on terms. Montrose, who had fought like a demon, was virtually dragged from the stricken field by his surviving officers and escaped on horseback.

Though the battle was over, the slaughter was not. Leslie gave way to the exhortations of the inevitable coven of ministers who were anxious that the Lord's work be seen to be done. By the Lord's work they meant the systematic massacre of prisoners who were marched to nearby Newark Castle and summarily shot in batches lined up against the ancient barmkin. (The bullet marks are still discernible.) In order to conserve valuable ammunition, the women and children were flung into the river and held under with lances till all were drowned. Only the three officers – Stewart, Laghtnan and O'Cahan – were spared.[82]

Montrose attempted to rally the survivors and those who had earlier fled at Peebles and with a battered and depleted band once again made for the secure fastness of the Highlands. For the rest of that year and into the next the indomitable marquis strove to raise another army but his cause, like the king's, was lost. In May 1646 Charles, conceding defeat, surrendered his person into the hands of his Scottish foes at Newark, sending his last royal command to his faithful vassal 'skulking in the heather' to lay down his arms and shift for himself. Montrose escaped to exile on the Continent.

The year of miracles was over.

Hamilton's Folly

As the Scots army began the long march to the Border, away from the beleaguered walls of Newark which had capitulated at the royal command, relations between the Committee and the English Parliament were becoming increasingly strained. At best a marriage of convenience born of desperate courtship, the alliance had no real foundation.

In creating the New Model Army, Parliament had fashioned a war-winning tool but in so doing created a monster which increasingly threatened to devour the parent. Riddled with radical sectaries, the army was becoming alarmingly vociferous and though Fairfax, its Commander-in-Chief, shunned political involvement, his General of Horse, Oliver Cromwell, did not.

The king was a valuable piece on the board and the Scots were only prepared to sell his person to Parliament on condition they received the first £400,000 of the promised £2,000,000. As usual the king was his own worst enemy, trying to play the Committee along but steadfastly refusing to sign the Covenant. On the streets of Edinburgh and other Scottish cities the worth of that document was wearing thin. Rampant bigotry and intolerance, an almost deliberate cruelty spiced with fanatical witch-hunts, had sapped popular enthusiasm and folk now muttered against the ministers' rantings.[83]

Whilst a prisoner of the New Model Army and ostensibly secure on the Isle of Wight, Charles, in the closing days of 1647, met with three Scots commissioners and came with them to a compromise or 'engagement' whereby Charles, in return for pushing Presbyterianism down English throats, would be supported by Scottish arms. It is doubtful if the king, clutching at straws, and conspiring more zealously than ever towards his own downfall, seriously intended to keep his side of the bargain but the pact gave credence to a resurgent royalist party known as the 'Engagers'.[84] Hamilton, as spokesman and leader, was able to sway the Estates when the members met the next year, and, as an ultimatum was ignored, found himself leading an army southward, over the Border, with the unlikely objective of restoring Charles to his throne.

Hamilton dragged his blundering force down the west side of England. His numbers, originally 6000 foot and 3000 horse, were swollen by a further draft of 7000 foot and a contingent of northern English gentry some 3500 strong led by the irrepressible cavalier, Sir Marmaduke Langdale. An ineffectual commander at best, Hamilton was soon hopelessly out of his depth, his intelligence patchy, his lines of communication over-extended. He ignored warnings from the experienced Langdale who discovered that General Lambert, in falling back, was simply feigning retreat, drawing the Scots deeper into Lancashire and into confusion, whilst Cromwell gathered his forces for the inevitable counter-stroke.[85]

On 17 August the blow fell, the New Model confronting Langdale and Scottish foot on Ribbleton Moor. There were sporadic and savage encounters over the soft moorland and amidst the stone dykes, but the relentless pressure broke Langdale's northern horse and the Scots, now in full retreat, fell back across Preston Bridge to put the Ribble between them and the New Model Army. Cromwell was not deterred and, retaining the initiative, stormed the bridge. By the end of the day 500 Scots were dead, wounded or captive.[86]

The remnants of the foot, still in some order, but without any semblance of higher command, marched north seeking to join with their own cavalry, but the horse were themselves soon mauled by Cromwell's troopers and the invading army steadily collapsed. Hamilton fled, taking the remains of the cavalry with him; the foot, now totally isolated, made a final stand at Warrington before laying down their arms.[87] The battle was over and the Scots utterly defeated. Lambert was left to mop up any stragglers and netted the unfortunate Hamilton at Uttoxeter. England had, by now, endured years of internecine strife and the new breed of general – men such as Cromwell, Lambert and even the chivalrous Fairfax – no longer considered war a gentlemanly pastime, to be ritualised by the courtesy normally shown towards a defeated foe. Hamilton's next and final journey was to the block.

Argyll, never one to despair at an opponent's ruin, took the opportunity to resume the reins of power and oust the Engagers, hopelessly discredited by the Preston débâcle. The duke found an unexpected ally in the shape of Cromwell himself, heartily sick of the war and looking for bedfellows north of the Border. This unlikely entente, born of opportunism, did not thrive. England was moving too far and too fast in a radical direction and when Charles made his final public appearance on the scaffold at Whitehall on 30 January 1649 the Scots were appalled. The Estates promptly hailed the exiled Stewart heir as Charles II.[88]

The young king proved a difficult negotiator, though he needed Scottish broadswords to carry him to Westminster. He refused the Covenant, wisely perhaps, for too fervent an embrace would have alienated English royalists. Cynical and ruthless, he was prepared to allow his father's unfailing champion, Montrose, to mount a fresh expedition to secure the northern kingdom by force of arms.

Ardvreck: The Deadly Refuge

On the northern shores of Loch Assynt in Sutherland a slender spur of rock juts out from the shore to form a miniature peninsula. The narrow waters are hemmed in on all sides; Bein Gharbh and Canisp to the south, Ben Mor Assynt and the Inchnadamph forest to the north and west. A solitary spire of masonry, showing the remains of a corner turret or bartizan, crowns a ruin of tumbled stones and half-filled basement chambers. This fallen keep is called Ardvreck – within its now shattered walls was enacted the final drama in the life of James Graham, marquis of Montrose.

It was five years after the catastrophe at Philiphaugh when he came to the castle by the water's edge, but he was again defeated and again in flight. Ardvreck must have appeared as a veritable oasis in the harsh glens of Sutherland, all the more so as he knew it was to be the demesne of Neil Macleod of Assynt, Seaforth's man and an ally who had been out with him earlier at the abortive siege of Inverness. He was greeted at the door by the laird's young wife, who had earlier welcomed his comrade Major Sinclair, whose case was little better than his own. The fugitives were taken down to the same tumbled basement visible today and there were fed and rested, like cattle before the slaughter.

Little is known of Neil Macleod of Assynt or of his wife who, as the legend relates, acted the part of Lady Macbeth, playing upon her husband's weaker nature and obvious greed. It seems Macleod's finances were none too healthy and the reward money of £25,000 was a huge temptation, fit ransom for a king by the standards of the day. It was the lady of the house who apparently had the thankless task of balancing the accounts and swiftly saw the monetary worth of her guests.

Some say in the laird's defence that he met the fleeing royalists on the high moors and arrested both upon the spot before any duty of hospitality could be laid upon him. Macleod's defenders are very much in the minority, however, and there can be no doubt that he harboured Montrose and Sinclair for just as long as it took his ghillie to ride to Tain and summon troops to effect the capture. Finding himself betrayed, it is said the marquis begged Macleod to kill him rather than let him be taken alive but Macleod refused, doubtless unwilling to damage so valuable a catch.

This sad, treacherous end to Montrose's last campaign was a far cry from its noble beginning. He had first made landfall in Orkney with 500 Danish troops he had brought from exile, soon to be supplemented by a levy of 1000 Orcadians, willing recruits but totally untrained in war. He had no more than 50 cavalry, gentlemen volunteers. The opening moves of the campaign of 1650 involved the deployment of a flying column in a swift dash across the Pentland Firth to seize the strategically important Ord of Caithness, some five miles from the coast, but whose tenure by the Covenanters would have constituted a major threat.[89]

Once the road ahead was secured, a flotilla of fishing craft conveyed the bulk of the army to the mainland shore. The infantry were given a black standard whereon was shown the bleeding head of Charles I with the motto *Deo et victicibus armis*; the cavalry also bore a dark banner with three pairs of clasped hands holding drawn swords and the words *Quo spietas, virtus et honor fecit amicos*.[90] The marquis had his own personal standard of white damask that held two peaks and a gorge below with a lion poised to leap the void; *Nil medium*[91] was the simple motto.

Montrose's intelligence, or wishful thinking, indicated that the country was tired of the harsh rule of the Kirk and of his old enemy Argyll. The once formidable army of the Solemn League and Covenant had been smashed at Preston two years before. To a man of Montrose's romantic zeal, the time seemed ripe for another year of miracles. He was, alas, deluded, caught in the deadly paradox that only the support of the Lowlands could guarantee a restoration, whilst only the swords of the Highlanders could win the fight. The Lowlanders' hatred of their Highland contemporaries by far exceeded any degree of loyalty to the exiled House of Stewart.

Even the amount of support the clans would give had been exaggerated and the scant welcome his little army received at Thurso must have sounded warning bells amongst Montrose's officers. Enmeshed in his own quixotic vision, the marquis remained undaunted by the fact that Sutherland and the far north had very little to offer him; it seems he was planning to move towards Inverness, where he hoped to draw men from the MacKenzies. In fact, he would probably have done better to march directly into Badenoch in Inverness-shire, in Aberdeenshire or Perthshire, where he could operate a guerilla war on ground he knew intimately; throughout this, his last campaign, he was never to demonstrate the *élan* that had so marked his generalship before.[92]

Two hundred men, drawn from his slender forces, were left in the far north, whilst the remainder were led south to besiege Dunbeath Castle, which consumed a further 100 as a garrison, when it fell. Montrose now found that all of the holds around the Dornoch Firth were garrisoned against him, forcing a move inland, past Lairg where a few Scottish reinforcements joined him from Tongue. From here he moved south-west, fording the Oykel at Rosehall and pushing down river towards the Kyle of Sutherland.

On 25 April he called a halt and the army dug in around the hill at Carbisdale, a good defensive site whose left flank was protected by the Kyle, the right and rear by the steep incline. These natural advantages were strengthened by a line of trenches to protect the front. Until now the campaign had achieved but little, fruitless sieges and precious men frittered away in useless garrisons. Evidence would suggest that the elements of his small army were all equally unhappy, the fierce, barren terrain was unnervingly alien to the Danes and the inexperienced Orcadians were becoming increasingly restless the further they moved away from their island home, which virtually none had left before.[93]

Montrose was waiting at Carbisdale for reinforcements to come in from the royalist clans and in so doing had passed the initiative to his enemies. It was a bitter irony that 400 potential allies from the Rosses and Munros had fallen in with a body of Covenanting troops and, with a practised eye for the main chance, had thrown in with them, even though they had been active in the royalist cause only the year before.

The Covenanters in question were an experienced cavalry unit under the command of Colonel Strachan, who had been ordered, together with Hackett's, to harry Montrose in Sutherland, whilst Leslie dragged slow-moving conscript infantry up from the south. Strachan was a vitriolic and bigoted officer but extremely bold and capable, one who was determined to fight this war his own way in spite of superior orders and who was not prepared to wait for lumbering columns of foot. When he met Hackett at Tain his force included Ker's regiment and a troop of musketeers from Lawlers, a total still of only 156 men, less than a fifth of Montrose's army, but what the Covenanters lacked in numbers they made up for in experience.

With his new and dubious allies 'scouting' in the van, Strachan's force approached Carbisdale at around 3.00 p.m. on 27 April. Once his skirmishers had reported the strength and disposition of the royalists he swiftly realised that a frontal attack would be futile and that his only hope lay in drawing the enemy onto lower ground, where he could exploit his superiority in cavalry. The Rosses and the Munros, meanwhile, had prudently withdrawn to a neutral eminence overlooking the Firth, there to await the outcome. Strachan now halted his horsemen in thick cover some four miles short of the royalist camp and sent a single troop forward as bait.[94]

Montrose proceeded to behave in a singularly rash manner. Though assured by his own Munro scouts that this single troop cantering into view was the sole Covenanting force in the area, he first sent Major Lisle's troop forward to drive them back and then struck camp and advanced his whole brigade. No one has satisfactorily explained why so experienced a commander should abandon a strong position on such flimsy provocation. Had he sensed that a stronger force was in the offing? His scouts were utterly unreliable and he may have felt it unwise to rely upon their intelligence. Some have suggested that he was only intending a show of force to impress the dithering clansmen.

No sooner had the royalists moved than Strachan cantered his main body across the Carron to halt again in thick cover. Meanwhile his vanguard was falling back before Lisle and his 50 troopers. Holding his men in check until the last moment, Strachan launched his entire command into the attack, spurring forward in a classic cavalry charge, stirrup to stirrup, broadswords flashing in the pale sunlight. Major Lisle and his stunned volunteers were instantly overwhelmed. Most died, the few survivors bolted back towards the illusory safety of the main body. The sudden shock of this terrible onslaught proved too much for the raw Orcadian levies who instantly broke and fled, flinging themselves into the waters of the Firth, pursued by the hacking, merciless blades of the Covenanters. The rout finally decided the loyalty of the wavering clansmen who now pounced on these hapless fugitives, slaughtering at will.[95]

Montrose, deserted by his legendary genius, reeled, impotent, as his tiny army was decimated around him. The Danes managed to hold formation, retiring in good order to a small wood Montrose is said to have marked earlier in the advance as a possible line of defence. Rattled and demoralised by the wreck of their erstwhile comrades, they swiftly lost heart and capitulated in droves. The marquis and his bodyguard fought with reckless valour, his horse was shot from under him, he and most of his surviving officers wounded. A fresh mount and a desperate spurt took him and a handful from the carnage – he was free, wounded and ruined. Hundreds of his followers were killed, 61 officers and 386 men were taken, his cause was finished. The Covenanters had lost one man only and he had died in the savage pursuit through the Firth.[96]

It would appear that Montrose's first thought was to re-join the garrison at Thurso but the exhausted and wounded men swiftly became lost in the wilderness of Strath Oykel. Their horses foundered and at least one succumbed to exposure. Pain, hunger and the bitter cold of the harsh mountains weakened them further; they separated and Montrose struggled on alone. Some time on 29 April he reached an isolated shieling near Loch Urigill (probably not far from the present Altnacealgach Hotel), some eight miles south of Loch Assynt. Here he was fed and sheltered, but forced to hide when a patrol appeared. Strachan had won a resounding victory, but his triumph meant nothing until he had captured Montrose. Always the true child of chivalry, the marquis had refused to hazard his humble hosts yet further and stumbled on until at last he sighted the lonely keep at Ardvreck.

The treatment of the captured Montrose by the vengeful Covenanters and his subsequent degradation are as infamous as the steadfast courage and dignity with which he bore them. The crowning irony of the whole sorry episode was that on 1 May Charles had signed a draft of the Treaty of Breda with Argyll's commissioners; he also agreed to sign the Covenant and enforce the rule of the Kirk in England. It would appear that Sir William Fleming was about to leave for Sutherland to halt Montrose's operations. The captive marquis was an embarrassment all round and was thus to be dumped as soon as possible.[97]

When he was, at length, arraigned before the Estates, a public letter from his Sovereign ordering him to disband his troops was already in the members' hands. A further letter of unproven provenance, but purported to be from the same source, was also in circulation; in this Charles affirmed '. . . he was heartily sorry that James Graham had invaded the Kingdom, and how he had discharged him from doing the same, and earnestly desired the Estates of Parliament to do him that justice as not to believe that he was accessory to the said invasion in the least degree'.[98] Such was the reward for loyalty to the House of Stewart.

The inevitable sentence was death and in the most horrible manner; he was to be hanged upon a gibbet with a Wishart's *History* and his own Declaration tied round his neck and to hang three hours thereafter in view of the people; then beheaded and quartered, his head to be fixed at the Prison House of Edinburgh, and his legs and arms to be fixed at the ports (town gates) of the towns of Stirling, Glasgow, Perth and Aberdeen.

On 23 June Charles landed in Scotland. When the king rode into the Scottish capital, his route passed up Canongate and beneath the towers of the Tolbooth where the skull of his most faithful servant was still affixed.

Road to Dunbar, 1650

With Montrose callously abandoned and speedily forgotten, Charles could concentrate upon more pressing matters; particularly pressing was Cromwell who, in July, had crossed the Border with a force of 16,000 men, supported by the fleet cruising the east coast.

It is probable that the Lord Protector, though resigned to further conflict, would have preferred to negotiate; his excellent intelligence network would have advised him that the alliance between the Stewart prince and the Estates was paper thin and hedged about by mutual distrust – Charles would not submit to the Covenant and doubtless never viewed his northern kingdom as anything other than a stepping stone on the road south.

'I beseech you in the bowels of Christ think it possible you may be mistaken,' he entreated, but to no avail – the Estates favoured a resort to arms. Leven was judged too enfeebled by age and the baton passed to David Leslie – the army he was to command as plagued with religious counsellors as Baillie's ill-fated command was saddled with politicians.[99]

Recruitment was now to be determined by religious rather than military qualifications and those falling below the exacting standards set were not welcome – existing formations were purged of 'malignants'. It was not an auspicious start; the ministers, blinded by their own brand of hysteria, looked more to the Devil than to Cromwell.

In spite of this, Leslie handled the opening stages of the campaign with panache. The Lord Protector was repulsed at Leith and seeking to secure Queensferry was blocked by the Scots, strongly posted on Corstorphine Hill. Frustrated and with his army becoming increasingly enfeebled through hunger and sickness, he retired on Dunbar.[100]

Cromwell had little cause for joy: his own army comprised no more than 7500 foot and half as many horse. The men were tired, hungry, demoralised and in many cases weakened by sickness. Cautious and with reason to be satisfied with the result of his Fabian tactics, Leslie drew up his army on Doon Hill, the last outrider of the Lammermuirs before the ground melts into the coastal plain. His position was virtually impregnable. He knew that the wounded tiger is most dangerous when at bay and, left to his own instincts, would probably have been happy to see Cromwell's depleted force taken off by the fleet, in itself nearly as humiliating as an outright defeat.

Leslie's spiritual and political advisers were not content. The enemy must be driven from Canaan by the swords of the righteous. Giving way, the Scots commander abandoned his position of strength and descended to the lower levels, from where on the morning of 3 September he could launch his attack.[101]

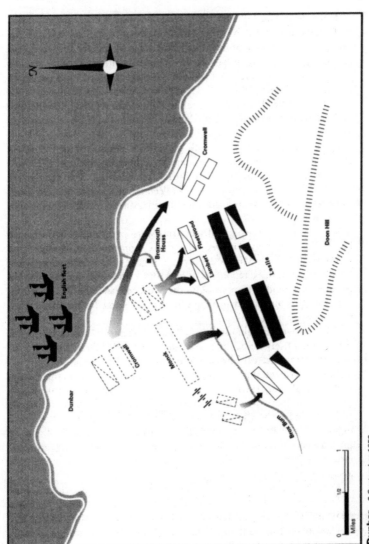

Dunbar · 3 September 1650

Miles

0   1/2   1

English fleet

Dunbar

Cromwell

Monck

Broxmouth House

Fleetwood

Lambert

Cromwell

Leslie

Broad Burn

Doon Hill

N

The night was wild and stormy. Unseasonal rain lashed the Covenanters, who, for the most part, were without the luxury of canvas and such few snug billets as may be found were quickly appropriated by officers. By 4.00 a.m. an uncertain dawn was filtering through the rainclouds. Cromwell, at his most lethal when seemingly cornered, had already spotted the fatal flaw in the Scots disposition. Though ideal as a springboard for attack, the position was too cramped for a sustained defence. Accordingly, it was the Lord Protector who now planned to take the offensive, the greatest gamble of his military career and ultimately the most successful. A council of war held at Broxmouth House seconded his plan.[102]

Leslie had positioned the bulk of his foot regiments on the lower slopes of Doon Hill along a frontage stretching inland from the coast with the ravine cut by the Brox Burn directly ahead. The horse were jammed into a relative bottleneck between the coast road leading south to Berwick and the shore. The guns were leaguered towards the base of the spur.[103]

Before 6.00 a.m. the New Model Army was on the move. In the centre Lambert and Fleetwood moved off with six regiments of horse supported by the English guns. Monck deployed a brigade of foot in support while Cromwell, with three regiments of foot under Pride and one of horse led by himself, intended to pounce on the Scots restricted flank, advancing over the Brox Burn and smashing into Leslie's cavalry crammed onto the narrow ground above.

The Scots were caught totally unprepared, regiments mustered beneath the ranting of sergeants, officers dashed from their billets. Leslie frantically sought to order his lines, battle was joined.[104]

Lambert crossed the stream unopposed and formed up on the eastern side. His first charge struck home into the still disordered Scottish horse, but their numbers saved them from rout. Monck with the foot brigade closed up on Lambert's right, but for all the unexpected fury of the attack the defenders held firm. Cromwell with this single regiment had crossed the burn near Broxmouth House and supported by Pride's brigade drove into the gap between Lambert and Monck who now renewed their own assault with grim determination.[105]

After desperate fighting the English horse finally punched a hole in the right of the line. Cromwell, repulsed several times, led one final, irresistible charge against Leslie's cavalry which thundered like the wrath of God and drove the Scots disastrously into the packed ranks of their own foot. The sun, breaking through the thinning cloud, glinted on harness and steel. Many Scots found the damp night had spoiled their powder and their matchlocks refused to discharge.[106] Only two regiments, armed with the superior snaphaunce, gave effective fire.

Thereafter, it was pure slaughter. As their right wing crumpled, the Scots line was rolled up and defeated in detail. Their position, jammed between the steep-sided burn to the front and the encroaching slope behind them, became a perfect trap, a killing ground, and the English plied their trade in earnest. By mid morning it was all over; 3000 Scots lay piled upon the bloody ground and a further 10,000 had laid down their arms.[107]

By heeding the pernicious counsels of his too many advisers, Leslie had unwittingly presented Cromwell with his most astute tactical victory. After the battle the English, now freed from any fear of ignominious evacuation, marched on the capital and consolidated their grip on the Lowlands. In the Assembly, however, the moderate Presbyterians and the royalists united in their support for Charles who was duly enthroned at Scone, the ancient seat of Scottish Kingship, on 1 January 1651.[108]

Cromwell remained unimpressed. Edinburgh Castle fell to him, though Leslie still defied him from the walls of Stirling. A detached command under the energetic Lambert won a sharp fight at Pitreavie near Inverkeithing and Cromwell descended on Perth. The king, his flank thus exposed, resorted to a bold stategy of his own, to march directly into England and raise the royal standard once again, the banner beneath which so many had already fallen.

The road south proved disappointingly bare of recruits and the army was relentlessly harried by Lambert and Major-General Harrison. By 22 August Charles was at Worcester, his

16,000 hemmed in by 28,000 of the New Model Army. Six days later Lambert seized the vital Severn crossing at Upton Bridge. Cromwell could now push towards the beleaguered city along both banks of the river. Charles met the Lord Protector's double thrust with some panache, but the veteran English proved invincible. With the royalist horse routed and in flight, Charles galloped for safety and renewed exile, whilst his abandoned foot surrendered.[109]

In Scotland Stirling finally fell to Monck who neatly captured the Committee of Estates virtually as a job lot at Alyth. On 1 September 1651, his troops stormed and sacked Dundee with wholesale massacre. Dunnottar Castle, the last royalist bastion, lowered its colours on 25 February the following year. The civil wars, at last, had ended.[110]

The Killing Time

Having stamped his will upon the Scots, Oliver Cromwell proved, in some ways, a benevolent dictator. His power was writ in blood, his garrisons commanded virtually every stronghold and even sought to wring obedience from the wild clansmen of the west; taxation was burdensome, and yet the nation prospered. The judicial system functioned and the Kirk, though politically impotent, was not oppressed. Factions were rife, particularly the 'Resolutioners', who had earlier supported Charles II, and their vociferous opponents, the 'Remonstrants' or 'Protesters', who had been sceptical of the young king's intentions. Though a minority, the Protesters were particularly active in the universities.[1]

The enigmatic Monck was instrumental in the Restoration; having agreed terms by the Declaration of Breda, the king returned to a tumultuous welcome from his travels in April 1660. The universal joy in England was mirrored in Scotland. The austerity and enforced saintliness of the Protectorate had worn thin and Cromwell's death exposed a hollow shell.

Anticipation was to prove more rapturous than arrival. Beneath Charles's genial exterior lay a shrewd, calculating intelligence, motivated, above all, by a desire not to return to a nomadic exile but also by a desire to boost his own power. In this the Kirk must prove an obstacle as it had been to his father and so the ministers must be brought to heel.

In the quarter-century of his reign the king never ventured into his northern kingdom. The throne of his ancestors was filled by a series of commissioners: Middleton, Rothes, Lauderdale and, latterly, his brother James, duke of York, the future James VII. Initially the Committee of Estates, rudely interrupted by the wholesale capture of the members at Alyth in 1651, was reinstated.[2] One of its early dictates was to forbid the holding of meetings or 'conventicles' without express royal authority.

As a coronation offering, the Estates discovered four traitors, including Argyll, whose deaths absolved all of complicity with the Protector. Others, particularly among the Protesters, were arrested but soon released.[3] One measure of particularly sinister import was the Act Rescissory which sought to cancel out all legislation since 1633 and, by so doing, removed the statutory protection which the Scottish Church enjoyed. Charles's promise to uphold the Church suddenly took on a wholly different complexion, for the ecclesiastical establishment of 1633 was not the creature of the Solemn League and Covenant.[4]

The episcopal system was an anathema to all good Covenanters, the back door to popery, and Charles found the perfect instrument in the ambitious and opportunist minister James Sharp, who, by December 1661, had connived his way to the archbishopric of St Andrews and primacy of Scotland. Two years later the episcopalian noose was further strengthened when a fresh edict excluded any ministers who had not been collared by a bishop. Some 270 abjured and their vacant parishes were parcelled out amongst the more malleable or 'King's Curates'.[5]

Such appointees were not popular and in November 1666 resentment spilled into armed insurrection: a body of Galwegians, perhaps 3000 men, mustered in Dumfries and seized the king's man, Sir James Turner, who, though doubtless humiliated, was not roughly handled. Men from Ayrshire and Lanarkshire joined the Protesters, led by an individual named Wallace, who proposed to march on the capital.[6]

As they moved eastward, however, support evaporated and desertions mounted. Snapping at their heels were several troops of dragoons under the Commander-in-Chief of the king's Scottish forces, Sir Thomas (Tam) Dalyell of The Binns. A fanatical adherent of the House of Stewart, Dalyell had been 'out' in the civil war and had quit the realm in disgust at the regicide. He had sought, and won, fame and a considerable fortune in the service of the tsar which had paid for his fine house at The Binns (where a collection of his Russian pieces may still be seen). His eccentricities extended to a flowing white beard, left uncut in memory of Charles the martyr, and a penchant for a style of dress which had last been fashionable during his reign. His enemies, who were many, perceived him harsh and ruthless and the more extreme believed him to be in league with the Devil, with whom he regularly played cards.[7]

By the time the rebels had advanced as far as Colinton, on the southern outskirts of Edinburgh, their numbers had dwindled to below a thousand and they sheered off westward through the Pentland Hills. At Rullion Green on 23 November Dalyell's dragoons finally caught up with them. Though possessed of no artillery and few firearms, the Covenanters made a brave stand, repelling two charges before a third dispersed them. Discipline and firepower defeated fervour – some fifty rebels were killed and many captured.[8]

The Protesters believed that Dalyell, having sold his soul to the Devil, enjoyed a charmed life, 'shot proof', an accusation they flung at other enemies, particularly Claverhouse, who proved impossible to kill; perhaps the superstitious explanation proved more palatable than a more pragmatic reflection on the quality of their marksmanship. During the fracas, Paton of Maidenhead blazed away at Dalyell to little effect, until, recollecting the old general's diabolical pact, he loaded a silver coin and took aim. Seeing the pistol raised, Dalyell dodged smartly behind a servant who in turn received the fatal lucre. Needless to say, this escape was blamed on unholy intervention.

For the prisoners retribution for the 'Pentland Rising', as it was called, was swift and savage: 33 men were hanged, more were transported. The viciousness of the reaction was evidence of extreme nervousness in government circles. The king was inclined to leniency and, displeased by the slaughter, appointed the duke of Lauderdale as commissioner, with a brief for conciliation.[9]

For a while the iron hand of repression was lifted, excluded ministers were allowed to return, and moves to strengthen the creeping power of the bishops were halted. It became increasingly obvious, however, that matters had gone too far for friendly relations and the fears of the more extreme Presbyterians ran too deep.

By 1678 the west was in turmoil and the government sought to contain the rapidly deteriorating situation by a show of force which amounted to a legalised *chevauchée* by 6000 Highlanders and half as many Lowland levies.[10] The Highland host was not popular and the pillaging of the west, exacerbated by Lauderdale's corruption and rampant nepotism, provoked a violent backlash.

A party of disaffected gentry led by Balfour of Kinloch, 'Burlie' and Hackston of Rathillet lurked on Magus Muir in wait for one of the detested deputies of the universally loathed Bishop Sharp. In the event they scored a far greater prize when they intercepted the archbishop's own coach. The unfortunate prelate was hauled out, then unceremoniously and enthusiastically dispatched, despite the entreaties of his distraught daughter. Hackston would not bloody his blade, abstaining from the actual act of murder on the grounds that he was too much charged with personal hatred. Intoxicated by bloodletting the murderers rode west.[11]

Drumclog, 1678

An armed conventicle was due to assemble on Loudon Hill on 1 June, essentially a martial rather than a religious gathering, the rebels divided into three companies of horse, and four battalions of foot, perhaps 1500 in all, armed with a motley of pikes and edged weapons, a few firearms, fowling pieces and an abundance of zeal. A crowd of wives and families completed the gathering, together with the requisite array of preachers to attend to the army's spiritual needs. Militarily they were led by an able young firebrand named William Cleland, a sometime poet who was later to command Angus's regiment and die heroically – like his enemy, Claverhouse – in the very moment of triumph.[12]

John Graham of Claverhouse – 'Bluidy Clavers' to the Presbyterians, 'Bonnie Dundee' to the Jacobites – was determined to nip rebellion in the bud, trusting to his troopers' cohesion and marksmanship. In his early thirties, slightly built, handsome in an effeminate way, Graham's portrait by Kneller shows studied arrogance with a hint of petulance. A superb rider and natural swordsman, he embodied to the full the *élan* of the *beau sabreur*. Charismatic but notoriously quarrelsome, he was loyal to his friends, amongst whom he numbered the duke of York and the murdered Sharp, who had taught divinity at St Andrews whilst Claverhouse was a student.[13]

Cleland had chosen his position well. His zealots were drawn up around the farm of Drumclog, their front protected by a deep and miry ditch with marshy ground beyond and extending around the flanks. Seeing his enemies so strongly posted, Claverhouse immediately abandoned any hope of a mounted charge and advanced his men, dismounted, in a skirmish line. The fight began with a desultory fusillade as the dragoons, armed with flint carbines, worked their way forward, almost to the ditch, their steady fire galling the untrained and unblooded defenders, though few were actually hit.[14]

Judging the moment, Cleland led one or more of his battalions round the sheltering ditch at the double and struck Claverhouse's line along the left flank and centre. Rallying his shaken troopers, Claverhouse had his horse badly gored by the thrust of a pitchfork and the crazed beast bolted, carrying its rider some way from the fight. Perhaps believing their leader had deserted, the dragoons began to fall back and by the time Claverhouse regained control his men were in rout. This proved fatal, for the rebels, with their vastly superior numbers, simply rolled over the line, hewing and slashing. Thirty-six soldiers died, seven more were taken. Of these five were released unharmed, an act of clemency which so enraged Robert Hamilton, a leading preacher, that he pistolled a sixth on the spot. This was not the only atrocity; the body of Cornet Graham, a relative of Claverhouse, was savagely mutilated.

In his subsequent report Claverhouse objectively described the nature of the disorder:

> In the end (they perceiving that we had the better of them in skirmish), they resolved a general engagement, and immediately advanced with their foot, the horse following. They came through the loch, and the greatest body of all made up against my troop. We kept our fire until they were within ten paces of us; they received our fire and advanced to shock.[15]

The rebel horse now followed up the victory chasing the demoralised troopers across country to Hillhead, where Claverhouse, his wounded horse now dying beneath him, managed to rally survivors. That evening the saddlesore and dispirited troop met up with Ross's Life Guards and retired into Glasgow. Besides Ross and the remnant of Claverhouse's command there were a further two royal squadrons under Airlie and Home. The troopers furiously flung up barricades, loopholed walls and generally prepared to meet an assault.

They were not kept waiting. Next morning the victorious rebels approached the outskirts and launched an immediate escalade, a strong party under Hamilton pushing up Gallowgate, another breaking in from the environs of the University. The rattle of musketry filled the usually crowded thoroughfares, the rebels came on valiantly, but the superior firepower of the government troops prevailed and every attempt was repulsed. Even the rabid Hamilton had to concede defeat and the attackers withdrew, shaken in arms but still unshakeable in faith.

Bothwell Brig, 1678

The defence, though stalwart, scarcely counted as a victory. Barely half a dozen rebels had died and it could, at best, be no more than a respite. The government fell into a panic and frantically sought to raise men wherever. The earl of Linlithgow, as Commander-in-Chief, advised Claverhouse and his brother officers to abandon the hard-won streets of Glasgow, which they left on 3 June, to a general muster at Stirling.

Despite the frantic plea for volunteers, few responded. The militias of Fife and Lothian were raised, giving the government some 5000 men. Charles sent his favourite bastard, James, duke of Monmouth, to take command, furnishing him with an expansive if unlikely commission to raise two new regiments of foot, three of horse and 800 dragoons. Though the bulk of his troops were both raw and unenthusiastic, the duke at least had good officers; as well as Claverhouse, Home and Airlie, he had experienced horse soldiers in Theophilus Oglethorpe, Major Edmund Maine and Captain Henry Cornwall.[16]

Whilst the government gathered its reserves and its resolve the rebels were split by factionalism and military preparation was ignored. The moderates, led by John Webb, wrangled with the fanatics, led by Hamilton, who also feuded with the party of Donald Cargill.[17] By 22 June Monmouth's dragoons, supported by a foot battalion, were deploying towards the bridge just south of the village of Bothwell. Possession of the crossing was vital, for only here could the heavy guns be easily manoeuvred over the Clyde.

The rebels were gathered in strength along the opposite bank and, though devoid of any plan of action, were soon exchanging shots with the duke's men. On paper the odds were favourable: Hamilton had perhaps 2000 horse and twice as many foot. Most were drawn up half a mile from the bridge on rising ground known as Little Park. Two companies of foot, a squadron of horse and a single gun were left to cover the crossing.[18]

The rebel leaders – with the possible exception of Hamilton – suffered a collective loss of nerve and proposed terms. Monmouth was not averse to talking and showed a genuine desire to avoid bloodshed but he would not negotiate whilst the Presbyterians remained in arms and gave them half an hour to consider their surrender. 'And hang next—' was Hamilton's dry comment.[19] As the duke utilised the respite to bring up his guns the rebels once again gave fire, actually driving back the gunners and had they not been impeded by their own barricades, they might have stormed the bridge and taken or spiked the abandoned pieces.

The moment passed. Oglethorpe's dragoons sent their volleys crashing across the parapet, and the guns were recovered. For the next two hours an intense firefight raged. The bridge was strongly defended by James Ure and Hackston of Rathillet but eventually the weight of government fire forced the rebels back from the improvised obstacles and dragoons rushed across, winning a foothold.

Oglethorpe's advance shook the rebels but Ure managed to rally his men on level ground south of the crossing and, in turn, began to advance but, with the bridgehead won, Oglethorpe was soon reinforced by Linlithgow's and Monmouth's own squadrons. Fatally for the rebels, the duke was able to advance his guns which now proceeded to pound the whole length of the rebel line.[20]

The cannonade threw Hamilton's wing into confusion; prayer was no proof against roundshot and the rebels had never experienced the abundant horrors of bombardment, iron shearing limbs, collapsing whole files into bloody writhing bundles, the psalms of the faithful accompanied by the screams of the maimed and the dying, blood from severed arteries jetting over the survivors. It was too much, the rot began on the left amongst the horse, swiftly spreading to the foot on that wing and then engulfed the right under Cleland.[21]

The battle was over and a dreadful pursuit began. As the broken rebels streamed towards Hamilton or south to Strathaven they were mercilessly harried by the dragoons. Oglethorpe, Maine and Claverhouse were particularly active, strewing the rout with corpses. Innocent villagers caught up in the stampede were shot or sabred without discrimination. Many who tried to surrender fared no better. The butcher's bill finally totalled around 800 with over a thousand prisoners. The captives were roughly handled, rank and file for the most part. Hamilton, Cleland, Ure, Hackston and the other officers, including the rest of Sharp's killers, escaped.

On the day after the battle the ageing but still formidable General Dalyell arrived in camp with a commission to succeed Monmouth as Commander-in-Chief. The old warrior roundly abused the younger man for his attempts at clemency, averring that had he come but a day sooner, 'The rogues should never more have troubled the king or country.'[22]

War of Attrition

The rebellion finished Lauderdale's career and Monmouth succeeded in getting an Act of Indemnity through which undoubtedly mitigated some of the horrors of the aftermath. The unlamented duke was followed by the king's brother. Courageous, with integrity but without humour or diplomacy, a fervent papist, narrow and autocratic, James, duke of York, could hardly have been a worse choice. One of his early measures was to propose a 'test' for churchmen, which caused widespread outrage, so much so that even staunch Episcopalians resigned in disgust.[23]

In the west and in the hills a war of attrition went on, a time of persecution, misery and, all too often, summary justice. The Presbyterians were led by Cargill and Richard Cameron, who bequeathed his name to Angus's regiment, which became the Cameronians. In July 1680, Cameron was killed in a petty skirmish at Aird's Moss in Kyle. Hackston was finally captured, paying a fearful price for his complicity. In the following May Cargill was taken and, like so many others, choked out his life at a rope's end.[24] Claverhouse was the government's instrument in the field and Sir George Mackenzie, 'Bluidy Mackenzie', the Lord Advocate, the instrument of justice.

In February 1685, Charles died without ever having set foot in Scotland since the Restoration, and his brother was proclaimed James VII four days later without any great show of rejoicing. The new king, unlike the old, made no secret of his persuasion nor of his intentions. At the coronation he omitted to undertake the preservation of the Anglican Church and very soon thereafter it became a capital offence merely to be present at a conventicle.

His reign became totalitarian and focused on a return to Rome. Like his father, the king was indefatigable in conspiring towards his own fall and English eyes turned towards Holland where the Stadtholder, William of Orange, was waiting in the wings.

The Dutchman sent a careful message to willing ears in Scotland, a promise to uphold the Presbyterian church and deliver the nation from the popish tyrant. The intimation fell on fertile soil and an unstoppable tide of anger and frustration swelled mainly from the south-west, enough to overawe the Privy Council, now deprived of troops, most of whom had marched south to bolster the crumbling regime. Once William had made his triumphal landing, driving his father-in-law into embittered exile, he sent letters to the Estates summoning a Convention, which assembled on 14 March 1689. By 9 April they had voted to abandon James and support the Williamites.[25]

Midway through the proceedings one member stormed out in protest and refused all summonses to return and by 30 March had been publicly proclaimed a traitor at the Mercat Cross in the capital. This man was John Graham of Claverhouse, now Viscount Dundee, whose loyalty to the House of Stewart remained unshakeable.[26]

Gone for a Soldier

One of Charles II's earliest tasks had been to dismantle the military machine created by the Protector, whittling the establishment down to a mere five regiments, intended as little more than the royal bodyguard but forming the core of a standing army. Several of these regular battalions were Scots: the Coldstreams, raised by Monck; the 1st Foot (Royal Scots), originally raised as Hepburn's regiment in 1633 for the French service; and the Scots Guards (1685), who could trace their origin to 1639 when Argyll mustered a battalion to fight in Ireland.

Both the Scots Guards and Royal Scots carry the battle honour 'Tangier' in honour of their service from 1662, which saw some savage fighting in the stifling heat of North Africa. The Royal

Scots Greys were raised by Dalyell, originally as a dragoon regiment. Dragoons were paid less and mounted on inferior beasts so they were more cost-effective than cavalry and amongst the hills and mosses of Galloway proved more versatile. The term 'dragoon' is derived from 'dragon', an early form of firelock, though by the last quarter of the seventeenth century all carried smoothbore flintlock carbines and pistols.[27]

A standing army meant that regular soldiers were needed and every winter recruiting parties cruised the towns and villages offering the king's shilling to anyone desperate enough to accept. Enlisting in His Majesty's armed forces could not, at this stage, be described as a 'career choice', more of a last resort. Poverty, hunger, crime and despair were the prime motivators. As recruits were difficult to find, even when economic conditions were poor, the sergeants frequently had to rely on the twice-yearly emptying of the gaols when malefactors found themselves in uniform for the good of the realm and the rate-payers.[28] Not infrequently abused or neglected by his officers, the redcoat was prone to desertion, rapine and pillage, and, if caught, he faced the lash or the firing squad.[29]

Despite the draconian punishment for desertion, 'bounty jumping' – enlisting, absconding and then re-enlisting elsewhere – was rife. Disease killed far more men than enemy action. British battle casualties during wars of the eighteenth century were never more than a fraction of those who succumbed to sickness and neglect.[30]

In the earlier years of this period foot regiments included both pike and shot, though the latter gradually came to predominate. Musketeers wore red tunics under buff jerkins, pikemen wore coats of the regimental colour; the famous scarlet was by no means universal and even by the end of the century a number of battalions still sported blue and grey.[31] The pike was made effectively redundant by the introduction of the bayonet, said to derive from the French place-name Bayonne. Early bayonets were of the 'plug' type which screwed into the muzzle, converting the musket into a kind of hybrid pike, the obvious drawback being that the weapon could not again be discharged. This proved disastrous at Killiecrankie and by the early eighteenth century had been replaced by the 'socket' bayonet whose hollow cranked handle slotted over the end of the barrel.[32]

Even after the demise of the pike, officers retained half-pikes or spontoons and sergeants carried halberds. Muskets gradually became more standardised and less cumbersome; by 1700 the William III Land-musket, forerunner of Brown Bess, had been introduced. With a calibre of .85 in., a barrel length of 5 ft and weighing 11 lb, these flintlock guns could fire two 1-oz balls a minute. Maximum range was 250 yards, though volleys were not usually fired at a range in excess of 60 yards.[33] The infantryman carried two dozen pre-wrapped paper cartridges in a pouch or 'cartouche'. When fully accoutred and complete with weapon, spare clothing and utensils, the private soldier packed a load of 50 lb or more.[34]

By the end of the seventeenth century a typical foot battalion comprised 12 companies, 11 of which contained 60 men and the twelfth, the grenadier company, an extra file of ten, a total complement of 44 officers and 780 NCOs and other ranks. The regiment had a surgeon's mate, quartermaster and solicitor, a drum major and deputy marshal. Each line company was commanded by a captain, lieutenant, ensign and two sergeants or corporals. The grenadier company, in addition to a greater number of men, also had a second full lieutenant rather than an ensign. Three, or perhaps four, companies would be under the direct orders of the colonel himself who, with his captains, drew wages of ten shillings per day.[35]

When preparing to engage, the regiment deployed from column into line, the ranks marching in step, bands playing, the foot flanked protectively by the horse and guns, the files dressing by beat of drum, NCOs marshalling with levelled halberds. Once formed up in line, the band, regimental officers and NCOs took up position. The opposing sides would exchange volleys at 60–70 yards. Though wildly inaccurate, the massed fire could create fearful casualties among bunched targets, the heavy leaden balls flattening in the air to inflict horrific wounds. Great palls of smoke swiftly obscured the field, the heavy air rent by stabbing flame and the fearful noise of discharge, men's faces swiftly blackened by powder. Muskets levelled, the survivors would advance steadily to close with the bayonet.[36]

Grenadiers were specialist troops, first introduced around 1678. They were an élite, their particular weapon, as the name implies, was the grenade, a circular bomb roughly the size of a cricket ball and ignited by a projecting fuse, itself lit from a length of slow match wound round the left wrist. The grenades were flung in volleys. Grenadiers were particularly in demand for storming parties, and as a badge of distinction wore their tall mitre-shaped caps. They were also the only troops to have slings for their muskets and carried longer bayonets and hatchets, the latter for hacking away at obstacles.[37]

Armour, at least for the foot, was going out of vogue. Restoration pikemen still wore breast and back, though without tassets and pot helmets, whilst plate defences had all but vanished by the end of the century. An echo survived in the use of the gorget, now an ornamental device worn by officers, which continued until well into the nineteenth century.[38]

Another development was the formation of fusilier battalions, which were originally enlisted to give protection to the artillery train, which was staffed primarily by civilian contractors and who frequently displayed a propensity for rapid desertion in stressful situations. Fusiliers were the first to be armed with flint guns, the mechanism of which relied upon a sharpened flint held between the jaws of the cock, which was controlled by a spring, drawn back once to safe or 'half-cock' – hence 'going off at half-cock' – and twice to full, ready for firing. The flint, when the trigger was depressed, struck against a steel, or frizzen, which was hinged over the pan, containing fine powder. The resultant shower of sparks fell onto the pan, lighting the powder and, through the touch-hole, the main charge.[39] Flint guns were to dominate battlefields from Blenheim (1704) to Waterloo (1815), the famous Brown Bess doing service throughout, and the age of flint provided some of the finest examples of the gun-smith's art, such as Jaeger rifles from Central Europe, 'Pennsylvania' or 'Kentucky' rifles from the American colonies, sleek duellers by Manton, Mortimer and Egg.

The horse, naturally, considered themselves a cut above the plodding infantry, though cavalry regiments were organised along very similar lines with nine troops of up to 60 men, usually under strength and commanded by a colonel, three troops forming a squadron. Dragoons were similarly organised, individual troop strengths between 40 and 50 troopers, with a greater proportion of non-commissioned officers and hautbois (oboe) players rather than trumpeters.[40]

Military fashion, particularly amongst the mounted arm, tended towards the extravagant, a reaction to the deliberate drabness of the Protectorate. Body armour was worn by curassiers till 1698 and, though wide-brimmed hats replaced pot helmets, steel 'secrets' were sewn within. Coats were worn long and loose-waisted with deep cuffs. Officers brimmed with lace. Stiff black leather thigh boots with bucket tops encased the leg. Every troop was commanded by a captain with a cornet, who bore the guidon and a couple of corporals. Standards were gorgeous, double silk damask, embroidered and fringed with tassels of silver or gold.[41]

As mentioned, the guns were serviced by civilian contractors who also furnished the army with pioneers, smiths, armourers and farriers. Artillery was slowly becoming more standardised from the heavy 24-lb siege pieces to diminutive 1½-pounders. A great quantity of horses was needed to drag these monsters, the heavier weighing up to three tons and requiring as many as 30 beasts. The late sixteenth century witnessed a peculiar breed of light or 'leather' guns, such as General MacKay carried on his ill-fated expedition to Blair. An example of this type survives from Sweden; the lined iron barrel is stiffened with alloy and splints, bound with iron wire and ropes, coated with several layers of canvas wrapping, profiled in timber and finally shrouded in leather.[42]

Bonnie Dundee

Having abandoned the Convention, Claverhouse, with a hard core of sympathisers, rode for the haven, albeit a temporary one, of his castle at Dudhope, near Dundee. Pursued by the Estates, he retired to the Highlands, where loyalty to the House of Stewart still prevailed.

Now a rebel himself, he journeyed first to his wife's people in Glen Ogilvy, where he began to preach the Jacobite gospel. After three days he rode on to Keith, again rallying the faithful of Banffshire. At Elgin he was welcomed by the burgesses; at Forres he met the proud chieftains of the western clans and received intimations of support from the Lowlands. At Cairn o' Mount he captured a government runner and learnt the Williamite commander, Hugh MacKay of Scourie, was at hand with three foot regiments and one of horse. Foiling his plan to capture the rebels, Dundee turned aside and made a run for Castle Gordon where the earl of Dunfermline and a body of gentry came in.[43]

So did the Highlanders. Graham had the magic name and possessed that rare strength and charisma that could weld the disparate clans into something resembling an army, his colourful following having a romantic gloss next to the dour pragmatism of the Williamites. The reality was somewhat more difficult. MacDonald of Keppoch, particularly, saw the rebellion as a prime opportunity for some imaginative freebooting and a general settling of scores. Inverness was MacDonald's first target. Claiming an unpaid debt, he extorted a ransom of 4000 marks. The outraged citizens protested to Dundee who, mightily embarrassed, could offer only a receipt in the name of James VII. The reaction of the impoverished burgesses is not recorded.[44]

From Presmukeroch, near Dalwhinnie, he issued a summons in the name of his king bidding the clansmen to muster at Lochaber on 18 May and then, slipping past MacKay, he ambushed government tax collectors at Perth and diverted their funds to the Jacobite cause. Having 'discouraged' some local lairds from raising men for William, he attempted to reach the men of his old regiment, stationed at Dundee. Despite the best endeavours of Captain Livingstone, the proposed defection was baulked by the watchful eyes of Williamite troopers, obviously suspicious of their comrades' true affiliation.[45]

The gathering at Killiecrankie was impressive: Cameron of Lochiel, MacLean of Duart and the MacDonald septs each mustered a thousand, there were contingents from the Stewarts of Appin, MacNeil of Barra, MacLeods of Skye and Raasay, Frasers, MacNaughtons, MacAllisters, MacLachlans and Lamonts. With these swift-footed Highlanders and his own troop of horse, Dundee began to stalk MacKay, who prudently withdrew. The Jacobites took Ruthven Castle and the incorrigible Keppoch paid off another old score by burning the MacIntoshes out of their hold at Dunachton. A further four days of intermittent skirmishing ensued, until MacKay's forces reached more open country round Strathbogie. Fearing their superior cavalry, which would have more room to deploy, Dundee called off the hunt.[46]

Presently MacKay was reinforced by a further pair of foot battalions and felt sufficiently strong to take the initiative, forcing the Jacobites to withdraw to Badenoch. On 9 June government dragoons engaged a body of MacLeans, 300 or so, marching to join the rebel army. A sharp encounter saw the Williamites put to flight, leaving most of their weapons and gear strewn behind the rout. Despite this success, even Dundee's charisma could not prevent an increasing toll of desertions, as the clansmen, replete with loot, slipped away homeward. Bowing to the inevitable he led the dwindling host back into the relative safety of Lochaber where the bulk of the army dispersed.[47]

For the next month, there was little activity. Dundee resisted an offer of truce mediated through his brother-in-law and was declared an outlaw with a bounty of £20,000. He wrote to Lord John Murray, castellan at Blair, which he held for his absent father, the marquis of Atholl, urging the young peer to declare for the king. The fortress was of considerable strategic value and its loss to either side would be a grievous blow. Murray did not reply. It was feared his sympathies lay with the Dutchman, and so Dundee decided to play safe, by ordering the marquis's factor, Stewart of Ballochie, a known Jacobite, to raise the Athollmen and seize control. The value of Blair was not lost on MacKay who chivvied his battalions on to win the race that was fast developing. It was the Jacobites who won, Dundee reaching the castle on 26 July with perhaps 2500 Highlanders. MacKay was left struggling past Dunkeld, his force comprising some battalions of foot, four troops of horse and four of dragoons, some 4000 in all.[48]

At Blair the Jacobites held a council of war. Though they commanded the castle, the Williamite army was known to be fast approaching and many of the chiefs urged caution, preferring to refuse battle till all of the scattered clans came in. Dundee was more bullish, stressing the men's high morale, and found support from Lochiel, the most respected of the clan leaders. The Highlanders girded themselves for battle.

Killiecrankie, 1689

The following dawn the Williamites marched out of Dunkeld and by mid morning the van was approaching the pass of Killiecrankie, a narrow and treacherous defile, enough to cause alarm in any commander of regular troops, the tumbling waters of the Garry plunging amid a cascade of boulders, the steep slopes crowded with a tangle of bushes and trees. The track, little more than a pathway, wound for two miles through the pass and, after a halt of two hours, the troops began the long ascent.

Once clear of the pass, MacKay made his headquarters at Urrard House and deployed his battalions to meet the expected attack. On the extreme left he posted a commanded party of 200 shot under Lt-Colonel Landers. Next to these stood the regiments of Balfour, Ramsay and Kenmure. The horse formed the centre and Leven's regiment, together with MacKay's own and Hastings's, stood on the right. The light 'leather' guns were all the ordnance that had been dragged through the pass.[49]

Killiecrankie · 27 July 1689

The government troops were not kept waiting for long; over the high ground from Blair came Dundee's Highlanders, gaudy in saffron and plaid, pipes skirling. On skirting the shoulder of Craig Ealloch, the Jacobites presented a superbly intimidating spectacle and MacKay realised at once that his men were at a serious disadvantage, and promptly sent his battalions scrambling up the slope to their front in order to deny Dundee the advantage of rising ground. Having conquered this obstacle, the government troops found another ridge beyond, 'but a short musket shot away', as MacKay noted, 'a ground fair enough to receive the enemy but not to attack them'.[50] Even this cautious observation was to prove over-optimistic.

As the clan regiments spread across the hillside MacKay was obliged to echelon his whole line to the right which effectively meant he now had the swift-flowing Garry behind and rising ground before. If his line was broken any form of orderly withdrawal would be difficult in the extreme.

On the right of Dundee's line stood the MacLeods and next to them an Irish unit under Colonel Cannon, then came the might of Clan Donald, men of Clanranald, Glengarry and Glencoe flanked by the Grants of Glenmoriston. In the centre there were a bare 40 mounted men under Walter of Craighie whilst on the left stood Cameron of Lochiel, more MacLeans, MacDonalds of Kintyre, the MacNeils and MacDonald of Sleat. Dundee took up position on the left.[51]

Whilst the strong sun still shone in the eyes of his clansmen, Dundee would not advance, and MacKay could not. Instead he began a rather desultory cannonade from his light guns – the strain of which prompted at least two to disintegrate. No casualties were inflicted. A body of Cameron sharpshooters worked their way forward, menacing MacKay's left, and the Williamite general dispatched a commanded party under his brother to drive them back.[52]

At 8.00 p.m., when the fierce glare of the summer sun began to wane, Dundee shouted the charge. Whilst redeploying earlier MacKay had been concerned that his line might be outflanked and, to compensate, he divided his foot battalions, advancing the three rearward ranks into extended line. To compound this folly, he allowed a distinct gap to open between Kenmure's and Leven's, relying solely upon the horse to hold the centre. Dundee was also worried about being outflanked and merely increased the distance between his clan regiments, in the event a far less dangerous expedient. Meanwhile, he had targeted his Highland regiments against particular battalions in MacKay's now much attenuated line.[53]

As the Jacobites, hurling their slogans, skimmed fleet-footed towards the Williamites the lie of the ground caused them to edge to the right. Consequently they exposed themselves to a devastating enfilade from MacKay's right; his regiment, Hastings's and half of Leven's avoided the fury of the onslaught. On the left, however, the charge struck home, the raw levies parrying the swinging broadswords with clumsy bayonets, the evening air ringing with the clash of steel. Lauder's fusiliers, Balfour's and above half of Ramsay's broke, spewing a torrent of fugitives fleeing the merciless blades.

In desperation MacKay hurled his squadrons against the Highlanders' flank but Belhaven's troop were contemptuously flung back, their rout disordering Kenmure's shaken foot, who, in turn, dissolved in flight. As the fugitives bolted towards the river they earned an unexpected reprieve when their pursuers paused to plunder the baggage.

MacKay managed a fighting retreat with such men as he could muster, the dazed survivors falling back through the pass in the gathering dusk and making for Stirling. Behind he left more than half the force dead or taken. The victors had also suffered. The opening volleys had torn great gaps in their ranks and as many as 600 had fallen, including Sir Donald MacDonald of Sleat, the Camerons in particular losing heavily from the flanking fire of Leven's.[54]

Amongst their loss was one who was irreplaceable. Observing the attack on the left in difficulty, Dundee spurred towards his stalled clansmen and as he did so a random shot, possibly one of the last, struck him in the side. He fell and died shortly after. John Graham, like Nelson, died at the moment of his greatest glory and with him perished the Stewart cause in Scotland, for as Lochiel had predicted, there was none who could take his place. The survivors of the battle stood sorrowing as their leader, his body wrapped in plaids, was interred in the small chapel at Blair.[55]

End of the Rebellion

Command of the Jacobite army descended upon Colonel Cannon, a necessary if uninspired choice for the colonel had none of his predecessor's *élan* or rapport with the clans amongst whose ranks old feuds were never far below the surface. The army advanced down the valley of the Tay, heading, though with no great certainty, for Perth. At Dunkeld their way was barred by a Williamite garrison of 1200 men of Angus's regiment, the Cameronians, led by their former paladin, William Cleland, now Lt-Colonel.

In the early hours of 21 August 5000 clansmen attacked the town from all four sides, but the Cameronians fought back doggedly. Every house was loopholed, every street and wynd barricaded. For four hours the fight raged. When the Lowlanders ran short of ammunition they stripped the lead from roofs and, as they were forced back, fired the houses they passed.

Cleland had constructed a final redoubt based round the twin bastions of the cathedral and Dunkeld House and as the town burned his men stood off repeated rushes, piling Jacobite dead round their barricades. Cleland himself took a fatal bullet in the liver and another in the head, the dying officer struggled towards Dunkeld House so that his men might not see him fall. Like his old enemy, he died a glorious death for soon afterwards the Highlanders withdrew leaving the charred and blackened shell of the town to the exhausted but victorious Cameronians;[56] 300 Jacobites had been killed for a cost of 45 Williamites.

After the débâcle at Dunkeld the army began to disperse, Cannon and his Irish retiring into Lochaber for the winter. The following year, 1690, was to be a fateful one for the Jacobite cause. In Ireland the defeat at the Boyne led to James's flight and the ruin of his cause. His Scottish army mustered again in April, led by a Major-General, Thomas Buchan, sent from Ireland. A modest 1500 recruits came in, but Lochiel and many other chiefs wisely abstained from taking the field again.

MacKay, still in command, sent Sir Thomas Livingstone with a mixed force of horse and foot, including levies from Clans Grant and MacKay. At the beginning of May the Williamites surprised Buchan's force in camp at the Haughs of Cromdale by the Spey. Six troops of dragoons thundered amongst the startled Jacobites, scattering the rebels completely. Over 400 prisoners were taken, though both Cannon and Buchan escaped barely clothed and without most of their gear. With this, the Rout of Cromdale, the rebellion came to an inglorious conclusion.[57]

Blood on the Heather

James VI was a monarch who could never abide the sight of blood and a deputation from his loyal subjects, the Colquhouns of Luss, in 1602 must surely have caused a royal shudder when they presented him with the bloodied shirts of their kinsmen savagely slaughtered by their neighbours, the MacGregors.

These troublesome clansmen were an ancient tribe, claiming descent from Grogar, third son of King Alpin, 'Royal is My Name', proclaimed their motto and, at one time, they intimidated and blackmailed weaker neighbours in parts of Argyll and Perthshire including Glenstrae, Glenlyon and Glengyle. Arrogant and rapacious, they raided softer lands by Stirling and into Clydesdale, struck like lightning and then withdrew to their fastnesses above Loch Katrine and amongst the wild mosses of Rannoch Moor, safe from hot pursuit.[1] Their nemesis was Clan Campbell, cautious but equally rapacious neighbours, careful always to have the benefit of law before they drew, but swift and relentless in purpose and execution. Gradually the MacGregors saw their territories eroded. By the latter part of the sixteenth century they were driven from Glenorchy and Glenstrae, though more than a few of Clan Campbell felt the weight of their resentment.[2]

It may well have been the case that the bloodstained shirts laid before King James had, as the more cynical observers suggested, been splashed with sheep's blood but it took little to stir his fury against the MacGregors. Colquhoun of Luss, who had undoubtedly suffered loss, was given a commission to deal with his troublesome neighbours without reference to the earl of Argyll.

The following year, 1603, the two sides held a parley, though to little avail, and it may have been Colquhoun's intention to lure his enemy to a convenient field of slaughter. If so, then it was a serious error of judgement. The MacGregors were led by Alasdair of Glenstrae, a doughty fighter who was too old a hand for such a ruse. Colquhoun with his allies, the Buchanans, sought to fall upon the MacGregors in Glenfruin with a force perhaps 800 strong and comprising both horse and foot. To meet the onslaught Glenstrae divided his forces, half to meet the shock of the charge and the remainder, led by his brother John, to circle the enemy's flank while they were so engaged. Falling upon the rear of the Colquhouns, the wild clansmen wreaked havoc amongst their conventionally armed and accoutred foes. The victors subsequently claimed that 200 Colquhouns and Buchanans were left dead upon the field while only two of their own number died, including John MacGregor, killed by a random arrow.[3]

The wholesale butchery of the men he had sent to enforce his authority angered James and he outlawed the entire Clan MacGregor. Even by the flexible standards of the day this was considered an extreme and terrible penalty. Though Glenstrae himself paid the ultimate price for his brawling,[4] the clan survived and generally seem to have carried on much as before.

Such murderous incidents were frequent in the history of the Highlands. Since time immemorial the clans feuded openly in the ancient way of the warrior, the stubborn roots of their society buried in antiquity. The ancient kingdom of Dalriada merged into the province of Argyll, whose long and convoluted coast-line formed a hunting ground for the first generation of Norse raiders, whose fleet longships scourged the western seaboard. First the Norwegians and latterly the Danes stamped their heathen will on Shetland, Orkney and the Hebrides. Powerful Norse earls such as Thorfinn the Mighty in the mid eleventh century annexed wide tracts of the northern province, including Sudrland (Sutherland) and Katanes (Caithness). Kings of Man extended their sway over the Hebrides, challenged by Dubliners and finally overcome, in 1093, by the utterly formidable King of Norway, Magnus Bareleg.[5]

The spread of Norman influence, during and after the reign of Malcolm Canmore, insidiously undermined the virile Gaelic tradition which not infrequently erupted in open defiance – in 1215 Donald Ban MacWilliam and Kenneth MacHeth, with their eyes on the Scottish crown, invaded Moray with Irish arms, only to be defeated by Farquhar MacTaggart.[6]

Feudalism in Scotland spread from within rather than from external intervention, the distinctive motte-and-bailey castles, hallmark of Norman expansion, do not appear in the Highlands but ancient tribal forts were refurbished as knightly or baronial castles as traditional loyalties to tribal chiefs were transferred, sometimes uneasily, to feudal lords.[7]

The development of urban centres which occurred during the early medieval period, fuelled by the consolidation of royal power, stopped short of the Highland line. Even at Inverness, the future 'capital' of the Highlands, the townsmen, often of English or Continental extraction, were sharply distinguished from their contemporaries north of the line who spoke only Gaelic and whose way of life remained agrarian.[8]

Though a number of clans were pure Gael, claiming descent from the Pict, others were a fusion of Celt and Viking, the Norse-Gaels were sprung from the Dalriadic Scots, such as the MacAlpines and mighty Clan Campbell itself, whose wide lands spread from the western shore at Benderloch to the inland reaches of Loch Tay. Among the Gael was an ancient confederation, Clan Chattan, the 'Clan of the Cats', wherein Davidson and Farquharson joined with MacBean, MacGillvray, MacKintosh and MacPherson. Their union dates from the eleventh century and the virility of the hero Gilliechattan Mor.

As the influence of the Manx and Norwegian rulers declined and before the Scottish kings had fully extended their own sway the vacuum in the west was filled by that most romantic of titles – the Lordship of the Isles. Of Norse-Gael descent, Somerled succeeded where his father had failed and brought the whole of Argyll together with Arran and Bute under his sway.[9] After his death his wide lands, according to Gaelic custom, were divided firstly amongst his sons, one of whom decisively defeated Godfrey of Man at sea in 1156, and latterly amongst his grandsons, from one of whom, Donald, the branches of mighty Clan Donald all claimed descent.[10]

As Somerled grew older his rapacity and defiance swelled. At one point, in the autumn of 1153, he sparked wholesale rebellion in the west, quite possibly in support of his brother-in-law, Malcolm MacHeth, a rival for the throne who claimed descent through the House of Moray and as a response to the encroachment of Anglo-Norman adventurers.[11] In 1164, as relations with Malcolm IV deteriorated, Somerled suddenly appeared, sweeping up the Clyde, with a well-manned fleet of 160 galleys.

The swiftness of the raid seems to have caught the Lowlanders completely by surprise and the islesmen made landfall at Renfrew without encountering any opposition. Marching boldly inland, the Highland host reached a small hill, known as the Knock, located roughly midway between Renfrew and Paisley.

Walter Fitz Alan was a knight of Shropshire whose family had sailed from Brittany with the conqueror. Attaching himself to the Scottish Court he had risen to become High Stewart and now held several fiefs in Renfrewshire, with castles at both Renfrew and Dundonald. A Norman knight in the classic mould, the Stewart refused to be intimidated by a rabble of piratical islesmen and now blocked their advance. This is speculation, but providing a rough calculation of, say, 30 men per galley, Somerled's host, allowing for a reserve left to guard the boats, may have totalled about 3000.[12]

Fitz Alan's knights and local levies may have numbered only a few hundred but a proportion of his men would be well mounted. Armed with lance and shield, hauberks of mail, charging stirrup to stirrup they smashed into the Highland army. The Lord of the Isles and his son were killed in the fray and his ragbag army routed.[13]

Fearsome on their own ground, armed with spears, bows and well-barbed arrows, leather targes and the occasional broadsword, the clans fought for glory and for loot, with a bias toward the latter which, once amassed, generally removed the incentive for further campaigning. The 150 years which followed the final fall of the Lordship of the Isles became known as the 'Linn nan Creach' – the Age of Forays, a romantic epithet for a time of violence, usually brought about by cattle-raiding. To the perils of internecine strife were added the bitterness of the blood feud.

In 1396 Robert III, together with many of his Court as well as foreign visitors, gathered to watch the climax of a feud between Clans Chattan and Kay, when 30 champions from each set out to battle à l'outrance on the North Inch of the Tay at Perth. Such was the fury of the combatants that only one of Clan Kay survived death or injury and this only by leaping into the Tay. Eleven of Clan Chattan survived.[14]

Another instance of where a long-running vendetta was settled by ritual slaughter occurred in 1464 when the Keiths and the Gunns, bitter foes, elected to send 12 paladins each and settle the score in a single orgy of bloodletting. The Keiths, however, proceeded to bend the rules somewhat by arriving with two warriors on each horse neatly doubling the odds and utterly defeating the Gunns. Depleted, but underterred and outraged at this arrant treachery, the survivors stalked their seemingly victorious enemies and surprised them at their celebratory feast, killing the chief of the Keiths and numerous followers with a well-directed flight of arrows.

Sixty years later the Keiths and the Gunns were still regularly at each others' throats when a grandson of the Gunn chieftain cut down another chief of the Keiths together with his son and a dozen or so clansmen.

After the Treaty of Perth in 1266 the ruler of the Isles accepted the sway of Alexander III – Angus Og MacDonald became a staunch ally of Bruce during the war of independence, unlike the powerful MacDougalls, who remained steadfastly opposed until roundly defeated at the Pass of Brander. The disaffected became the disinherited and many crossed to Ireland where they became progenitors of a mercenary caste, the Galloglas.[15]

John of Islay, son of Angus Og, married Margaret Stewart in 1350, a powerful alliance which gave the Lord of the Isles a pivotal role in the politics of the time, being courted by both Edward Baliol and David II.

During the captivity of James I, when Albany was regent, Alexander, earl of Buchan, a younger brother of Robert III, was appointed as justiciary of the northern Lowlands. Buchan, aptly nicknamed the 'Wolf of Badenoch', had a particularly turbulent career. Despite being driven from office he remained active as an outlaw, sacking Elgin Cathedral in 1390, an atrocity which earned his excommunication.[16]

His natural son, Alexander, equally ruthless, forced the widowed countess of Mar, on the death of her first husband Malcolm Drummond, into matrimony, though the lady was probably far from unwilling as Alexander offered a challenge to the ruthless rapacity of the Albany Stewarts. About this time dispute arose over the earldom of Ross, when the incumbent died leaving only a daughter, Euphemia, who retired, wisely perhaps, to a nunnery. Donald MacDonald, son of John of Islay, had married the late earl's sister, Mariota Leslie, and through her he laid claim to the earldom which, since the days of Alexander III, had included Skye and Lewis. Before withdrawing from the world however, the regent Albany had persuaded a browbeaten Euphemia into agreeing that her dead father's lands should pass to her maternal uncle, the present earl of Buchan who, incidentally, was Albany's son.[17]

In 1411, gathering beneath his banner a substantial contingent of his own clansmen with detachments from Clan Chattan, Cameron of Lochaber, together with MacLeans of the Isles, Donald pushed aside local opposition from the MacKays and Rosses at Dingwall and, having sacked Inverness, advanced upon Aberdeen. This MacDonald was no mindless freebooter, a cultured magnate with more claim to gentility than the swashbuckling mar.

Alexander, now finally established as earl of Mar, refused to be daunted and collected what forces he could. Volunteers were raised by the Provost and burgesses of Aberdeen, augmented by a smaller force of Lowland knights. Despite the obvious disparity in numbers – Donald's force is said to have numbered at least 10,000, though this may have been an overestimate – Mar marched boldly out of the city towards Harlaw in Garioch by way of Inverurie and there, some 14 miles north-west of Aberdeen, battle was joined.

There seems to have been little time for manoeuvre. Both armies simply rushed upon each other. The van of the Lowland force was led by the hereditary standard-bearer Sir James Scrymgeour, while Mar commanded the centre. In the ranks were knights from several of the leading Lowland families: the Murrays, Straitons, Leslies, Stirlings and Lovells.

'Red Harlaw', as the fight was known, became a bitter slogging match in which neither side could gain the advantage. Fuelled by numbers and contempt for their Lowland adversaries, the clansmen charged time and again to break against the armoured ranks of the knights or be spitted on the pikes of the Aberdonians. At dusk Donald withdrew his bloodied remnants and fell back through Inverness to Dingwall, leaving, according to some contemporary chronicles, as many as 1000 killed upon the field. The following day the host melted back into the west, the chiefs of both the MacLeans and MacKintoshes being among the dead. Some chroniclers, notably Bower, who was no friend to the islemen, award the victory to Donald, and say that less than a hundred Highlanders died in the fight, whilst Mar lost five times as many. This seems unlikely, given that the tribesmen were unarmoured and doubtless rushed into the attack with their customary reckless valour.

Though the honours went to Mar, the cost had been heavy. Gallant Scrymgeour; Sir Alexander Ogilvy, sheriff of Angus; Sir Alexander Irvine of Druoch; Sir Robert Maule of Panmure; Sir Thomas Murray; Sir William Abernethy and Sir Alexander Straiton of Lauriston, with many of the apprentices and gentlemen of Aberdeen and Buchan, had died. Donald may even have regarded the outcome of Harlaw as some kind of Pyrrhic victory and might have hoped that Albany would feel obliged to grant him the coveted earldom. In any event, Albany remained implacable and raised further forces of his own to finally frustrate the MacDonalds' aspirations.

Though defeated in the east, Donald survived in the west, dying some time around 1420. His son, Alexander, was one of half a hundred Highland chiefs invited by James I to Inverness in 1428. Determined to stamp his authority on the Highlands, James had the truculent chiefs gaoled, some he even executed. Alexander was one of those imprisoned but he successfully escaped and torched Inverness by way of retaliation. His spree was short-lived, however, for he was soon retaken and forced to undergo a humiliating submission.

In 1431 his uncle and cousin raised a rebellion in the west and routed a royal army at Inverlochy. This time it was the ageing paladin Alexander of Mar who was bested. Alexander received his pardon and his liberty. Four years later he was recognised as earl of Ross.[19]

Alexander's son, John, learnt little from his father's misfortunes and championed the overmighty Douglases against James II, though he survived the ruin of the Douglases after Arkinholm in 1455. After the death of James he continued to conspire against his successor. In 1464, after a preposterous alliance with Edward IV of England, and the exiled Douglas, the near-risible Treaty of Westminster-Ardtornish', he was partially reconciled with the king but, ten years later, when the full extent of his duplicity became known, he was stripped of the earldom of Ross and the title to the lordship was vested fully in the crown. John's later years were no less turbulent – his illegitimate son, Angus Og, rebelled against him and defeated his father in an epic sea battle at Bloody Bay. Only Angus's assassination in 1490 cancelled his ambitions.[20] Finally in 1493 the lordship was forfeited.[21]

The forfeiture of the lordship left a vacuum which has become known as the Lin na Creach, 'the age of forays'. The clan was ruled by its chief who parcelled out land by way of leases or tacks to tenants, who became known as tacksmen and who in turn sublet to the clansmen. The patriarch retained his own mesne lands for personal use. Occasionally parcels of land were gifted in perpetuity, say, to the clan bard or to a favourite piper. The clan system appears to have fully developed by the early sixteenth century and was clearly in decline by the opening decades of the eighteenth.

The Highlands are a harsh landscape and life was hard. The ground supported little husbandry and the clansmen were by nature herdsmen and drovers. A chief would count his wealth in the shaggy black cattle grazing in his straths and in the numbers of broadswords that made up his clan regiment, of which he, invariably, was colonel, with his sons and tacksmen as officers.

Feudalism could frequently strengthen a chief's control over his clan – if he was granted a feudal charter then, as tenant in chief, he gained clear title to his lands. As a feudal lord he could establish the idea of primogeniture rather than having to rely on the often bloody uncertainties of tainistry. On his death his lands would pass intact to his eldest son without the need for subdivision. If the heir was a minor, then a mature kinsman became guardian, or captain, till the lad came of age. Certain of the clans, most notably the Campbells and the MacKenzies, practised 'aggressive feudalism', seeking charters that extended their own lands, often at the expense of their less enlightened neighbours. The slow decline of Clan Donald was mirrored by the inexorable rise of Clan Campbell and a bitter rivalry developed.

The government of James VI, in 1598, attempted to plant a group of colonists who rather grandly styled themselves the 'Adventurers of Fife' upon the island of Lewis, a stronghold of the warlike MacLeods, with results nearly as disastrous as the later Darien expedition. By 1605 pressure from the MacLeods forced the settlers to withdraw.

Earlier in the sixteenth century, in 1516, a dispute over ownership of certain MacKay lands between, on one side, John and Donald MacKay, bastard sons of Roy MacKay, and on the other, their uncle, Neil, erupted into clan warfare. The disputed territory lay in Strathnaver in Sutherland and Neil was supported in his bid by the earl of Caithness. Initially successful, he was soon caught in an ambush laid by his aggrieved nephews, themselves allied to Clan Chattan. Though Neil escaped, his sons and many of his followers fell. John MacKay finally settled the account with his uncle the following year in an encounter which cost Neil his head. Growing bolder, the brothers invaded Sutherland but were defeated by the earl's forces in a savage fray that left 250 dead. Undaunted, John MacKay continued his career in arms and fought against the Murrays throughout the 1520s.

Despite this martial heritage, it has been suggested that a relatively small percentage of those who lived north of the Highland line were natural warriors in the true sense. Many in the remote isles and in the barren wastes of the north-west were too scattered and too poor. It would undoubtedly be wrong to think of every Highlander as a 'Rob Roy' figure. Most were poor herdsmen and drovers who can have had little time or energy for extensive forays. Such adventures were better suited to the sons of chiefs and tacksmen, less ground down by daily necessities and better able to afford expensive arms.

General Hawley, Cumberland's General of Horse, seen as a loutish and ill-tempered martinet cordially detested by all those who had the misfortune to come under his command, though this may be an overly harsh assessment, has left us with a description of Highlanders arrayed for battle. A more hostile witness would be hard to identify but his description, however grudging, has an edge of reality:

> They commonly form their Front rank of what they call their best men or the Highlanders, the number of which being always but few when they form in battalions they commonly form four deep and these Highlanders form the front of the fore, the rest being Lowlanders and arrant scum.[22]

One assumes that Hawley penned this contemptuous summary before these Highlanders, ably assisted by the 'arrant scum' and brilliantly led by Lord George Murray, gave Hawley's troops a severe mauling in the sleet at Falkirk.

What, in England, may have developed as a long-running case in chancery, developed in the third decade of the sixteenth century into a murderous internecine feud, when in 1534 Ian Moydertach, the captain of Clanranald, was granted a charter recognising him as head of the clan. Ian was a bastard son of Alistair, successor to the former chief of Clanranald, Dugal, who had been assassinated by his disgruntled kin, grown weary of his authoritarian habits. Alistair, being more amenable, was set in his stead and, on Alistair's death, Ian was accepted as chief.

Dugal, however, had left a son called Ranald who had been raised by Lord Lovat, head of the powerful Frasers. When Ranald, known to his estranged clansmen as Ranald Gallda or 'Ranald, the Stranger', came of age his uncle sought, on his behalf, to assert his birthright. Moydertach negotiated an alliance with Keppoch and Lochiel and, in 1544, with their aid, drove out Ranald and for good measure laid waste his stepfather's lands and relieved him of possession of Castle Urquhart on Loch Ness. Lovat now called upon his own ally, the earl of Huntly, who, in turn, routed Clanranald. The 'Stranger' enjoyed a further brief sojourn as chieftain before Moydertach, rallying his supporters, ambushed the Frasers near Loch Lochy and accounted for some 300, including Ranald, Lord Lovat and his son, the Master.

Huntly now entered the ring on behalf of his fallen vassal and, with the aid of the MacKintoshes, defeated Clanranald, capturing and executing both Keppoch and Lochiel. Moydertach was outlawed and forced to 'skulk' in the heather while MacKintosh and Huntly fell out with each other, leading in 1549 to the execution of the former. The sentence of outlawry was eventually lifted and Moydertach, now pardoned, was able to resume the chieftainship.[21]

The weapons which these Highland warriors wielded became, latterly, as distinctive as their dress. Throughout the medieval period the rank and file relied upon spears, bows and axes, introduced by the Vikings, and by the fourteenth century the long-handled axe had reached its fully developed form. The use of the term 'Lochaber axe' is not recorded until the sixteenth century and appears to describe a long-shafted weapon with a distinctive head, a sweeping cutting edge, greater in length than in breadth and finished with a hooking device embedded in the head of the shaft.[23]

Swords were a rarity and not for the commonality. By the sixteenth century a peculiar Highland variant had developed: essentially a two-handed weapon with a heavy double-edged blade distinguished by its downward sloping quillons terminating in pierced quatrefoils, the slender grip surmounted by a wheel-shaped pommel. This great sword or *claidheamhmor* was a fearsome weapon.[24]

The later form of Highland blade, the basket-hilted broadsword, is often mistakenly referred to as a 'claymore', a bastardised pronunciation of its distinguished forebear. English chronicles refer to early basket-hilted weapons as having 'Irish' hilts. These hilts developed from simple beginnings in the sixteenth century to a highly distinctive and superbly crafted form by the early eighteenth. By this time the original framework of vertical bars had assumed rectangular shape and the spaces between filled with a variety of designs: circles, diamonds, clubs, and other shapes. The finest hilts were made by the craftsmen of Stirling and Glasgow, amongst whom John Allan of Stirling is particularly famed.[25]

The Highland dirk or 'widowmaker' in all probability was descended from the earlier 'ballock' knife, a long-bladed dagger intended to be held left-handed and as long as a man's forearm. The blade, often salvaged from a cut-down sword, was single-edged and tapering, the upper edge sometimes set in brass. Bog-oak or myrtle was favoured for the stubby pot-bellied handle, surmounted by a disc-shaped pommel, finished in silver and brass.[26]

Very much the Highlander's choice and usually crafted in the dark glens themselves, the targe or target was a survival from the round bucklers of an earlier era. Two layers of oak or fir 2 ft across were laid with the grain opposing and covered in supple hide, the basic form embellished with brass studs and intricate tooling, finished with a central projecting boss which itself could often be threaded with a slim spike, intended mainly for parrying.[27]

Early firearms had little appeal to Highlanders whose main tactic in battle was the charge, that wild onrush as fierce as breakers on the Atlantic shore. Such guns as they possessed were discharged before the final rush and cast aside. In hand-to-hand, the average infantryman of the period, especially in the era of the 'plug' bayonet whose insertion automatically prevented reloading, had but scant prospect of survival. Trained since early manhood to the use of his weapons – flashing broadsword and hacking dirk – the Highlander was a formidable opponent.

A survivor of the rout at Killiecrankie in 1689 described the terrifying speed of the Highland charge and how the clansmen cast aside their plaids to rush, clad only in shirt and doublet, onto the redcoats.

Though the cumbersome matchlock never gained favour the development of the wheel-lock and snaphaunce mechanisms spurred the production of both pistols and long arms. Early Highland handguns or 'daggs' are distinguished by their all-metal construction, stubby triggers, absence of trigger guards and highly distinctive 'fishtail' or 'lemon' butts. The Highland pistol fully came of age with the introduction of the flintlock. Though retaining the stubby trigger and all-metal stocking, these later weapons have the equally distinctive heart-shaped butt. The weapon was finished with a belt hook as the use of holsters was eschewed and the guns, usually carried as a pair, were suspended from a belt worn high across the chest.[28]

The customary dress of the clans was a highly distinguishing factor and one which was noted by most outsiders. An Englishman, William Sacheverell, writing at the end of the seventeenth century, has left the following description of Highland costume:

> The usual habit of both sexes is the plaid ... the men wear theirs after another manner ... it is loose and flowing like the

mantles our painters give their heroes. Their thighs are bare with brawny muscles. Nature has drawn all her strokes bold and masterly. What is covered is only adapted to necessity, a thin brogue on the foot, a short buskin of various colours on the legs, tied above the calf with a large shot pouch on each side of which hangs a pistol and a dagger . . . A round target on their backs . . . in one hand a broadsword and a musket in the other.[29]

In 1589 the great Catholic magnates of the north were busy conspiring with Philip II to provide a forward base for military operations against the troublesome English. The earls of Huntly, Errol and Angus did all but flaunt their treachery, much to the irritation of Elizabeth who demanded James VI take action. Despite the arrogant manner in which the earls had behaved, the king, after forcing their submission at Brig o' Dee, was disposed to treat them with extreme leniency. Undeterred, Huntly and Errol continued plotting, though warned in 1593 to renounce their faith or forfeit their estates. In the event they lost neither, remaining secure and aloof in their northern territories.[30]

The following year, finally, they overstepped the mark and sprang a papal agent from gaol in Aberdeen. Stung into action, James prepared to march but before the royal army could be marshalled, Argyll, aided by the MacLean and his islesmen, advanced to the attack, a combined force of about 7000, against whom Huntly was able to field about 1000 of his own Gordons, with a further 3000 horse under Errol.

The two sides clashed and despite the apparent odds the northern earls won the day. Huntly had bolstered his foot with the addition of a small train of artillery, some six guns in all. The 'whiff of grapeshot' proved decisive and Argyll fled discomfited, leaving several hundred dead upon the field. The victory of Glenlivet was hardly decisive, however, for when faced with the king's full power they submitted meekly.[31]

Above the desolate rim of Rannoch Moor looms the hunched majesty of Buchaille Etive Mhor, the 'Big Herdsman', the guardian of Glencoe. Once beyond the petrified edge of the moss, the mountains rank like sentinels, crowding the narrow valley floor, where the waters of the Coe pelt, tumultuous, down to Loch Leven. The Glen is forever linked with the name MacDonald and the grim happenings enacted on 13 February 1692, a night when nature's fury rose to equal man's inhumanity.

MacDonald of Glencoe was a small sept of mighty Clan Donald but the mischief they created belied their numbers and few were better versed in slaughter and pillage. Alistair MacIain was the twelfth chief and, entering his seventh decade, could look back on a career replete with banditry, latterly legitimised by his adherence to the exiled House of Stewart. His clan, perhaps 500 in all, lived in a necklace of scattered hamlets, mostly on the fertile shores of Loch Leven, at Invercoe, Carnoch, Achnacone and Achtriochtan, overlooked by the rough-hewn ridge of Aonach Eagach. Though Clan Donald were not the original inhabitants, they were by now the most numerous and MacIain could probably count on 150 broadswords.[32]

Glencoe has been labelled romantically the 'Glen of Weeping' and, apt as this may appear, it derives form a mistranslation by Macaulay. It is more likely to mean the 'Glen of Dogs', after the wolfhounds of the legendary hero Fionn MacCumhail, whose deeds were sung by his son, the poet Ossian. The Feinn, as his warband were known, were said to have slogged it out with a Viking force whose long-oared galleys, 40 in all, had swept up Loch Leven. So furious was the fight and so merciless the pursuit of the defeated Norsemen that a mere two ships sufficed to evacuate the survivors.

In 1690 King William, mindful of the slaughter Jacobite clans had wreaked at Killiecrankie, devised a scheme to guarantee the loyalty of the chiefs by binding them to him by formal oath. By the middle of the following year the architect of this plan, Campbell of Breadalbane, fixed a deadline, 1 January next, by which date all must submit or face the consequences. Exactly what these consequences were to be was not defined; it is doubtful if Breadalbane intended a massacre.[33] 'Grey John' harboured a particular animosity towards Glencoe but was too canny a politician not to see the fallout from attempted genocide.

MacIain, punctilious in his roguish honour, insisted on waiting until he received formal intimation, from the exiled Jacobite court at St Germain-en-Laye, that he was released from his earlier oath to James VII. This proved a protracted business and the year was fast waning when the old bandit turned up at Fort William to submit. The garrison commander, Colonel Hill, an ageing but still formidable figure and one who emerges from the unholy affair as essentially a decent man, was unable to administer the oath. Undeterred, MacIain battled through 60 miles of appalling weather to give his uneasy pledge in the Campbell stronghold of Inveraray.[34]

His journey, dogged by inclement weather, was halted when he was first wrongly arrested and then frustrated when a sheriff empowered to administer the oath could not be found. By the time he finally placed his hand upon the Bible his submission was five days beyond the deadline. Technically it was thus too late and, arguably, invalid.[35]

Pedantic as this argument may seem, given the circumstances, it was fully sufficient for the needs of Sir John Dalrymple, Master of Stair and Lord Advocate. Dalrymple favoured a more forthright approach to the problem posed by the recalcitrant clans and found a willing tool in Major Duncanson, Hill's second-in-command, who, doubtless, felt that Hill himself would baulk at the orders he proposed to issue.[36] It has to be doubted whether Stair, however much he despised these embarrassingly backward clansmen, intended a slaughter. Much depends upon the exact interpretation of the word 'extirpate' which has a clearly defined meaning in Scots' Law.

And so it was that on the night of 13 February in near blizzard conditions Captain Robert Campbell of Glenlyon prepared to carry out his unequivocal instructions which concluded with a scarcely veiled threat should his conscience seek to intervene. Glenlyon, in some ways, was the perfect choice; already in late middle age, he had been forced to seek a commission when, burdened with drink and debt, he was ruined when the MacDonalds laid waste his mortgaged estates. The plan called for a co-ordinated attack by three columns of foot, to one of which, led by Duncanson, was assigned the unenviable task of marching through the freezing darkness over the difficult mountain path from Kinlochleven, known appropriately as the 'Devil's Staircase'. The columns were to sweep down the glen, mopping up the string of hamlets and cutting off all avenues of escape.[37]

The MacDonalds were totally unsuspecting, yet the botched death-toll of 38 recorded slayings, mostly of the old and infirm, was a consequence partly of the foul weather and lack of visibility. MacIain was shot down as he struggled into his breeches, shouting for whisky to be brought to his assassins, who had but lately been his guests. His sons, however, and most of the clan escaped, stunned, fleeing through the snow. Many found shelter in a remote eyrie, the Coire Gabhail, but others died of exposure on the merciless slopes of Bidean Nam Bian.[38]

Jacobite propagandists were not slow to capitalise as news of the horror spread. Though few had much sympathy for the MacDonalds, whose own record was scarcely exemplary, many were revolted by the idea of murder under trust where government soldiers appeared as murderers in the night amid the very folk upon whom they had been billeted and with whom they had previously fostered cordial relations. Glenlyon seemed anxious to blab his story around the coffee houses and taverns of Edinburgh to all who would listen and public disquiet grew.

As a result of this increasing unease, an official inquiry was instigated, soon followed by another. The second investigation did not publish its findings until June 1695 and succeeded in fully clearing all the participants save Dalrymple and Duncanson, neither of whom was made to suffer for his sins.

The massacre of Glencoe has held the public imagination ever since but it was by no means an isolated incident. Far from the 'Rob Roy' image, many Highland affairs were brutal and one-sided. In 1578 a marauding band of MacDonalds of Uist locked the MacLeod inhabitants of Trumpan on Skye in their timbered kirk and fired the building – only one young girl, horribly burnt, staggered clear and lived just long enough to raise the alarm. Big with vengeance, MacLeod of Dunvegan tracked the killers to Ardmore Bay and spared none. The dead clansmen were laid out along a turf dyke, toppled onto the bodies by way of burial, an incident which became known as the 'battle of the Spoiling of the Dyke'.[39]

By the third decade of the eighteenth century the Highland way of life was becoming increasingly anachronistic. The more sophisticated inhabitants of the Lothians and south of the Highland line found their northern contemporaries an embarrassment. Though Martin Martin had produced his 'Description of the Western Isles of Scotland' in 1703 the romancing of the Highland way of life was still some time away. Since the Restoration the chiefs, whose prominence had been enhanced by the Civil Wars, were tending to rely upon lawyers rather than swords. James II, whilst Duke of York, intervened on their behalf or ostensibly so, to curb the power of Clan Campbell. It was this which fuelled the chiefs' loyalty to the Stuarts.

Oliver Cromwell was perhaps the first who planned a formal policing of the Highlands. He built forts at Inverlochy and Inverness, with additional battalion posts whose garrisons could stamp the government's will on the troublesome clans. This forward policy lapsed with the Restoration but Dundee's rebellion of 1689 concentrated King William's mind on the governance of his wilder northern subjects.[40]

In 1690 Hugh MacKay, presumably still smarting from the débâcle at Killiecrankie, successfully advocated the rebuilding of the fort at Inverlochy, now to be called Fort William. Twelve hundred men with 12 guns were soon crammed in disease-prone proximity within the earth and timber ramparts of the new works.[41] The fort provided garrisons for outlying posts at Invergarry and Urquhart to the north, Tioram to the west, Duart to the south and Ruthven in the east.[42] For the first time since the Protector's day the Highlanders were presented with a tangible symbol of central authority. Not to be outdone, Campbell of

Breadalbane remodelled the fifteenth-century castle of Kilchurn on Loch Awe, adding barracks for 'independent' companies or militia.[43] Grey John was in competition with Argyll for seniority within the clan, which for all his long and devious endeavours he never attained. After the abortive rising and Jacobite scare of 1708 Fort William was itself substantially rebuilt in stone.[44]

Once the smoke had cleared from the '15, the government was bound to accept the need for further policing of the Highlands. It was, therefore, proposed to bolster the larger and existing garrisons by constructing fortified barracks at key locations – Inversnaid was built under the lee of Ben Lomond, largely to curtail the excesses of Rob Roy MacGregor; Bernera barracks were raised in Glenelg, Kiliwhimen or Kilcumein, astride the Great Glen (the future site of Fort Augustus), and Ruthven in Badenoch.[45] Typically these garrisons or fortlets consisted of two, four-square barracks of three to four stories linked by a loopholed curtain with a parapet walk. They were intended to resist neither siege nor bombardment, though Ruthven did, in fact, defy the Jacobites for a considerable period during the '45.[46] In a purely subjective sense these isolated platoon-sized posts are oddly reminiscent of the embattled patrol posts of Northern Ireland where sandbags and wire have replaced solid ashlar.

General George Wade, who after the fiasco of the '19 was appointed to conduct a thorough review of the policy of the Highlands, was not impressed with such limited measures. He reported that the clans were potentially both restless and hostile and that considerable expenditure of both effort and treasure was needed. Writing in 1724, Wade recommended that the recruiting of independent companies from the Whig clans was to be encouraged; the defences of Inverness (the future Fort George) were to be radically strengthened as were the barracks at Kiliwhimen and an armed sloop was to be permanently stationed in Loch Ness.

Suitably impressed, the administration accepted the fiscal burden of the 250 miles of roads and 40 bridges that Wade went on to construct – work which was continued by his successor,

Major Caulfield.[47] Fort Augustus became the headquarters of the government forces in the Highlands.[48] The line of forts along the length of the Great Glen, the new roads stretching over virgin heath, the garrison outposts, all served to undermine the ancient superiority of the chiefs, to pare away the insularity and remoteness of the clans. Tangible proof that the dark glens were no longer free and sovereign territory, that a powerful central government existed, a government that could and would stamp its will on even the furthest of its north British subjects.

Kings over the Water

On 25 July 1745 in the heat of summer, a French frigate, the *Du Teillay*, made landfall near Arisaig on the wild and beautiful shore of Loch-nan-Uamh in the western Highlands. On board was a young man, who, with only seven companions, was determined to wrest the throne of Britain from its Hanoverian incumbents and restore the flagging fortunes of the House of Stuart.

Few episodes in history have left an afterglow so soaked in romance and even though much has, in recent years, been said or written to 'debunk' the myth of the '45, a shadow of that aura remains and will probably always remain. Prince Charles Edward, son of the 'Old Pretender' and grandson of James II, did have charm, charisma, youth and good looks, but the outward shell of the young chevalier masked his abundant failings. He had no real talent either for politics or for war. He was shallow, petulant, self-centred and mercurial. Ruthless in his true indifference to the welfare of his men, he was easy prey for weak-minded sycophants and bitterly resentful of opinions contrary to his own. Even in his mid twenties, he displayed that fondness for the bottle which finally ruined him completely. The vibrant, almost effeminate beauty of his early portraits are in marked contrast to the empty, sagging despair shown in middle age.

His crusade was quixotic, noble in parts, squalid in most others and ultimately tragic. Its only immediate consequence was the savage destruction of the clans and their ancient, if decayed, way of life. The slaughter on Drummossie Moor was one of the nastiest in our history and, at the end, Charles abandoned the survivors without compunction. None-the-less, with what was perceived as a mere rabble of Highlanders he virtually drove the government forces out of Scotland, shattered one regular army, marched his ragged host to Derby and back, bloodied Cumberland's nose and roundly thrashed a sizeable force of regulars in the blinding sleet at Falkirk, all before that final and terrible reckoning.

The Union of Parliaments, 1707

If William III was, on the one hand, generally broad-minded and tolerant, he was, on the other, narrow, authoritarian and obsessive, particularly in his lifelong enmity with France. As Stadtholder he had sought to resist the expansionist aims of Louis XIV and he saw England and English bayonets as but a useful tool in this great struggle. His relations with his Scottish Parliament were not always entirely cordial as France was, after all, a traditional ally, even if, by now, the links were purely mercantile.

Though Dundee's rebellion petered out the Jacobite flame was never wholly extinguished. After the rout of Cromdale MacKay rebuilt Cromwell's old fort at Inverlochy and appointed Colonel Hill, that old but capable Cromwellian, to command. Breadalbane subsequently came to an understanding with the chiefs at Achallader in August 1691, promising amnesty to all who submitted and took an oath of loyalty by the following 1 January. This nicety of timing provided, as we have seen, the excuse for the slaughter in Glencoe. William's joint secretary, Sir John Dalrymple, who was implicated in this horror, clearly hoped the tardiness of the chiefs could be used as a pretext for a bloodbath.

The Kirk was determined to savour its return to power and though the king was by no means anti-episcopalian, the bishops, in many cases, were tainted by Jacobite affiliations. William was minded to maintain episcopalians who openly espoused his cause but the Kirk, brimful of repression and bigotry, was in full spate. Clergy and academics were thoroughly purged. Harsh new measures curbing such perceived ills as profanity and blasphemy were enacted and enforced with rabid power. Thomas Aikenhead, a student who fell foul of this regime, was hanged in 1696.[1]

The late seventeenth century was a time of commercial opportunism. English traders were opening up new horizons and tapping into seemingly limitless markets; new colonies were being founded and developed. Scotland was very much the poor relation, anxious to make her own mark. In 1695 the king sanctioned the forming of a new company to promote trade with Africa and the east, capital for the venture being subscribed from both London and Edinburgh. Under the influence of the Scot William Paterson, founder of the Bank of England, attention turned to the isthmus of Darien in the New World – a more unsuitable choice would be hard to imagine. Folly was compounded by conspiracy when the English investors, afraid of Scottish success, withdrew. Southern opinion prevailed upon William who obstructed his northern subjects at every move.[2]

The colony, finally settled in 1698, was a stillborn thing, under-capitalised, ill chosen, the colonists at the mercy of an impossible fever-ridden climate. Despite initial losses, the Scots tried again the following year and besides all their previous trials had to endure the militant hostility of the Spaniards. Though defeated at Toubacanti, the Spaniards blockaded Fort St Andrew, the colonists' base, by land and sea, compelling the sick and exhausted survivors to capitulate in March 1700. Finally beaten, the Scots left nearly 2000 dead behind them and the nation £200,000 poorer.[3]

A further insult was the Act of Settlement which provided for the Hanoverian succession on the death of Queen Anne. The Scots were simply not consulted and there were many who might have preferred a Stuart ruler to an unknown German. The French had unhesitatingly recognised the prince – to be known to history as the 'Old Pretender' – on the death of James in 1701.

King William had toyed with the concept of a single Parliament but had found little enthusiasm at Westminster. The king's obsession with France continued to the day he died and within two months of his sister-in-law's accession, England was once again at war.[4]

In May 1702 the queen agreed legislation which paved the way for union and she encouraged her Scottish Parliament to embrace the idea. The sensibilities and complexities were enormous and another four years of negotiations and compromise were needed before an acceptable solution was found. Traditional distrust was fuelled by additional tensions created by such partisan legislation as the Navigation and Alien Acts. By July 1706, the commissioners of both nations, sitting at Whitehall, had reached agreement: the two assemblies were to be united with a common flag, a common seal and universal coinage. The Scots representation in the new unified Parliament was scarcely dramatic: 43 out of 513 commoners, a mere 16 peers out of 190.[5]

In Scotland the draft treaty was not rapturously welcomed; Darien still rankled, the Scots were understandably resentful of having to shoulder a portion of the English debt whilst being patronised – in short, they were not enamoured at the prospect of a Hanoverian succession. Stair, the unstinting champion of union, died just too soon to see his vision realised. Though the Jacobites fanned the flames of discontent as best they could the treaty became law on 16 January 1707 and the Scots Parliament voted itself out of existence.[6]

Meanwhile, in Marlborough's great war in Europe, Scottish regiments continued to fight, and with distinction. When Anne died on 1 August 1714 the Whigs, with Argyll prominent among them, moved with speed and certainty to secure the throne for the Elector of Hanover. A middle-aged, boorish and disinterested candidate who none-the-less succeeded, George I was at least a Protestant unlike his Scottish cousin who refused to abjure his staunch Catholicism. The Jacobite cause, however, was far from dead.

The 'Fifteen'

With the benefit of hindsight it would be possible to argue that the Jacobite cause was doomed from the outset, yet in the first half of the eighteenth century no less than four attempts were made, in 1708, 1715, 1719 and 1745. Any chance of success depended upon foreign aid. Even in Scotland Jacobite sympathies were always in the minority, the brand of Rome an anathema to most and in England, the Hanoverians, if hardly popular, were accepted.

In 1708 the Pretender, the chevalier de St George, attempted an invasion, supported by 6000 French bayonets, but bad weather at sea, one of the many crosses the Jacobites had regularly to endure, frustrated the attempt. A mere five months before the death of Queen Anne, James was given the opportunity, if he would but set aside his faith, to secure the accession ahead of the lumpen Hanoverian. Such a price was too high for a man as fervent as the chevalier and he refused. Taciturn and humourless, the Old Pretender was courteous, loyal and constantly temperate in the face of his many reverses.

The 'wee wee German lairdie'[7], as the Jacobite balladeer described him, entered his new realm, whose customs he did not begin to understand and whose language he did not speak, on 18 September 1714. James's supporters in England, led by the earl of Oxford and Viscount Bollingbroke, were outmanoeuvred and isolated by the Whigs, their botched plans for risings in the south-west soon exposed.

Jacobite philosophy always viewed a rising in Scotland as a mere sideshow which could be used either as a catalyst or to divert government attention whilst the main action occurred in England. As prospects for this faded, James became wary of an unsupported insurrection in Scotland but the affair was effectively taken completely out of his hands by the unilateral actions of his self-appointed lieutenant, John Erskine, earl of Mar. In his fortieth year the hereditary chief of the Erskines was recognised for his skill in politics and for his fickle loyalties. A total opportunist, he had held senior ministerial positions and had been a supporter of the Act of Union. Mar, if unscrupulous, was always a skilled orator and his words in support of the exiled chevalier, gilded with pious hopes of an uprising in England and promises of French bounty, bred conviction. Though the chevalier himself was far from convinced, Mar had gone too far to procrastinate further. On 6 September the 'Restoration' standard was unfurled.[8]

The English rising proved a total illusion, the plotters were arrested before their plans could be enacted and Mar had no more than 500 beneath his newly raised banner. The government, however, appeared more worried by possibilities in England than realities in Scotland and Mar, whose talents as a politician considerably exceeded his abilities as a general, remained in the field. Effectively unimpeded, he secured the Highlands and, though he failed to take Edinburgh, established a base at Perth where, by the end of September, his numbers, mostly clansmen, had swollen to over 5000.

Five days before the chevalier was proclaimed in Scotland, Louis IV died, a loss which removed any real prospect of French intervention. Under the terms of the Treaty of Utrecht, wrung from Louis by Marlborough's string of successes, he had accepted the reality of a Hanoverian succession obliging James to officially quit the realm and seek sanctuary in Lorraine. Secretly he had continued to promise support, but with his death, these assurances evaporated and the regency council undertook with England that they would frustrate James's attempt to join his rebellious supporters in Scotland.

Mar, having won the Highlands, now sat, indecisive, in Perth, giving the government time to rally. His opponent was John Campbell, second duke of Argyll, three years Mar's junior and a far more able commander. A champion of the Union, he had also championed the Hanoverian succession, though he had been swiftly disillusioned.

To oppose the growing ranks of the Jacobites, Argyll could muster barely 3000 but with an impregnable base at Stirling determined to block any southward advance. Mar was aware of support from amongst the hard-riding, Catholic gentry of Northumberland, but instead of summoning these to Perth and then sweeping southward he detached Brigadier MacKintosh of Borlum with an independent command of some 2000 broadswords to seek out and join with the Northumbrians.

The prime mover amongst these was the earl of Derwentwater, one of the more quixotic of the Jacobite adventurers, doomed to lose his treasure, his lands and his head in the Stuart cause. Though naturally suited to lead the rebellious northern gentry, he deferred to his cousin, Tom Forster, local Member of Parliament, and being Protestant, untainted by the smear of popery. Forster was a man cast in Mar's own mould, bombastic and optimistic. His volubility hid a total lack of ability. Derwentwater, Forster and Widdrington rode at the head of a following comprised mainly of their own tenantry. There was no real swell of popular support in northern England, an attempt on Newcastle proved a fiasco and the rebels were mighty glad to join with Borlum at Kelso.[9]

With the addition of MacKintosh's men, those who had not deserted, and a stiffening of Border lairds, Lords Kenmure, Nithsdale, Carnforth and Winton, the Jacobites could muster some 1400 Lowland foot, half as many horse and perhaps 1000-odd Highlanders. Kenmure was appointed to command the Scottish insurgents, Forster the English; by dint of his religious affiliation and glib tongue Forster was subsequently nominated as overall commander, a disastrous choice. Once appointed he unfolded his master plan for the coming campaign: far from moving towards Stirling and engaging Argyll in a two-pronged attack, Forster preferred the bolder strategy of a descent upon the north-west where, he felt sure, recruits would be quick to come in.

At this point, perhaps as many as 500 Highlanders sensibly decided to vote with their feet and decamped, soon followed by some of Lord Winton's men. Undeterred, Forster blithely led his shrinking force into the English west march on 1 November.

After spending their first night in and around Brampton the Jacobites easily shooed away some local militia raised by Lord Lonsdale, and progressed southward by way of Appleby, Kirby Lonsdale and Lancaster till, on 9 November, the horse entered Preston, two troops of dragoons under Colonel Stanhope withdrew without firing a shot and next day, the weary foot trudged into the town. Thus far the campaign had been distinguished by a singular dearth of recruits and many of the Scots would be aware of the disaster which overtook Hamilton's army at Preston 67 years before. Forster still entertained hopes of a further advance towards Manchester, but his scouting was as faulty as his intuition for the net was fast closing in.[10]

General Carpenter, with a sizeable force, was hurrying westward from Newcastle whilst General Wills with three foot battalions and five mounted regiments was but a few miles distant. Acquainted with this alarming intelligence, Forster dissolved in panic, issuing a stream of useless orders before taking to his bed in despair. One of his more intelligent directions had been to send Farquharson of Invercauld to cover the key bridge over the Ribble, an order he had immediately rescinded, leaving the vital crossing unguarded. It was by this route that the government forces approached the town and Wills could simply not believe that no attempt would be made to hold the bridge. As the lane beyond was narrow and hemmed in on both sides by high hedges, his natural instincts led him to suspect a trap. His caution bought the Jacobites some time in which to throw up rudimentary defences.[11]

Stripped to the waist, Derwentwater laboured alongside his followers, promising cash incentives to encourage toil, though it is unlikely that further encouragement was necessary. MacKintosh of Borlum commanded the first of four barricades, straddling the principal thoroughfare by the church and with an outwork further up. Derwentwater's volunteers, mounted alongside the Border lairds, occupied the adjacent churchyard. On the left flank of the town Lord Charles Murray blocked up the lane opening out onto open ground; at the third, or windmill barrier, another MacKintosh commanded covering the Lancaster road and with a fall-back position set up by the Mitre Inn. The final barrier secured the Liverpool road; the detachment here was under Major Mills and Captain Douglas. The Jacobites were possessed of half a dozen cannon, which, properly served, could have done some service. Allowing for desertions, the rebels were probably around 2000 strong.[12]

Having discovered his enemy's invisibility was due to negligence rather than guile, Wills, at around 2.00 p.m. on 12 November, began his attack, sending a detachment of foot with mounted dragoons to assault the Lancaster road barricade while Brigadier Honeywood was detailed to lead a similar commanded party against Borlum's post. The Highlanders gave their attackers a spirited reception, maintaining a steady and telling fire, not just from behind the barricades but from the vantage of two large town houses. The government troops suffered heavily, the narrow lane filling with a haze of smoke and a steadily mounting trickle of casualties.

With over 100 men dead and wounded, the frontal attack stalled, but Lord Forrester used the cover of gathering dusk to infiltrate men of his battalion through the gardens to the rear of the larger house to isolate these positions. Inexplicably, the Jacobite defenders were withdrawn from one and the other soon taken.

Wills's second attack was twice repulsed and a third sortie against Murray's barricade also failed after timely intervention from Derwentwater. By nightfall the Jacobite defence was still intact and at the cost of minimal casualties. However, their position was critical. Government troops surrounded the town and were expecting substantial reinforcements. Powder was running low and many used the cover of darkness to slip away before the noose was tightened.

The regiments camped in the open fields surrounding the beleaguered town and next day which, appropriately for the Jacobites, was the 13th, General Carpenter completed his march from Newcastle around noon bringing with him Cobham's, Churchill's and Molesworth's regiments. As the newcomer was senior, Wills offered to cede command but Carpenter, once he had provided for the complete encirclement of the rebels by sealing off the Fishergate exit, approved his predecessor's dispositions.[13]

The Highlanders were all for attempting a breakout preferring the chance of death with honour to the certainty of slow attrition. Forster was less resolute and sought parley, an unpopular choice. A clansman shot the drummer bearing terms, but the talking continued through the afternoon and on the following day the Jacobites surrendered unconditionally.

Most of Forster's talking had been aimed at saving his own skin and he had won no promises of clemency. Some 1500 prisoners were counted. Most of the rank and file were Scots with 140-odd officers; some 75 English gentry were amongst the haul. Only 11 Jacobites were reported killed and 25 wounded, though others, such as Derwentwater, would later go to the block.[14] On the same day that Forster talked his way into shameful surrender, the Jacobite cause suffered a further and fatal blow on a stretch of desolate moorland near Stirling.

Sheriffmuir, 1715

Despite his inactivity Mar had received a steady flow of recruits and by early November had some 10,000 men under arms. All Scotland north of the Tay now belonged to the Pretender and on the 10th he finally decided to move, the apparent strategy being to march southward and seek out Forster with his, by now, vast army of English recruits. Colonel Balfour with three battalions of foot was left to guard Perth and three commanded parties each of 1000 were detailed to mount diversionary crossings of the Forth to confuse Argyll. These detachments would all cross in the vicinity of Stirling whilst Mar with the main body moved higher. At Auchterarder the main rebel army was joined by General Gordon of Doune who was promptly given command of the smaller contingents and ordered to secure Dunblane.[15]

Argyll, however, was not so easily fooled. His intelligence appraised him of the likely Jacobite moves and, calling in his extended garrisons from Glasgow, Kilsyth and Falkirk, he prepared to march. Fearing, perhaps, that the river would freeze over, affording easy passage, he reached Dunblane ahead of Gordon, causing the Jacobite van to retreat smartly towards the main body.

The speed of the government advance and the hasty withdrawal of his own troops seem to have taken Mar by surprise. He had marched the main Jacobite army down the old drove road from Perth as far as Kinbuch on the banks of the Allan Water. The higher ground ahead, known as Sheriffmuir, a training ground for local militias, was a stretch of undulating and frequently waterlogged moorland with the government forces holding the southern rim, tapering to the confluence of Allan Water and the Wharry Burn.

A general mood of uncertainty prevailed. Mar outnumbered Argyll by a margin of three to one but was not by any means spoiling for a fight. His army was short of food and his strategy undefined. The next morning, as General Carpenter's battalions were approaching Preston, the Jacobites at Kinbuck were drawn up awaiting orders. Having kept the shivering files standing since first light, Mar made his appearance around 11 o'clock and treated the army to what – as even the bitterest of his detractors had to admit – was a superb and rousing address. Challenged by their general as to whether they wished to fight, the rank and file bellowed in martial defiance. Argyll, who had already had his men stand to arms, heard the shout and discerned its import.[16]

By beat of drum his 3500 men formed up for battle. The duke believed the icy winds would have frozen most of the normally wet ground and would allow him to utilise his superiority in cavalry. He deployed his front line so that his left rested on high ground (just west of the present road), with the battalions stretched eastward on the downhill slope towards the Wharry Burn. The first rank, moving from the left, comprised Carpenter's and Kerr's dragoons on the extreme flank with the foot battalions of Clayton's, Montagu's, Morrison's, Shannon's, Wightman's and Forfar's. On the right flank were more dragoons, those of Evans and Portmore. The second line, dangerously thin, contained, on the left, a detachment of Stair's dragoons, then Orrery's and Egerton's foot with the rest of Stair's horse and a party of mounted gentry on the extreme right.[17]

From his vantage near the Gathering Stone Argyll caught glimpses of the rebel army as it drew nearer, the line of approach being frequently through dead ground so that at one moment the government troops might see nothing, then, at others, as Argyll reported, 'the dark cloud like masses of the clans as they wheeled into order'. Mar was also deploying into two lines, each comprising ten foot regiments with his horse covering the flanks.[18]

The right of the front line was held by MacDonald of Sleat with Glengarry, Breadalbane, Clanranald, MacLean, Glencoe, Cameron and Stewart of Appin. In the second line, from the right, Seaforth, Huntly, Drummond, Panmure, the Athollmen and Robertsons. On the far right nearest the Allan stood three squadrons of horse: Huntly's, the Stirlingshire men and the Earl Marischal's, a mounted contingent of Seaforth's formed a reserve. On the left were the Angus, Fife, and Perthshire squadrons. The Earl Marischal was in overall command of the horse, General Gordon led the right of the line and General Hamilton the left. Mar himself took up position in the centre.[19]

Though by now barely 700 yards apart the two armies were still largely ignorant of each other's dispositions. Mar delivered yet another rousing exhortation and gave the order to advance. Only when the rebels finally reached the ridge did each side realise their respective right wings were each overlapping the other's left. Argyll had also shifted position, fearing the nimble clansmen could rush his right where the sheltering morass had frozen. The duke himself was in command of the right, General Wightman the centre and General Witham the left.[20]

Mar also made a hasty attempt to extend his left, with his regiments advancing in battalion columns; this last-minute shuffle would cause the first and second lines on that flank to become fused as one. On Argyll's left both Witham and Wightman were hopelessly over-extended but the government line was stretched too thin to allow for any rapid redeployment.[21]

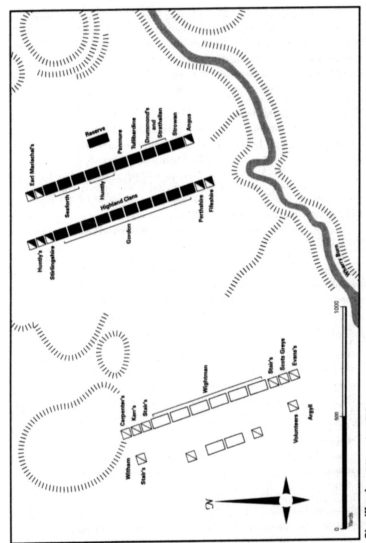

Sheriffmuir · 13 November 1715

Seeing the confusion opposite, Argyll seized his opportunity and attacked with all of the horse on that wing supported by five foot battalions. Though at a considerable disadvantage, the Highlanders fought hard and gave ground grudgingly, supported by their own cavalry. Inexorably they were pushed back, constantly under pressure, but never broken. The duke sent a squadron of dragoons under Colonel Cathcart, cantering round the soft ground to strike at the flanks. Assailed on two sides, the clansmen retreated steadily, falling back in a great semicircle towards the Allan Water. In three hours they battled stubbornly over three miles of bloody ground. Argyll was too experienced a commander to relax the relentless pressure, though he undoubtedly found the job of killing fellow countrymen repugnant, and personally intervened to save some survivors of a Lowland company from being butchered.

Though he had vanquished on the right Argyll had neglected his left and had virtually abandoned his subordinates. The clans fell upon the Government left in a Highland charge, flinging off their plaids and pausing only to discharge their firearms. It was not entirely one-sided: Wightman's battalions managed at least one volley bringing down a number of Jacobites, including the popular Captain of Clanranald. Seeing the MacDonalds waver, Glengarry himself leapt forward, yelling the slogan and putting fresh heart into Clan Donald: 'Revenge, revenge. Today for revenge and tomorrow for mourning.' As the merciless broadswords swooped and fell, the government left collapsed, broken regiments streaming back towards Stirling.[22]

Appraised of this disaster, Argyll regrouped his victorious troops from the right, together with three surviving battalions from the centre which had not succumbed to the panic afflicting the left. His position appeared precarious, with barely a thousand men on the field. Mar, equally shaken, also regrouped. His forces now occupied the higher ground running north-east from the Gathering Stone. Argyll's survivors were technically at his mercy. The Jacobite general, however, appears to have had enough and the rest of the short winter's day passed without battle being rejoined. As dusk fell both sides tacitly withdrew, the Jacobites back towards Ardoch and the government forces to Dunblane.[23]

Next morning Argyll led out a patrol to reconnoitre the ground and to prepare for what he was sure would be another day of combat. To his surprise he found himself master of that bleak and empty field. Though he claimed a victory the real result was, at best, a draw. From the government's viewpoint this was enough, for the Jacobites had badly needed to win and in that they had failed utterly. Argyll had lost 290 men and another 200 wounded. Mar admitted to 60 dead and 80 taken prisoner, though his real losses were undoubtedly much higher, perhaps 300–400 dead.[24]

The drama of the '15 was entering its final and almost farcical act. Despite the best efforts of the French and a plot hatched by the English ambassador to procure his assassination, the Pretender set sail from Dunkirk on 16 December, landing at Peterhead six days later. He stayed in his native kingdom for a total of six unhappy and unhealthy weeks doing little service to his failing cause. A coronation at Scone was planned for 8 January 1716 but Argyll, substantially reinforced, was again on the march.[25]

The Jacobites remained immobile at Perth whilst Huntly, seeing how matters stood, sought terms. James was foolish enough to agree to a 'scorched earth' policy as a last-ditch expedient to slow Argyll's inexorable advance. Although he was replaced as Commander-in-Chief Argyll could not be swayed to the Jacobite cause. The rebels withdrew, passing through Dundee towards Montrose and the coast. Mar persuaded James that the situation was hopeless and he should take ship back to France. He did not need a great deal of persuasion and on 4 February bade farewell to the kingdom of his ancestors. Mar had argued that with James gone his supporters could more easily seek terms from the government, a somewhat fatuous point as Mar, himself, together with the earl of Melfort and Lord Drummond, fled overseas.[26]

Abandoned by its leaders, the Jacobite army, still in surprisingly good order, continued its retreat north. Once amongst the

hills and glens, the clan regiments simply melted away and the
'15 was over. An Act of Pardon was passed in 1717, officially
recognising the end of the rising.

The 'Nineteen'

James's return to the Continent was no happier than his sojourn
in Scotland. After a brief, nomadic existence he was invited to
reside in Rome as a guest of the Vatican, a move scarcely likely
to enhance his popularity in Britain. The Jacobite cause was an
anachronism, to be dusted off and considered should expediency
dictate.

The Treaty of Utrecht had resulted in Spain suffering a number
of territorial losses and Philip V, advised by Cardinal Alberoni,
sought revenge for England's increasing rapacity. Relations deteriorated and war was declared on 8 December 1718. Admiral
Byng defeated a Spanish naval squadron off Cape Passaro, and
Alberoni, fuming, dreamed of an invasion. The Pretender was
the obvious tool for the job and it was proposed that the duke
of Ormonde should lead the descent on south-west England
whilst a diversionary rising would be staged in Scotland. George
Keith, the tenth Earl Marischal, was nominated to manage the
proposed rebellion. Summoned to Spain to receive his orders, the
Earl Marischal was to recruit a force of Jacobite exiles, including the marquis of Tullibardine and his brother, Lord George
Murray.[27]

The main armada, 5000 troops with 30,000 muskets in 29
ships, did set sail from Cadiz but, almost inevitably, experienced typical Jacobite conditions and the expedition was ruined
before it managed to stagger even as far as Corunna where
Ormonde was waiting. The lesser flotilla fared better, creeping
out of various French harbours with a total complement of 307
Spanish soldiers, besides the Jacobite officers and a quantity of
arms. Having tacked round Caithness and braved the unforgiv-
ing rocks of Cape Wrath, the invaders made landfall at Eilean
Donan Castle at the mouth of Loch Duich on 2 April.[28]

Once ashore the rebels fell to bickering. Tullibardine disputed the Earl Marischal's right to command and an unsatisfactory compromise was proposed: the former should command the land forces and the latter the ships. So acrimonious was the dispute that the two 'generals' set up separate camps for their own partisans some two miles apart. This was hardly an auspicious start and doubtless Lochiel, who had returned with the exiles, and Clanranald were glad to escape on recruitment detail. The results of these labours were far from encouraging.[29]

Believing themselves open to attack, with the Royal Navy sealing up the back door and, as yet, no news of Ormonde, morale amongst the rebels plummeted. Tullibardine was all for seaborne evacuation, but the Earl Marischal sent his ships away empty, prompted more by spite than by tactical considerations.

Spies now brought news from Ormonde. Though he had failed even to pass beyond Spanish waters, he urged the Scottish Jacobites not to lose heart, to advance and raise the clans whilst he, for his part, promised a further supply of arms. Though these exhortations took little account of practical difficulties, the rebels struck their camp by Eilean Donan and prepared to march inland, leaving behind a token garrison. An advance supply base was set up at Crow of Kintail, though a substantive cache was left at the castle. It was now May and English frigates were operating in Lochalsh. They missed the main Jacobite contingent but compelled the surrender of the garrison and pounded the ancient castle into rubble.[30]

Orders had been sent to Lochiel and Clanranald to bring as many men as they were able. Meanwhile the main body marched towards Glenshiel in two contingents, the first passing along the east flank of Loch Duich and the other by Loch Long, crossing the high fells north of Loch Duich. On 4 June Lochiel came in with 150 broadswords. Seaforth had raised another 400. Small bands from a motley of clans probably amounted to a thousand more. Three days later a party of Chisholms reached the pass bringing intelligence that a government force under General Wightman had passed through Fort Augustus and was advancing down Glen Moriston.[31]

By 9 June Wightman had reached the head of Loch Cluanie and would be level with the pass the following day. He could dispose some 850 foot, including a Dutch contingent, a commanded party of 200 grenadiers under a Major Milburn, a couple of squadrons of dragoons and 130-odd clansmen. In addition, and by way of ordnance, he brought six coehorn mortars.

The Jacobites determined to stand and strengthened the centre of their proposed line with a series of entrenchments. Lord George Murray, savouring his first taste of command, took the right flank position on the south bank of the Shiel. Moving to the left, on the north bank, stood the Spaniards, 250 in all, on their left Lochiel's men, then the legendary Rob Roy MacGregor with 40-odd reivers, next Sir John MacKenzie, Campbells of Ormidale and of Glendaruel, the redoubtable MacKintosh of Borlum and on the extreme left some 200 yards up the steep incline, Seaforth's men.

Wightman continued his advance and was deploying by noon. On his extreme right, opposite Seaforth, he positioned his own Highlanders, MacKays from Sutherland. Running downhill he placed Milburn's grenadiers, two foot battalions, the Dutch foot, and covering the drove road, his dismounted dragoons. South of the fast-flowing water, on the left, stood Colonel Clayton's regiment, led by Lt-Colonel Reading, with Munroe's on the far flank. On this wing Wightman placed his handy mortars.[32]

Though hostilities began soon after midday with a popping of carbines and a desultory rattle of musketry and a driving in of the Jacobite picquets, battle was not begun in earnest until late afternoon. The six coehorns soon proved their worth lobbing shells towards Murray's men, who were obliged to retire from their exposed vantage, laying open the rebel flank. Now the mortars were turned against the Spanish regulars, and though the range was too great for any serious damage, the thump and crash of the stubby weapons was disconcerting, and the projectiles fired the bone-dry heather.[33]

The government Highlanders had meanwhile moved round to outflank Seaforth and a brisk firefight ensued. Uniquely for a clan battle, neither side came to close quarters. The Earl Marischal took a ball in the arm and his men, being worsted, fell back. With both flanks gone, the Jacobite centre began to waver and though the Earl Marischal, aided by Campbell of Ormidale, steadied the line, the withdrawal soon became general with Tullibardine and the Spaniards following. Funnelling through the high pass round the base of Sgurr na Ciste Duibhe, the Jacobites faded into the long summer's evening.[34]

Murray, as well as Seaforth, had been wounded, though fatalities on both sides were few – each may have lost a score with as many injured. The rising was effectively over and the Spanish regulars, with no sheltering glens, surrendered. Even if the rebels had managed to brush Wightman aside, a victory would still have led nowhere. In short, the '19 was a sideshow without a main event. Ormonde's failure doomed the exiles before they ever quit France.

The Pretender himself, having stoically endured a rash of hardships, reached Madrid in time to learn the full extent of the fiasco. The trip was not entirely without profit for on 1 September he married Clementina Sobieska, a descendant of the kings of Poland. In the next year his bride bore him a son, the heir to his cause, Charles Edward Louis Philip Sylvester Casimir Maria – to be known to history as 'Bonnie Prince Charlie'.

The Young Pretender

In the 1720s and 1730s, Marshal Wade embarked on a major road-building programme through the Highlands, diluting the distinctive territories of the clans, and strengthening the grip of the three royal garrisons – Fort George at Inverness, Fort Augustus and Fort William – that straddled the impressive length of the Great Glen. His infantry were paid an extra 6d a day for navvying but were still too slow and heavy to catch fleet-footed Highlanders. Consequently, Wade, considering the value of poachers turned gamekeepers, enlisted independent Highland companies as a form of native police. In 1729 he raised six companies, whose worth proved such that by 1739 the government proposed raising a further four and creating a new regiment, destined to become immortal as the Black Watch.[35]

Having fought through Marlborough's bloody triumphs, the Royal Scots Greys broke the Regiment du Roi and took their colours at Ramillies. At Dettingen in 1743 the Royal Scots Fusiliers held and then broke another French cavalry regiment, storming the shaken horsemen with the bayonet. On 11 May 1745 Cumberland led a British army to disaster at Fontenoy; completely out-generalled, he left thousands dead. The Scots Guards alone suffered 437 casualties. The Black Watch, present at this defeat, adapted their Highland tactics to the European theatre, firing and dropping flat to receive fire, then sweeping forward with the broadsword.[36]

The Rising of 1745

For 20 years the Jacobite cause languished whilst a dwindling band of exiles clung to a fading dream. The failure of the '15 and the fiasco of the '19 had made it abundantly clear that a rebel crusade could be viable only if backed by foreign troops. By 1740 it might have seemed that the Pretender had run out of time, but the outbreak in that year of the War of Austrian Succession, which saw Britain and Austria pitted against France and Prussia, infused new hope.

Having been badly beaten at Dettingen the French cast around for fresh inspiration which surfaced in the handsome form of the Pretender's son Prince Charles Edward. Worn out by frustration and failure, James was happy to entrust the crumbling fortunes of his dynasty to his heir. In December 1743 Louis XV invited Charles to France and the Young Pretender, as he was to be known, after much journeying and subterfuge, arrived on 10 February the following year.

His welcome was less fulsome than he had expected and a wiser man might have drawn his own conclusions, but Charles was optimistic to the point of delusion: troops, under the formidable de Saxe, were assembling; there was talk of a descent upon Britain's shores; the main force of 12,000 invading the south-east, led, at least in name, by Charles; and a diversionary force of some 3000 under the Earl Marischal landing in Scotland. These heady proposals were tempered with caution; the French wanted assurances that the country was ready to rise, and the Scottish Jacobites needed sureties that the promised legions would materialise.[37]

These rumblings were taken seriously enough in England. Troops were mobilised, as were the militia. As usual, the weather chose to support the House of Hanover and the available French transports were severely damaged by gales. In the spring of 1745 de Saxe roundly and bloodily beat Cumberland at Fontenoy. French interest in Charles Edward began to wane. The prince, too naïve to sense the underlying political realities, believed the time ripe for an invasion. King George was in his German fief, most of Britain's regulars, those who had survived Cumberland's generalship, were in Flanders, and Charles was always ready to believe the pious hopes of his agents in Scotland.

Undeterred by French disinterest, the prince set about mounting an expedition of his own, funded by cash raised from sympathisers in Europe. He raised sufficient monies to fit out two vessels and to procure a quantity of arms and ammunition, including a score of cannon. On board the frigate *Du Teillay* Charles was joined by Tullibardine, now a gouty 60-year-old, and by four of his Irish toadies, including his old tutor Sir Thomas Sheridan and Colonel John William O'Sullivan, a soldier, on his own account, of some distinction but generally perceived by most who knew him as an intemperate and bombastic fool.[38] Sullivan may have received a bad press. Most writers prefer to elevate Lord George Murray, who, whilst competent, lacked any degree of patience and O' Sullivan has suffered in the comparison.

The Irish, as a group, were distinguished by their eager willingness to support their young general even in his wildest and most outrageous fantasies. Like him, they had nothing whatsoever to lose.

Glenshiel · 10 June 1719

In preparing for his great adventure, Charles had by far exceeded the brief from his father, who knew only too well how vital major support from France would be. Charles's fleet comprised the *Du Teillay* and the 68-gun *Elisabeth*, which also carried the Jacobite army, all 700 of them. Predictably, the seas were unkind. *Elisabeth* ran into HMS *Lion* off the Lizard and a lively engagement followed, the French vessel generally getting the worst of it and, much damaged, limping back to Brest. She did not venture out again.

If the expedition had been ill advised at the outset, then to continue was clearly madness but the prince refused to be deterred by such a minor reverse as the loss of his whole force and by the middle of summer the *Du Teillay* was cruising amongst the Western Isles. On 23 July the prince came ashore on Eriskay to reclaim the throne of his ancestors. Besides himself, he had a total of seven followers. He did not receive a rapturous welcome. Even the MacDonalds of Sleat, noted for their Jacobite sympathies, saw little promise in a Pretender with no French battalions at his back. The *Du Teillay* later tacked towards the mainland and by the 25th had entered Loch-nan-Uamh and was lying between Arisaig and Moidart.

Initially there was little comfort to be had; again the MacDonalds were wary and yet Charles was able to win them round by his infectious enthusiasm and potent charm. Unloading *Du Teillay*, the Prince and the legendary 'seven men of Moidart' discharged the vessel and committed themselves irrevocably.

Support was still lukewarm. Overtures were made to John Murray of Broughton, James Drummond, titular duke of Perth and, most influential, Cameron of Lochiel. The prince went to work on the chief, understandably reluctant to commit his people, his lands and his treasure to so foolhardy a venture. Yet Charles was persuasive, enthusing about the great host of English Jacobites ready to follow the Highlanders' lead and the promise of support from France. Now, whether he was guilty of total duplicity or of simply passing on his own delusions is unclear but what must be certain is that Lochiel 'came out' because he believed the clans would not have to fight alone. In this he was to be sadly disappointed.[39]

Glenfinnan

With Lochiel's support assured, the clans began to stir and a general muster was ordered for 19 August by Glenfinnan at the head of Loch Shiel. Meanwhile, on the government side, the commandant of Fort Augustus had detailed two companies of the Royal Scots to reinforce Fort William. These luckless infantry were ambushed and captured by Keppoch's MacDonalds and some Camerons. Despite this morale-booster, the gathering at Glenfinnan was poorly attended. After a couple of anxious hours the Camerons appeared and Tullibardine felt confident enough to unfurl the rebel standard and the tiny army was soon swollen by MacDonalds driving their prisoners.

Throughout this phase of the rebellion Charles remained anxious to cultivate his clan allies, affecting Highland dress and the odd phrase of Gaelic. He offered a spurious reward of £20,000 for the person of the king in retaliation for the administration offering such a bounty for his own golden head. In fact, his relationship with the Highland chiefs, final paladins of a dying breed, was never more than a marriage of convenience, born out of mutual desperation. Charles, having nothing, could afford to risk all on a single throw. The clans, threatened by the natural decline of their ancient way of life and steadily increasing pressures from government, were not inclined simply to fade away.[40]

It must be remembered that of the full fighting complement of the western clans, perhaps 30,000 broadswords all told,[41] only a relatively small percentage were prepared to hazard all in the Jacobite cause. Some credit for this reluctance must be due to the Lord President of the Court of Session, Duncan Forbes of Culloden, who kept a stern if avuncular eye on his Highland clients. Forbes was pro-active in the government cause and spread admonition tempered with reason.

Many took careful heed. As well as seeking to deter potential Jacobites, he sought to raise independent companies for government service.

Despite Charles's dramatic flourish at Glenfinnan, there was as yet no undue panic in Edinburgh; the Commander-in-Chief of government forces, Sir John Cope, transferred to Stirling to take charge of a proposed expeditionary force. This would consist of Lee's, Lascelles's and Murray's, with some Highlanders, and two companies from Guise's, Gardiner's and Hamilton's dragoons. Colonel Gardiner was a professional soldier of considerable experience, something of a *beau sabreur*, though latterly prone to depression. The quality of his and Hamilton's troopers may well have been a contributory factor.[42]

Cope's brigade marched from Stirling on 20 August, heading for Fort Augustus by way of Crieff and Tay Bridge. He had perhaps 1500 men, four 1½-pounders, as many coehorns and 1000 muskets to distribute amongst the independent companies the general was hoping to raise. But as he toiled north and west, he found support for the government scarcer than gold and most of the spare arms went back to Stirling.[43]

Marshal Wade's road-building programme had conquered the steep pass of Corryarrack where the track now climbed a dizzy series of hairpins. Whoever held the pass controlled the way to Fort Augustus, and the Jacobites, who had quit Glenfinnan on 21 August, won the race, the rebel ranks now swollen with men of Clanranald, Glengarry, Grant of Glen Moriston and Stewart of Appin. Outmanoeuvred and probably outnumbered, Cope hastily abandoned any thought of offensive action and diverted east towards the sanctuary of Inverness.

Cope's defection left the road to the south and the soft belly of the Lothians wide open. Such a glittering prize was more than sufficient for the prince and he ordered his fledgeling army south. Realising his error, Cope marched his footsore brigade to Aberdeen where transport would carry his battalions south by sea. The embarkation was not completed until 16 September by which time the rebels were knocking on the capital's door.

Edinburgh

Swift-footed, the Highlanders scorned the difficulties that so weighed upon the government armies and marched cross-country by way of Blair to Perth which they entered on 4 September, and where the prince welcomed Drummond and Tullibardine's younger brother, Lord George Murray.

This last was a momentous union. Lord George was everything the prince was not: in his mid-forties, a natural soldier, loyal, honest and temperate. A Jacobite through and through, he had lived quietly, tainted but still in possession of his estates since the débâcle at Glenshiel. Respected by the clans, he had a real understanding of how to use Highlanders in battle. Conversely, he tended to be authoritarian and was blunt to the point of rudeness. He could not abide fools, which instantly put him at odds with the prince's Irish cronies and his relationship with Charles became increasingly acrimonious as the prospects for success diminished.[44] The chevalier de Johnstone served as his lordship's aide and left a lively memoir of the Rising, in which he describes Lord George as 'tall and robust, and brave in the highest degree'.[45] Like Lochiel, he was seduced by intimations of French aid which, as usual, the prince conjured out of thin air and, like Lochiel, his awakening was to be a bitter one.

On 11 September, with morale soaring, the rebel army began the march to the capital. By now the Jacobites were being taken very seriously indeed and the city was in uproar. The walls, long neglected, were indefensible and Cope was still somewhere on the high seas. By the 15th Charles was at Linlithgow, the palace of his forebears and by the following day had reached Corstorphine, a bare three miles beyond the city gates. Buoyed by Cope's landing at Dunbar on the 17th, the magistrates desperately sought to organise some sort of local defence. The performance of Gardiner's dragoons, the only regular unit available, was less than inspirational, no opportunity for hasty retreat had been overlooked and they had done nothing to deter the rebels' inexorable advance.

Before the day was out a Highland unit seized the gates and in a largely bloodless struggle, the Jacobites occupied the city. By nightfall all was theirs bar the great castle, which, under the surprisingly virile leadership of its 87-year-old governor, remained defiant.[46]

Though generally well behaved the Highlanders would never be welcome in the Lowland capital; they might be feared but would never be respected. Only the dashing figure of the young chevalier himself elicited admiration, particularly from members of the opposite sex. Though occupied, the city remained unimpressed with the rebel army. Their lack of firearms was particularly noticed, as one resident commented:

> I observed there armes they were guns of diferent syses, and some of innormowos length, some with butts turned up likk a heren, some typed with puck thread to the stock, some without locks and some matchlocks, some had swords over ther shoulder instead of guns, one or two had pitchforks, and some bits of sythes upon poles with a cleek some (had) old Lochaber axes.[47]

There were few arms to be had in the city, as most were safely locked up in the castle, and fewer recruits. The irony of Charles's crusade was that, whilst his fearsome Highlanders might win battles, they had not won hearts and minds. With the army camped at Duddingston, one mile to the south-east of the capital, the rebels were reinforced by a brigade of MacLachlan's and Athollmen, with mounted gentry under Lords Elcho and Balmerino, bringing the prince's strength up to perhaps 2400 foot and, say, 50 horse.

Cope had marched from Dunbar on the 19th. His foot and dragoons reunited, he intended to seek battle in the hope of utterly crushing the rising. That evening the government forces bivouacked in pasture just west of Haddington. By the next day the Jacobites, too, were on the move, Lord George Murray leading the van, and an encounter now seemed inevitable.

Loudon's scouts advised Cope that the rebels had reached Preston and would shortly be in view. The general decided to hold his ground, a level plain between the villages of Preston and Seton. On his right lay the hamlet of Prestonpans whilst nearer, on the same flank, crowded thick-walled stone enclosures. Between his extreme left and the straggling cottages of Seton, the ground dissolved into a morass, draining into a pond behind the village. To his front more soft ground with a sheltering ditch and tangle of hedges, to his rear Cockenzie and, beyond, the Firth of Forth.[48]

The rebels were crowded onto the higher ground around Fawside Hill, west of the government position. Lord George recognised the strength of Cope's dispositions and, though he might itch to be amongst the redcoat lines, any form of frontal assault seemed utterly impractical. As the late summer day waned, the armies shuffled and manoeuvred but the basic position remained unchanged. Frustrated, the rebels held a council of war that evening to decide their tactics for the following day, though the obstacles were great; an all-out assault, trusting to the nimble surefootedness and fighting spirit of the clans, appeared the only viable option. Lord George believed the government forces to be stronger than they were, when in fact he enjoyed a marked superiority in numbers. Cope could barely muster 2000 men.

Battle of Prestonpans, 1745

Matters took a dramatic turn when a local sympathiser, Robert Anderson, approached the Jacobite officers. He had been one of the few recruits to join the ranks in Edinburgh and knew the ground well, having shot snipe amongst the marshes, and more particularly he knew of a way through. This intelligence was not wasted and, in the dim hours before dawn, the rebel army, in slender columns, crept downhill to the fringe of reeds and, following Anderson, picked their way across the morass.[49]

As the men moved, like wraiths, a shallow shroud of mist hung over the flat and desolate marshland. In that chill hour before sunrise an alert dragoon discerned some hint of movement and bellowed a challenge. There was no attempt to reply and the rebels hastened through the fog. The duke of Perth was in charge of the van leading the column north through a shallow defile by the solitary steading at Riggonhead. Once the rearguard had safely passed over, the army deployed into line.

This proved unexpectedly contentious when Camerons and MacDonalds volubly contested that each was entitled to the honour of holding the right flank. At length this dispute was resolved in favour of Clan Donald and Lochiel's men, with bad grace, took the left.

Thus and from the right the rebel line comprised the regiments of Clanranald, Glengarry, Keppoch, the roguish MacGregors, Perth's and the Appin men, the Camerons. In the second line, also from the right stood the Athollmen, Robertsons and MacLachlans with the horse on the left flank in reserve. Perth led on the right of the front line, Lord George Murray on the left with the prince commanding the second.[50]

As the mist cleared and the day brightened General Cope, awakened and alerted by the earlier alarum, now found himself completely out-manoeuvred. With his flank wide open, he had to swing his whole line to the left. Sensing the tremors of fear amongst his raw troops, the general treated them to a rousing address, giving vent to his contempt for the Highland army as 'a parcel of rabble, a parcel of brutes'.[51]

He deployed his foot battalions, Lee's, Guise's, Lascelles's and Murray's, in the centre with dragoons on both flanks and in reserve. For ordnance he had his mortars and half a dozen light guns. So far the government dragoons, Hamilton's and Gardiner's, had failed to display any noticeable trace of martial vigour and did not seem likely to improve. Had Cope possessed aggressive cavalry, he could have sought to exploit the gap which had opened up between the two wings of the Jacobite front line. Perth had, in fact, deployed too far to the north, his view obscured by dead ground.

The moment, however, passed and suddenly the Highlanders were advancing, bounding over the level cornfield that lay between, a whirlwind of saffron and plaid skimming the golden stubble.

Colonel Whiteford, a volunteer from the Marines, commanded the government artillery, a lonely command as the makeshift gunners fled at the sight of Lochiel's men. Heroically, the Colonel managed to fire five of the six guns and all of the mortars which caused some casualties amongst the Camerons. The government line was hemmed by the morass on the right and the Firth of Forth on the left. Gardiner's dragoons were to the rear and left of the guns and quite probably suffered from that single cannonade. Panic swiftly spread. Gardiner, himself, despite a conviction that this battle would be his last, fought on and tried to rally his fleeing troopers. Left alone he continued to fight till a Lochaber axe hacked him from the saddle, his dread premonition coming true.[52]

Deserted by dragoons and gunners alike, the untried troops managed a single volley, before dissolving in rout as the clansmen also fired and closed for the kill. At close quarters the barely trained infantry had no answer for broadsword and targe, which cleaved skulls and sheered limbs like cornstalks. Though the fight barely lasted 15 minutes, the field was soon 'covered with heads, legs and arms, and mutilated bodies'.[53]

Some attempt was made to rally the dragoons, who briefly stood but soon wheeled about and galloped off towards Dalkeith. Cope, cursing the poltroonery of his men, tried to salvage what forces he could from the disaster but these were few, less than 200 foot. More than 300 lay mangled on the field, 1600 and more were captive and Cope had lost all of his ordnance arms and ammunition, together with his pay chest and the several thousand pounds it held. The defeated general with Loudon, Drummore, Home and the shattered remnants, made for Coldstream.[54]

Prince Charles Edward was now master of Scotland. With the exception of the garrisons of Edinburgh, Stirling and the Great Glen forts there were no government troops left to oppose him. The Jacobites, who had lost perhaps 30–40 dead and twice as many wounded, called the field Gladsmuir, ample revenge for the earlier defeat at Pinkie nearby.

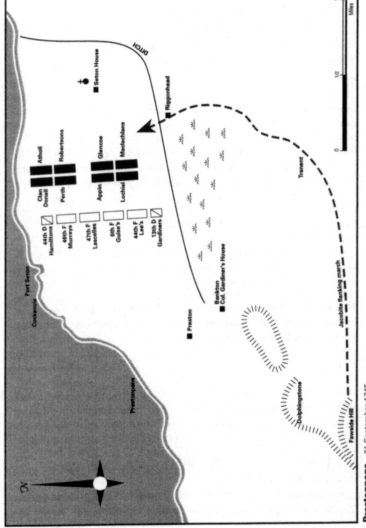

Prestonpans · 21 September 1745

Though the clans had fought ferociously they were quick to offer quarter to all who laid down their arms and every attempt was made to care for the wounded:

> Never was quarter given with more humanity by the Highlanders even in the heat of battle ... The wounded (who were mainly of the enemy) were taken as great a care of as possible.[55]

Into England

The victory fed Charles's delusion that his army was invincible. He did not dwell on the consideration that this was but one battle won against markedly inferior troops and with the benefit of a practical gambit that was unlikely to be repeated. He now wished, to the alarm of the chiefs, to pursue the defeated Cope and invade England. Lord George and Lochiel, however, were for remaining north of the Border and consolidating their hold on Lothian. Their political aims were limited to control of the north and an effective dismemberment of the Union. This was no good to Charles; he could not afford to antagonise support in England by being seen as a purely Scottish king – for the Scots were never more than the means to an end and that end lay not at Holyrood but at Westminster.[56]

For six weeks, whilst the evenings lengthened and the winds of autumn blew through the narrow wynds, the rebel army remained in Edinburgh. More recruits came in, but almost exclusively from the north: Lord Ogilvy, with men of Angus, Gordon of Glenbucket from Aberdeenshire, MacKinnons from Skye, Lord Pitsligo's northern horse. Bar the odd bout of sniping from the garrison, spiced with roundshot, there was little action. On 3 October three transports arrived from France, bringing further arms. The prince cited this fresh aid as evidence of quickening support from across the Channel, secure in his dream of significant French intervention.[57]

Meanwhile in England there was a fever of activity. Cope's defeat had forced the realisation that this was no mere local disturbance. Marshal Wade was at Newcastle whilst regional forces were being mustered in the midlands and south-east. On 19 October Cumberland was appointed Commander-in-Chief. The taints of popery and absolutism were sufficient to rally southerners behind the Hanoverians and volunteer units sprang up throughout the shires.

At a council of war on 30 October Charles was all for an immediate descent upon Northumberland and an early reckoning with Wade. The chiefs, with their regiments dwindling from the inevitable rash of desertions, were less sanguine. Lord George proposed, as an alternative, an advance through the western marches via Carlisle into the relatively undefended north-west where, it was supposed, the cause might find many sympathisers. Relations between the prince and his general were still at that stage where all seemed possible, not yet soured by bitter realities or the poisons of jealousy.

Largely as a result of Murray's effort, the rebel army that marched out of Edinburgh on 1 November was properly organised into 13 clan regiments, though many were below strength: five Lowland regiments, two troops of Horse Guards, a troop of Life Guards under Lord Elcho, together with a train of 12 pieces, half of which had been captured at Prestonpans, in all some 5000 foot and 500 horse. The planned invasion involved splitting the army into two columns, one of which would launch a feint to the east and hope to confuse Wade. The ruse was successful and the ageing marshal remained impotent at Newcastle whilst the Jacobite forces, now reunited, descended on Carlisle.[58]

The local militia under Colonel Durand made a show of defiance from the ancient citadel which, in its long history, had seen many a Scottish host encamped beneath its massive walls. On 14 November the town surrendered and the castle capitulated the next day. Though Durand succeeded in spiking most of the ordnance, a quantity of arms and powder fell to the rebels. On the 16th Wade belatedly struck his camp on Newcastle's Town Moor and began to march west. Hampered by bad weather and with news that Carlisle had fallen he soon returned.[59]

Though they had outmanoeuvred the government forces the Jacobites could not afford to be complacent. Wade would not stay bottled up in Newcastle forever. Sir John Ligonier was advancing from the midlands, whilst to their rear the garrison of Glasgow with some militia and dragoons had concentrated at Stirling. Again the chiefs, their men unhappy, counselled caution and advocated withdrawal and again the prince would have none of it. He insisted on a continued advance promising a flood of recruits as the army marched south, and the chiefs reluctantly concurred.

By 27 November the Jacobites were at Preston, not a place where they would wish to linger, the name heavy with past calamities. After an uneasy day's rest, and still without recruits, the army moved on again to Manchester. Here, as a result of exertions of a Sergeant Dixon, an enthusiastic and persuasive recruiter, the prince found 180 volunteers.[60] This was still a poor return for so many cold and footsore marches. Meanwhile Cumberland, having superseded Ligonier, was at Lichfield.

Lord George proposed another ruse to fool the duke and lead him to think the army was about to head west whilst the main body slipped round his flank and secured Derby. Cumberland had already, and incorrectly, assumed the rebels would make for Wales and veered away leaving the road to Derby open. On Wednesday, 4 December the rebel army entered the town.[61]

The Jacobites had done remarkably well, having maintained a steady advance and foiled attempts at interception. This happy state of affairs was unlikely to last. Cumberland must soon awaken to his blunder. A further government force stood between the Highlanders and London and a great swell of volunteers was said to be drilling on Finchley Common. If this was not bad enough the promised flood of recruits had totally failed to materialise, the Jacobites were isolated and fast becoming surrounded and they were a very long way from home. The chiefs were advised in their counsels by Dudley Bradstreet, allegedly a Jacobite but in fact in government pay. He painted an even blacker vision of the strength of likely opposition.

To turn back now was the ruin of all Charles's hopes. His was too fragile and shallow a character to bear the inevitable reverse with dignity. Retreat meant defeat and he behaved with sullen petulance, abandoning the outward show of comradeship he had cultivated on the road south. The local populace, sensing the change, swung from a nominal welcome to overt hostility; what is less well known is the part played by an English agent, Dudley Bradstreet, in persuading the Jacobite invasion force to turn back from Derby. On 6 December the long retreat began. With their leader a mere shadow and morale low, the discipline of the clan regiments began to waver but Lochiel and Murray rose to the occasion, the latter taking over effective command. Speed was their main hope, to escape the trap before the jaws closed.

Still there was some good news from the north. In Scotland Drummond's brother, the duke of Perth, had landed with troops from France – scarcely an army, however – the regiment of Royal Scots and a battalion of Irish picquets, 50 men drawn from the six regiments of Wild Geese in the French service. More local recruits had come in under Lord Strathallan.[62]

Relations between the prince, who had transferred the blame for his failure onto Murray and the other chiefs, and his general had deteriorated considerably. Lord George led the rearguard whilst Charles, now always on horseback and distant from his tired Highlanders, stumbled along with the main body. By 17 December the army had reached Penrith, miraculously without opposition, though Murray believed he must be attacked either on that day or the next.[63]

Clifton Moor

The rebel column straggled for several miles along the sunken way. The baggage wagons toiled through the freezing mud and made heavy going of the steep inclines. The rearguard consisted of the Glengarry men, a mere handful, and Lord George sent a request for reinforcements, preferably mounted. The prince sent John Roy Stewart's Edinburgh Regiment. Lord George was continually frustrated by stoppages and breakdowns amongst the cumbersome wagons but Charles had issued strict orders that nothing was to be left behind. By the time the main body had entered Penrith the baggage was still ten miles behind at Shap.

As the column inched its way up Thrimby Hill, some five miles north of Shap, a body of horsemen appeared, crowding the summit. Any hope that these were Jacobite reinforcements was soon dispelled. They were, in fact, a commanded party of Bland's dragoons and their objective was clearly to cut off the rebel rearguard. Leading the column was a Lieutenant Brown, an officer from Lally's regiment with two companies of Perth's men. In the absence of orders the lieutenant bade his men draw swords and charge. The MacDonalds, making light work of the hedges and enclosures, swarmed after – Bland's horse did not remain to dispute the issue.[64]

Despite this minor success the struggling column remained under constant danger of attack as increasing numbers of dragoons began to appear. It was, by now, about 1.00 p.m. on 18 December and it seemed that the government troops must seek to engage the column before they reached Penrith. About an hour later a body of the dragoons supported by a motley of local volunteers charged the MacDonalds and a running fight ensued. For an hour and a half the Highlanders met rush after rush, falling steadily back in good order and covering the last mile to the village of Clifton.

The Jacobites believed the enemy was upon them in strength but the pursuit this far had been ineffective owing to a confusion of orders and the fact that Colonel Oglethorpe had overslept, for which he was roundly berated by a furious Cumberland. It was nearly 4.00 p.m. and dusk was falling as the Hanoverian general rode up towards Clifton Moor, brushing aside an attempt at ambush from a body of Pitsligo's horse. A desultory rattle of musketry punctured the cold evening air as the two sides manoeuvred uncertainly on the difficult ground.

Charles had sent Perth with the Atholl brigade to cover the withdrawal from the north side of Lowther Bridge; Stewart of Ardshiel moved up with the Appin men and MacPhersons. Perth had come forward to confer with Lord George and may have had some idea of drawing out the rest of the army to mount a general flank attack but the prince's orders were to withdraw and avoid a general engagement.

Cumberland, meanwhile, had dismounted his dragoons and formed them into two lines: the first comprising Bland's, Lord Mark Kerr's and Cobham's; the second Lord Montague's and Kingston's. A commanded party was detached to cover the Appleby Road.[65] Having paraded numbers of his men up and down the single village street to confuse the enemy as to how few the Highlanders really were, Murray deployed the MacDonalds on the right, half concealed amongst the hedges fronting the moor to the west of Clifton, the line curving back towards Lowther – the Appin men nearest the village in the centre, and Cluny's MacPhersons on the left and eastern flank, again fronted by hedges. John Roy Stewart's regiment and other Lowland stragglers stood in reserve.

Murray took up station on the right with Clan Donald as an eerie fumbling fight began, the darkness and confusion lit by odd scudding patches of moonlight. On the left Bland's dragoons began to filter into the enclosures, to be met by a ragged volley from the MacPhersons. Better armed, the government troops returned fire. Outgunned, the Highlanders swept forward in a desperate charge, skipping over the ditches and hedges like wraiths and falling on the dragoons, who, after a sharp and bloody combat, fell back in disorder, their commanding officer, Colonel Honeywood, amongst the many wounded.[66]

On the rebel right Cobhams were trying to outflank the MacDonalds by beating through the enclosure to their rear whilst Kerr's troopers pushed along the road itself, seeking the Jacobite centre. A party of MacDonalds, concealed amid the enclosures, delivered a murderous flanking fire at virtually point-blank range.[67]

Having blunted these probing attacks Lord George sought to disengage. The Edinburgh men went first, followed by the Appin men, MacPhersons and Glengarry. By mid evening the fighting was done and Cumberland, though he claimed a victory, had little to show for it. Some 40 of his dragoons were dead and more wounded for the loss on the Jacobite side of perhaps a dozen.[68] There was no pursuit and so Murray, the last man to quit the field, retired. He might congratulate himself on a most effective afternoon's work.

With Cumberland encamped in the dismal rain on Clifton Moor, the rebels retired by an exhausting night's march to Carlisle. For the whole of the next day the tired men were allowed to rest, whilst their leaders resumed their habitual discord. Charles clung to the belief that he could maintain a foothold in England by leaving a garrison at Carlisle, undeterred by the patent unreality of such a proposal or by the fact that, in any event, the castle was indefensible. It was the unlucky Manchester regiment, the pathetic remnants of the great recruiting drive, who were left behind.

On 20 December, the day the prince attained his twenty-fifth year, the army marched northward again. At about 2.00 p.m. they halted by the banks of the Esk, swollen with autumn rain and for the next two hours, linking arms in files, the troops struggled through the freezing current which swept a pair of female camp followers to their deaths. When finally assembled on the Scottish side the men restored their circulation with dancing and horseplay. Against all odds the retreat had been successfully accomplished.[69]

Falkirk, 1746

One of the more furious wrangles at Carlisle concerned the baggage which the prince insisted on retaining but which Lord George was determined to dump – in the event all but three of the cannon were left. Once safely north of the border, the army split once more to confuse their pursuers and the van marched into Glasgow on Christmas Day, the main body the following evening. The Highland army had covered 600 miles in 56 days.

Cumberland had struggled on to Carlisle where the hapless garrison made an attempt to resist. Initially hampered by a lack of ordnance, the duke found some 18-pounders at Whitehaven and on 30 December the rebels were forced to surrender, no terms being offered. Having seen the Jacobites off his father's southern realm, Cumberland returned to winter quarters in the south, leaving his subordinate, General Hawley, to pursue the rebels into the northern kingdom. Hawley was a dour, ageing martinet, not much liked by his men. He utterly loathed the Jacobites and considered the noose as the most effective cure for any disturbance. Notwithstanding Jacobite successes, 'Hangman' Hawley maintained a total contempt for the Highlanders and their methods of waging war, convinced they would not stand against his seasoned regulars. He was due for a most unpleasant surprise.[70]

On 3 January 1746 the Jacobites marched from Glasgow in two columns, the prince leading the first by Kilsyth to Bannockburn and Murray the second through Cumbernauld to Falkirk. In each case the objective was Stirling, the main strategic town left in government hands. Reunited, the rebel army numbered some 9000 men, the fullest complement it was to achieve. By the 18th the town had submitted but the garrison, safe behind impregnable ramparts, and actively commanded by another sprightly septuagenarian, Major-General Blakeney, held out.[71]

Three days after the rebels quit Glasgow, Hawley's commission was confirmed and he marched his own and Wade's command by the eastern route to Edinburgh. On 13 January Hawley detached General Huske with a commanded party to carry out a reconnaissance in force, and two days later marched out with the rest of the army, his immediate objective being the relief of Stirling. Murray, too, was patrolling and, having sighted Huske at Linlithgow, began to concentrate Jacobite forces at Bannockburn, a mere 1200 men being left to man the entrenchments.

On the 15th, as the two armies converged, Lord George deployed for battle, in the expectation of an attack, but none came, neither on that day nor the next. On the 17th he determined to seize the initiative and proposed a further advance to the hill of Falkirk, a moorland waste whose rim commanded Hawley's encampment below. For the government troops to ascend and meet their foe on even terms, they would need to struggle up a steep and broken incline traversed by a ravine.[72]

By noon the rebels were moving forward. Lord John Drummond was sent with a commanded party to make a feint towards the government position: effectively screened by woodland, the diversionary force was mistaken for the main body and produced some admirable confusion.

Lord George, leading the main body from the camp at Plean and riding at the head of Clan Donald, knew the ground intimately and chose a wide sweep, under the shelter of Torwood, crossing the Carron at Dunipace. The fool O'Sullivan requested that the army should now halt and make camp but this fatuous advice was ignored and the advance continued. Murray had, in fact, completely outmanoeuvred Hawley, who having ridden over the ridge in the morning, had concluded that no offensive moves were likely. Consequently he had withdrawn for a long and vinous luncheon in the beguiling company of Lady Kilmarnock, wife of the Jacobite earl. For a man of Hawley's experience this was virtually wilful negligence.[73]

It was only when the alarm was raised that the reluctant general awoke to the danger, riding pell-mell and wigless from Callander House. The action that was about to be fought would be a race for the advantage of the ridge and the higher ground, and Hawley, by now nearly too late, realised he was trailing. Sending his dragoons to secure a foothold, he began the cumbersome process of getting his battalions marshalled and sent scrambling up the slope. The climb became a nightmare as passing squalls lashed the cursing, stumbling infantry, blinded by sleet, their powder damp – a disciplined ascent was impossible. The government artillery being hauled by civilian contractors became enmired at the base of the hill and was promptly abandoned.[74]

By now the rebels were drawn up on the moor, the wind and rain blowing on their backs, their lines ordered, their powder dry. On the right of the front line, their open flank protected by soft ground, the MacDonald regiments held their traditional stance: Keppoch, Clanranald and Glengarry. Next, Farquharson, MacKenzie, MacIntosh and MacPherson, on the left Fraser, Cameron and Stewart of Appin flanked by the cleft. In the second line stood the Athollmen, Ogilvy's, Lord Lewis Gordon's regiment, MacLachlans and Lord Drummond's men.[75]

There was some confusion, abetted by the ministrations of O'Sullivan, as to who should command where. Murray took the right and thought Drummond had the left but in fact Lord John was stationed with the reserves and the left wing remained effectively leaderless. The prince was with the rearguard, comprising the French regulars, Irish picquets and cavalry.

Inclement weather combined with uneven terrain to obstruct sight and neither army could be sure of the other. Hawley was frantically pushing his sodden troops into line. On the right he placed the Royal Scots, flanked by Ligonier's, Price's, Pulteney's, Cholmondeley's and Wolfe's. Barrells held the right of the second line with Battereau's, Fleming's, Munroe's and Blakeney's. Howard's were left in reserve. As the lines jostled for position Hawley's right came to outflank the rebel left, hemmed by the ravine which drove in towards the Appin men, but on the other flank it was the government soldiers who were in turn, and substantively, outreached.[76]

To an extent this deficiency was made up by the dragoons, Cobham's, Ligonier's and Hamilton's, who were echeloned forward on the left. Hawley had the benefit of several companies of Loudon's Highlanders, though he made little use of them as they straggled on the extreme right. As the battle began the 700 volunteers of the Glasgow militia were still toiling uphill on the left. Hawley had a total of some 7000 men, the rebels a few hundred more.[77]

Even before his men were in place Hawley gave his dragoons the order to advance. Two squadrons from each flank of the massed horse regiments were detached, without any noticeable enthusiasm. Why this rather bizarre order was given is unclear. Colonel Ligonier could discern no military logic as his unwilling men would be totally unsupported, a fact the hesitant troopers had not overlooked. Given the indifferent record of the cavalry, the order seems ill judged. Most likely the general was hoping the dragoons would check any rebel charge whilst he ordered his lines.[78]

If this was his intention, he was to be disappointed. The MacDonald regiments led by Lord George came on steadily, no mad rush of wildly disordered lines, and let fly their single volley at a bare 12 paces. With four score saddles empty, the dragoons wheeled about, some riding off between the lines, the less fortunate crashing into the MacDonalds whose lethal dirks eviscerated or hamstrung the horses before dispatching the riders.

The panic spread to the remaining dragoons. Ligonier's (formerly Gardiner's) and Hamilton's retired downhill, their rout disconcerting the Glasgow militia, at least one of whose companies dissolved. Cobham's seem to have galloped between the lines, raked by Jacobite musketry, though this was largely ineffective. As the rebels were chronically short of powder they abandoned any attempt to reload, drew swords and charged the government right. The Appin men, Cameron's and Fraser's hacked at the Royals, Ligionier's, Price's, and Pulteney's, inexorably driving the redcoats backward.[79]

With the horse in flight the MacDonalds fell upon the government foot, who with their powder soaked could manage only the feeblest of volleys. The battalions on the left did not stay to fix bayonets, but streamed after the dragoons, carrying most of the second line with them. As the left flank gave way only the staunch veterans of Barrells stood firm. Though the swift-footed Highlanders could have swept down upon the mass of fugitives doing fearful execution, they did not. There was no immediate further advance. Murray and the other officers simply could not believe they had so easily vanquished Hawley's veterans and suspected, wrongly, that they were being offered a trap.[80]

Neither of the rebel wings could clearly see how matters stood with the other and, though the government right had given ground, the ravine prevented the clansmen getting round the flank and it was Cobham's dragoons who, having rallied, attempted to slip round the Highlanders and fall on them from the rear. Seeing the danger, the prince sent in the Irish picquets and the dragoons retired, though in relatively good order, with Barrells, latterly the King's Own Royal Regiment, making a disciplined withdrawal. With the Irish plugging the gap between the wings and order restored on their left, the Jacobites were masters of the field though, as most of the second line had charged with the first, there were no real reserves left to exploit their success.

One wonders if General Hawley, penning his dispatch that evening to Cumberland, still held the clans in such lofty contempt. The dispatch was a masterpiece of understatement. As not all of his regiments had been broken he preferred to describe the battle as a draw and remained economical with the truth when reporting his losses. The battle, whilst unsatisfactory, was not a calamitous defeat and though it must rank as a Jacobite victory did little more than delay the inevitable reckoning.

Due to the lack of pursuit these were less severe than might have been expected. Between 300 and 400 government soldiers died and a further 200 were taken, including many officers. As O'Sullivan ironically observed, 'Gold watches were at a cheap rate.'[81] The rebels lost perhaps 50 killed and as many or more wounded. Darkness concealed the carnage upon the field where the injured were left to moan and shiver till the cold, their wounds or a stroke of the looter's knife, ended their ordeal.[82]

Next day the pallid, stiffening corpses were bundled into mass graves without undue ceremony. Johnstone, overseeing this grisly chore, noted that 'the rustics who stood around easily distinguished the English soldiers from the Highlanders by their comparative nudity and by the deep gashes which scarred their shoulders and breasts – the dreadful work of the broadsword.'[83]

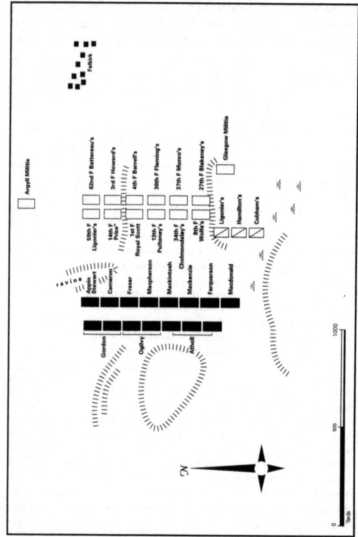

Falkirk · 17 January 1746

Though the battle had been, from the rebel viewpoint, both well conceived and bravely executed, the victory achieved little. The government army remained intact, if shaken; Stirling Castle remained defiant and the Highlanders, bored with siege work, were beginning to drift away. No further support had come from France and Hawley was swiftly superseded by Cumberland.

The duke has not enjoyed a good press. His corpulence bred ridicule and his military career was at best undistinguished and ended in acrimonious ignominy. Though he defeated the prince in the field romantic history labelled him a butcher and he presided over a campaign of ruthless terror unleashed on the Highlands. None-the-less, he was a competent if not gifted officer and, though strict, was immensely popular with his soldiers. Hawley meanwhile had enjoyed something of a religious conversion, blaming his officers for misleading him as to the true fighting skills of the Highlanders and his men for running away. Several were hanged, others flogged and more cashiered before the general's equilibrium was restored.[84]

In the Jacobite camp there was now a palpable rift between, on the one hand, the prince and his Irish, particularly O'Sullivan, and on the other Murray and the chiefs. The former wished to continue the siege of Stirling, blind to the fact that they lacked the means or the skills for the task, whilst the latter advocated a further retreat to the north, there to regroup and make the most of the respite. After a right royal tantrum the sullen prince was obliged to submit and on 1 February the army splashed over the Forth and headed north.[85]

Culloden, 1746

In bitter winter weather, the rebels, again divided into two marching columns, battled towards Inverness, where they arrived on the 21st, Loudon's companies beating a hasty retreat. Again they were baulked by the castle but the garrison, commanded by Colonel Grant of Rothiemurchus, proved less resolute and soon capitulated.

For the next six weeks, the prince enjoyed such sport and society as the Highland capital had to offer. Fort Augustus finally fell, whilst Murray with Cluny MacPherson beat up government detachments in Atholl but failed to take Blair Castle. In the far north, Lord Cromarty was active if somewhat ineffective in the Pretender's cause. Drummond kept busy around Fochabers. As March drew out and the iron grip of winter began to relax the rebel forces were widely scattered: Murray still at Blair, the Camerons investing Fort William, Cluny and his MacPhersons in Badenoch, the Master of Lovat recruiting more of the Frasers. In the event, neither MacPherson nor Lovat took any part in the ensuing action.[86]

With his forces reduced to no more than 5000, the prince shifted his headquarters to Culloden House, home of Duncan Forbes. His cavalry and artillery were particularly weak. Elcho and FitzJames combined could barely fill 150 saddles.[87] Cumberland was at Aberdeen, having taken command at the end of January. He had relieved Stirling and then moved eastward through Perth, where he had been reinforced by a division of crack German mercenaries, Hessians, under Prince Frederick of Hesse-Cassel.

In March he sent a commanded party under Major-General Bland to Strathbogie and, leaving Aberdeen with the main body on 8 April, caught up with the van at Cullen. Crossing the Spey unopposed, by the 19th he had pushed as far as Balblair, only a mile south-west of Nairn. Though he had not brought his Hessians, he still had 15 foot battalions, three regiments of dragoons and several companies of Campbell militia. His guns were served by the Royal Regiment of Artillery and the fleet kept the army well provisioned.[88]

The duke commanded a force of 9000 men of which 2400 were mounted; his foot battalions were equipped with iron ramrods enabling them to fire three volleys per minute and a new bayonet drill had been taught whereby each man in the line engaged not the screaming enemy to the front but the man to his right. The principle here was that where a man with musket and bayonet could be deflected by an opponent parrying with a targe, he could lunge unhindered at the exposed ribs of the next, striking below the upraised arm. The tactic was similar to that employed by the Romans who had campaigned over this same ground 1700 years before.[89]

In the rebel camp was much confusion as scattered units continued to come in. Under O'Sullivan's inept management the commissariat had broken down completely, the men were unpaid, unfed, unclothed and unhoused. Tired of Murray's caution, the prince was determined to prove his own worth as a battlefield commander and had elected to face his Hanoverian cousin on the high ground south of his headquarters, a largely flat, gently rolling plain some 470 feet above sea-level, spotted with humble steadings and enclosures, virtually devoid of trees – Drummossie Moor.

Murray bitterly opposed his choice, considering the ground ideal for regulars and unfavourable for Highlanders. He had already spotted rougher and more suitable terrain near Dalcross, between Culloden and Nairn. When this site was ruled out he sent Brigadier Stapleton and Colonel Ker to view the land south of Nairn and again found more favourable ground. Lord George was, once more, overruled – the prince now listening only to O'Sullivan.[90]

Perhaps more in desperation than hope, Murray now proposed a night attack. The government troops had spent 15 April toasting their general's health; he, too, was now 25 and it was thought that drink might dull the English sentinels. The plan was bold and daring, verging upon the reckless. The exhausted Highlanders were to advance silently and swiftly, marching through most of the hours of darkness to be in position by dawn on the 16th. Murray was to lead the first and larger force; Charles, with the duke of Perth, the other. The night was dark, only the MacIntosh guides knew their ground, the path led over rough and broken terrain. By 2.00 a.m. the van was at Knockanburie, still three miles short of the government camp. There was confusion but the sound of signal drums was unmistakable. Cumberland's guards were far from fuddled, surprise was lost and the rebels, indescribably weary and extremely hungry, stumbled back towards Drummossie Moor.[91]

The Jacobites seem to have hoped or prayed that the government army would not attack that day, but by first light the long lines of scarlet-coated foot, the squadrons of dragoons, guns and limbers were on the march. By 10.00 a.m. Jacobite scouts reported the royal army a bare four miles distant. A hurried council of war was held: Lord George argued that the men were in no state to fight, the ground was wrong, they were outnumbered and outgunned, but the prince was adamant that the army must stand. There could be no further retreat. By 11 o'clock the armies were in sight of each other across two miles of open moorland, a dismal cold and dreary day, the grey skies still heavy with intermittent squalls.

Despite their fear and exhaustion the clans still found sufficient stamina to argue over who should have the right. As a placatory gesture the prince awarded the honour to Murray's Athollmen, who drew up flanked by the Camerons, Frasers, Clan Chattan, Farquharsons, MacLachlans, MacLeans, John Roy Stewart, Chisholms and Clan Donald, with bad grace, Clanranald, Keppoch, Glencoe and Glengarry on the left.[92]

The second line comprised, from the right, Lord Lewis Gordon, Glenbucket, Perth, the Royal Scots and Irish picquets. The remnants of the horse were drawn up behind, Murray commanded the right, Drummond the centre, Perth the left, the Jacobite guns were positioned in batteries of four on each flank and in the centre of the line, the gunners were volunteers who barely knew their trade, a sad contrast to Cumberland's dedicated professionals. The rebels were positioned so that both flanks rested upon, on the right, the walls of the Culwhiniac enclosure and on the left those of Culloden Park. Beyond the Culchunaig and Culwhiniac enclosures lay the course of the Nairn and a bare 500 yards beyond the Jacobite front the government troops were deploying.[93]

Some time before the duke had ordered the shift from column into two lines, each of six battalions with three in reserve. On the left his position rested on Leanach farm and the secure barrier of the river. He had hoped to have a morass on his right, but, finding that he had advanced beyond, ordered up two of the reserve battalions to take the extreme right of both the first and second lines. To consolidate his position on the left, he ordered Wolfe's regiment to move slightly ahead of the front line and redeploy at right angles to it, their backs to the gaggle of buildings at Leanach. The redcoats could pour enfilading fire into any immediate attack upon the line.[94]

Brevet-Colonel Belford had supervised hauling the guns over the rough march from Nairn. He had 16 3-pounders, which were sited in pairs between the front-line battalions. The trusty coehorns were split into two batteries of three and positioned ahead of the flanks. Lord Albemarle was to command the first line, General Huske the second, Hawley was allowed the cavalry, with Kingston's horses covering the right. More dragoons crowded the extreme left and guarded the flank of the second line which from right to left comprised Battereau's, Howard's, Fleming's, Conway's, Bligh's and Sempill's with Blakeney's in reserve.

The swift-footed Campbells, for whom this was a clan affair, had begun to infiltrate the Culwhiniac enclosure, the obvious possibilities of which Murray had not overlooked. He had also requested that the regiment on the right should tear down the walls of the Culloden enclosure to give them more space to manoeuvre. Other officers suggested that the walls be lined with marksmen. Both of these ideas were dismissed out of hand by the prince who, despite his insistence on fighting on Drummossie Moor, had failed to reconnoitre the ground to his front, which was extremely soft and waterlogged, heavy going even for Highlanders with the wind and rain beating in their faces.[95]

Shortly before one o'clock Cumberland addressed his troops, a short and soldierly oration, where he advised his redcoats to remember that they fought for King, Country and ancient liberties. Looking across the expanse of that dismal moor, few on the rebel side, with the obvious exceptions of Charles and O'Sullivan, can have had many illusions as to the likely course of the coming battle.

Viewing the long lines of scarlet and gold, the forest of gleaming bayonets, the black muzzles of the guns, many must have quailed, but they did not flee. Lord George is said to have muttered, 'We are putting an end to a bad affair.'[96] At one the rebel guns began a desultory cannonade and the royal gunners responded in kind. The last battle to be fought on British soil had begun.

It is said that the rebel gunners were provoked by the elegant figure of Lord Bury who had cantered to within 100 yards to mark their dispositions. If his lordship was the intended target, then he remained quite safe, for the ball passed clean over his head, over the heads of the first-line battalions, before pulping some unfortunate in the rear. Another ball struck a few yards away from the duke, missing his ample figure but killing another two almost directly in front.

Belford's gunners totally outclassed their scratch opponents, most of whom were soon dead or in flight. With the brief unequal duel ended, the Royal Artillery concentrated their fire on the clan regiments, the roundshot tearing great gaps, strewing the heather with bloodied plaid and mangled limbs. This was not warfare as Highlanders understood it. It was not in their nature to stand helpless and exposed while being shot down like rabbits. The carnage was dreadful. Mingled with the cries of the injured and dying was the order to close up, close up, repeated as every ball found its mark.[97] Whilst the number of actual casualties caused by the government guns was likely quite few, the psychological effect was considerable.

Charles had taken up position on a slight eminence north of Culchunaig, and behind the centre of the second line, an unsuitable vantage. His view was restricted, his mood indecisive. Lord George and the chiefs pleaded for the order to charge, to be allowed to close with the enemy, sweep across that dreadful kill-ing ground before the regiments were utterly decimated by the relentless and galling fire.

The prince was guarded by the scant remains of the horse and several were killed around him as the gunners found the range. At last Charles gave the order, sending his young aide Lachlan MacLachlan towards Perth on the left, but the youth was struck down before he could deliver the message.[98] Lord George had earlier sent Ker to Graden to Charles, begging that those of the left should echelon forward to close the greater gap on that wing – the opposing lines funnelled towards the right.

Cumberland had taken station towards the front of his second line ahead of Howard's. From here he could see exactly how the battle was developing, at this point satisfactorily. Belford's sweating gunners were winning the day for him.

Around 1.30 p.m. a sudden squall flung wind, rain and sleet in the rebels' faces; Murray could barely control the fury of his Athollmen, 'so impatient they were like to break their ranks'.[99] With a defiant roar the MacIntoshes and Clan Chattan burst from the centre, followed by the Athollmen and the Camerons into the stinging sleet. As the Highlanders burst over the moor the first rank of the government battalions dropped to one knee, the remaining ranks remained standing, firing by platoons, dense rolling volleys flaying the clansmen as Belford's men began load-ing grape. The wet ground and the pelting rain made the going hard. Those in the centre crowded onto the old drove road, where the surface was harder but this channelled them to the right, where they blundered into the struggling regiments on that wing. And the fire never slackened; 18 officers of Clan Chattan and a score from the Atholl Brigade fell before they even saw the government troops, so thick was the smoke of battle. Archaeology has indicated that the walls of the enclosure were only knee height, and no impediment to Highlanders, but that the government mortars, contrary to previous opinion, delivered a continual 'stonk'.

As Clan Chattan closed with Barrell's and Munro's the fury of the onslaught pushed the 'Old Tangeerers' back but they held, flickering bayonets clanged and scraped, Price's and Cholmondeley's blasted the attackers' flanks whilst Wolfe's men raked the Athollmen. Over a thousand Highlanders were hacking at the redcoat lines with Barrell's and Munro's bearing the brunt. Officers and men fell beneath vengeful broadswords, but the cry of 'Give them the bayonet' still sounded and the veteran infantry lunged and parried, striking to the right, driving the needle-sharp points through flesh and bone, their white gaiters spattered with blood.

With his front line under such enormous pressure Cumberland ordered up Sempill's and Bligh's from the second; unbloodied these battalions fired and fell on with the bayonet. Lochiel had already been carried off, both ankles smashed by grape; Murray charging at the head of the Athollmen had his horse shot from under him and received several gashes in the savage mêlée. Seeing that his men could make no headway, he dashed back to entreat the second line to advance – pleas that were were greeted with a marked lack of enthusiasm.[100]

On the left, and with more ground to cover, Clan Donald never reached Pulteney's and the Royals, whose rippling volleys punched great gaps in the charging lines. Still sulking from their relegation to this wing, hampered by the uncertain ground and mercilessly pummelled by shot and cannister, the advance past the sheltering walls of the Culloden enclosure opened their flank and for once the government dragoons did not miss the opportunity. Keppoch and many of his officers were killed and the clan regiments would have been completely cut to pieces if Stapleton had not led forward his Royal Scots and Irish to give covering fire.[101]

Murray had previously noted, with alarm, that the Campbell militia were encircling the Jacobite right by breaking down the rough masonry of the enclosures and cleaving a path for Hawley's dragoons. To counter this Lord George ordered some of Lord Lewis's Gordons men to face about and guard the flank. This still did not prevent some Campbells from lining the northern walls of the Culwhiniac enclosure and blazing away at the Athollmen now streaming back in disorder.

To add to the rebels' growing load of difficulties, five squadrons of dragoons had been lurking along the line of track that ran up from the Nairn past Culwhiniac farm, the obliging militia heaved a mass of stones out of their way and the horse cantered towards Culchunaig and the Jacobite rear. Alert to this fresh peril, Murray dispatched Gordon of Avochie to hold the Campbells with FitzJames's horse in support. Another posse of Campbells struck at the retreating Camerons who still had sufficient fight in them for a vigorous riposte.

Hawley, with ten full squadrons, was finally established in the Jacobite rear, but as his men advanced along the track, sunken through generations of use, Elcho's Life Guards and FitzJames's horse bravely barred the way. A spirited charge could have annihilated the handful of rebel horse, but Hawley's men had difficulty in manoeuvring, impeded by the lane and both sides merely swapped pistol shots. This would not be to the general's liking.[102]

The rebel cavalry, pathetically few as they were, did their comrades good service buying vital minutes whilst the broken regiments fell back. The prince, the wreck of his army about him, may have attempted to rally the MacDonalds on the left but was persuaded by Sheridan and Hay of Restalrig to quit the field – he had had his try at generalship.

Lord George Murray was left to salvage what he could, rallying Ogilvy's and some of the Angus men. He, together with Stapleton's battalions, formed a screen, keeping the threatening dragoons at bay whilst the defeated Highlanders either splashed over the Nairn towards Badenoch or fled along the road to Inverness.

Over a thousand lay dead on that terrible field, piled in heaps before the survivors of Barrell's and Munro's. Barrell's alone had lost 17 killed and 108 wounded out of a roll call of 438. In total Cumberland had lost around 50 dead and many more injured. He had, however, utterly crushed the rising and secured his father's crown.

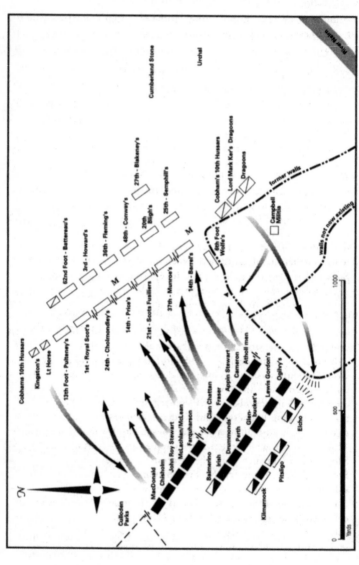

Culloden · 16 April 1746

Beyond the battlefield the fields and lanes were choked with rebel wounded enthusiastically sabred by dragoons who, drunk with slaughter, cantered down the Inverness road cutting down any they encountered, including a number of luckless civilians.[103] A host of captives were taken, including Balmerino and Kilmarnock. Strathallan had preferred to cheat the headsman by a suicidal charge into the midst of Cobhams. More prisoners were dragged from refuge in the cottages and barns. Most got no further than the nearest convenient wall. The Royal Scots and Irish, being regular French units, were allowed honourable surrender. Brigadier Stapleton died of his wounds.

Indefatigable Murray, together with Drummond and Perth, had managed to keep some 2000 together and under arms. A rendezvous was arranged at Ruthven but their prince did not appear. Instead he sent a note which contained some helpful advice: 'Let every man seek his own safety the best way he can.'[104] For some, including Murray, this was the beginning of a life in exile, for others a career 'skulking' in the heather; for the prince a short interlude of wandering, to be followed by a wasted life of acrimony, despair and dipsomania.

For the Highlands and the clans that spring and summer were to be an ordeal by fire, slaughter and terror, their dress and weapons proscribed, their steadings ruined, their byres empty. Barely a generation later, absentee lairds and the more profitable farming of sheep finished what Cumberland's men had begun.

Postscript: The Thin Red Line

'Rally the Highlanders'[1]
Sir Thomas Picton

The 'pacification' of the clans which followed the débâcle at Culloden – and that term must, as a savage euphemism, rank alongside such loathsome modernisms as 'ethnic cleansing' – destroyed the ancient life of the glens. This and the Clearances, almost equally traumatic, which followed barely a generation after, completed the ruin.

Before the '45 the bulk of Scots regiments had been drawn almost exclusively from the Lowlands, where hatred of the Gael ran deep. Aside from those independent companies raised by Wade later in the eighteenth century, Highlanders had been viewed with about as much sympathy and understanding as, say, the Pathans or Zulus a century later.

It was not long, however, before Whitehall realised that, in the Crown's turbulent northern subjects, whose traditional dress and weapons were proscribed under the Disarming Act of 1747, they possessed a reservoir of available manpower, accustomed by tradition to the use of arms, brave beyond compare and, above all, expendable. Surely it was preferable that these uncouth clansmen be encouraged to take the king's shilling and fight and die for him abroad rather than be left idle in their own dark glens, where conspiracy and rebellion had been seen to flourish.

Pitt the Elder, in a celebrated speech to the House in 1766, cannily praised the martial vigours of the Highlanders and stressed the advantages of recruitment.

The unequivocal loyalty the clansmen demonstrated towards their chiefs and tacksmen translated quite easily into the regimental system, especially when units were raised locally. The duchess of Gordon is said to have boosted her husband's recruiting drive by offering a kiss to every red-blooded Highlander contemplating taking the king's shilling.[2] The 100th and 92nd, immortalised as the Gordon Highlanders, brought nothing but honour to the name. The natural valour of the Highlanders, once safely channelled, brought respectability, paid for in blood such as the furious assault of the Black Watch (42nd) on the French fortress of Ticonderoga in 1758, an epic defeat where the regiment lost 314 killed and more wounded. The hit-and-run nature of warfare in the American wilderness suited the Highland temperament, whilst their contemporaries in other regiments, such as the KOSB (25th), won fame at Minden in 1759 when six foot regiments marched against the French army, their disciplined volleys savaging horse, foot and guns. Of the 11 regiments raised in Scotland for service in the Seven Years War (1756–63) only one battalion was from the Lowlands.

Duncan Campbell was one of those who took part in the disastrous attack ordered by General James Abercrombie against the defences of Fort Carillon in July 1758. This was one of the many actions fought in the course of the Seven Years War (1756–1763) in the vast arena of the North American wilderness. Ten days after the fight, Duncan Campbell, serving with the 42nd, succumbed to his wounds. Some three years beforehand Campbell is said to have provided shelter to one who turned out to have been his brother's murderer. This was a fine choice for a Highland gentleman; to deny the call of vengeance or the obligations of the host. A humane man, he spared the assassin and gave him refuge. A little while after his dead brother appeared to him in a dream in which he promised they would meet again at a place called Ticonderoga, which at that point and, unsurprisingly, Campbell had never heard of. On the very afternoon of the day on which the fateful engagement had been played out in New York State, a ghostly panoply of fighting men appeared in the clouds over Inveraray Castle. Clan Campbell was thus given notice it would soon mourn many of its lost sons.

The name Ticonderoga derives from the Iroquois expression *tekontaro:ken* – 'at the junction of two waterways', an entirely pragmatic description for the place stands astride the strategically significant narrow passage of Lake Champlain, where a short traverse cuts through to the northern flank of Lake George. Thus the fort dominated the busy trade highway between English-held Lake Hudson and the French-controlled St. Lawrence River. Such was the importance of its location that four major combats were fought out there within a mere two decades. When the French began to build in 1755, they named their new work Fort Carillon, the choice inspired by the almost musical resonance of tumbling falls nearby. Construction was spread over a period of two years, and the ramparts were not completed until 1757. By then local rivalry between France and England had flared as a wider consequence of the Seven Years War – Pitt the Elder's expansionist triumph that a later populist leader, Winston Churchill, branded as 'The First World War'. It was from there the French launched a successful campaign against Fort William Henry, an episode familiar to all readers of James Fenimore Cooper's *Last of the Mohicans*.

By the following year the British in North America had been substantially reinforced whilst the French, under Louis-Joseph de Montcalm, were forced back onto the defensive. Two campaigns were planned: General Amherst would lead an attempt on the great French bastion of Louisbourg, whilst Abercrombie, as Commander-in-Chief, would assault Fort Carillon. His forces were considerable, comprising some 7000 British redcoats and 9000 colonial militia, well supported by a formidable artillery train. His regular battalions included the 27th, 44th, 46th, 55th and the 42nd Highland regiment (The Black Watch). For the difficult and dangerous business of scouting and skirmishing he could count upon over a thousand of light infantry. Colonel Gage, commanding the 80th foot, was a devoted student of that celebrated exponent of irregular warfare Richard Rogers, whose

Rangers had already made a name for themselves as masters of commando-style operations.

Against this formidable deployment Montcalm could muster no more than 3600 defenders all told, made up of seven battalions of French regulars, supported by marines, French colonials and native allies. He knew the blow must fall upon the bastion of Ticonderoga and thus looked to his defences. The site enjoyed a superb tactical position, pushed out on a spur that jutted, like a salient, against the course of the river, the rushing waters providing additional cover on three sides. The fourth flank was partly screened by a bog and covered by a timber outwork, a substantial palisade nine feet high, the timbers soundly buttressed, and the ground before sown with stakes and other obstacles. The fort itself was a classic star-shaped construction with four corner strengths or bastions, two freestanding works, or ravelins, guarding the most exposed flanks and the whole built upon a swell of higher ground. It was altogether a most commanding position.

Any successful assault could only be prepared after the major logistical effort needed to transport men, their equipment and supplies, the great guns, ammunition and quantities of powder, had been competently undertaken. The officer responsible was Brigadier Viscount George Augustus Howe, one of several remarkable brothers, all of whom were destined to leave their mark on North America. Howe, colonel of the 55th, had made a particular study of the irregular pattern of warfare that so suited the terrain and had spent time with Rogers. The many lessons learnt he put to good effect, stripping his fellow officers of much of their more luxurious baggage, lightening the men's load, adapting their uniform, weapons and drill. He went so far as to be seen washing his own linen in rivers, a chore normally undertaken for officers by the regimental women whom he'd sent back. This was indeed novel!

In the warm flush of a continental summer, at the end of June, Abercrombie's task force was mustering on the banks of Lake George, where the ruins of Fort William Henry served as a potent reminder. Thanks to Howe's efficiency, some 800 barges or

bateaux, plus 90 whaleboats had been laboriously hauled over-
land. Each of the boats would carry 22 troops with all their gear
and 30 days' supply of foodstuffs. On 5 July, with commendable discipline and *élan*, the regiments embarked and the great
flotilla of heavily laden craft proceeded sedately down the length
of Lake George. It was indeed a sight of awesome majesty, the
might of the burgeoning British Empire, a rich tableau of scarlet
and gold, the deep blue of the colonials, the latent power of the
great guns, lashed to rafts, the silken standards lifting in a gentle
breeze. Around them the sylvan glories of an untouched wilderness – tall stands of pine and fir, the light glancing from the calm,
burnished waters of the lake, hills rising on every side.

By dawn the following day, 6 July, the long passage of Lake
George had been accomplished without mishap and the battalions were approaching the narrows; ahead of them was the
expanse of Lake Champlain but, rising in its headland, reared
the great mass of Fort Ticonderoga, an unconquered citadel.
Montcalm, however outnumbered, was still vigilant and the
shoreline was held by a commanded body of skirmishers; fire
from the boats drove these back beneath the shelter of the trees
and the attackers disembarked without further opposition. Once
ashore, the men were detailed into marching columns but this
terrain was not the level arena of Flanders, it was rather a dense
web of tangled undergrowth, fallen trees and confusing slopes.
Abercrombie's guides proved less than competent and the British
were soon in difficulties. In the confusion the right, commanded
by Howe, became involved in a running fight with the French,
taking casualties; amongst these was their gallant commander,
one whose loss would be keenly felt. Major-General Stewart,
writing of the action some decades after, commented:

> The march was continued in the same order [July 7th], but the
> ground not having been previously examined, and the guides
> proving extremely ignorant, the columns came in contact, and
> were thrown in confusion. A detachment of the enemy, which
> got bewildered in the wood, fell in with the right column, at

the head of which was lord Howe. A smart skirmish ensued, in which the enemy were driven back and scattered with considerable loss. This petty advantage was dearly purchased by the death of Lord Howe.

Abercrombie, deprived of his subordinate's wise counsel, now took a fateful and disastrous decision. Sensibly, he could have deployed his colonials to interdict communications between the beleaguered fort and possible reinforcement from Fort St Frederic (Crown Point). He could then have begun the laborious process of dragging the guns from their barges to the eminence of Mount Defiance and, from there, commenced a bombardment, which given the weight of shot he disposed would surely have soon battered the fort into submission. He chose instead to rely on the distinctly unsound advice of a junior officer of engineers, who opined that the impromptu defences covering the approach were flimsy and could be rushed with the bayonet. With drums beating and banners unfurled, the regular battalions of foot moved into the attack with purpose and precision, but the defences were far stronger than had been suggested, and the line of the breastwork was held by Montcalm's veterans.

A withering hail of fire greeting the leading ranks who were flensed away as their comrades behind struggled to fight through the lines of obstacles – this was grim, close-quarter work which presaged the horror of the trenches. The men could make no headway:

Masses of infuriated men could not go forward and would not go back; straining for an enemy they could not reach, and firing on an enemy they could not see, they were caught in the entanglement of felled trees. Shooting, yelling and cursing, they were assailed all the while with bullets, which killed them by scores, stretched them on the ground, or hung them on jagged branches, in strange attitudes of death.

Thus far the 42nd, with the 55th, had been kept in reserve but, as the assault faltered, they were now sent in. Formed nearly two

decades beforehand, the 42nd (Lord John Murray's Highlanders
– the Black Watch) were proud of their natural elitism. Drawn
mainly from the ranks of Clan Campbell, the soldiers were men
of quality and some standing. Their *élan* was ferocious, and
they fell upon the defences with gusto. The battle now reached
its savage denouement as the Highlanders fought and clawed
their way forward. Captain John Campbell and a handful of his
company became the only British forces to gain a lodgement in
the enemy position but, unsupported and disdaining retreat, they
were cut down to a man. As the celebrated historian Francis
Parkman wrote:

> Then the Highland soldiers of the 42nd could endure no
> longer. Impatient of their position in the rear, they rushed
> forward, hewed their way through the obstacles with their
> broadswords. Since no ladders had been provided, they made
> strenuous efforts to carry the breastworks, partly by mount-
> ing on each other's shoulders and partly by fixing their feet
> in holes, which they had excavated with their swords and
> bayonets in the face of the work. The defenders were so well
> prepared that the instant an assailant reached the top, that
> instant he was thrown or shot down.

Losses were frightful. The 42nd, which had suffered most
grievously, had lost eight officers, nine NCOs and 297 other
ranks killed, 17 officers, ten NCOs and 306 men hurt – a total
loss of 647. The regiment was reduced to a mere shell. The attack
was a disastrous failure though, in recognition of its sacrifice the
42nd was awarded by George II the designation 'Royal' – never
was such a distinction better merited.

Though they might be content to take the king's shilling, the
Highlanders were never prepared to be taken for granted and ill
usage produced a rash of mutinies between 1778 and 1783.

'Ninety-second, you must advance! All in front of you have
given way.'[3] With such stirring words Sir Denis Pack exhorted
the Gordons at a crucial moment amidst the carnage of Waterloo
as D'Erlons' massed columns threatened to engulf the crumbling

allied line. Long before the final confrontation, Highland regiments had distinguished themselves in the Peninsular War through a score of savage battles. Present at Waterloo were some 6070 Scots including the three Highland battalions. Out of 1061 members of the Scots Guards nearly a quarter became casualties and the furious charge of the Scots Greys, immortalised in oils by Lady Butler, became the very stuff of legend, Gordon infantry clinging, in an unlikely manner, to the stirrups of the cavalry. The redoubtable Sergeant Ewart hacked his bloody path to glory by capturing the Eagle of the 45th Infantry.

Steadfast valour, an effusion of blood and the new wave of romanticism, pioneered by Sir Walter Scott, transformed the Highlander from unruly barbarian into noble savage. The clansmen became respectable and respected. The long peace of the 1830s and 1840s ended in the freezing stalemate of the Crimea. In the midst of this ill-starred campaign three celebrated volleys from the Argyll's, under the tough generalship of Sir Colin Campbell, smashed a horde of Russian cavalry. Highly impressed, William Russell for *The Times* wrote that the resolute Highlanders resembled a 'thin red streak tipped with a line of steel', a flight of poetic fancy later corrupted and accidentally immortalised as 'the thin red line' of popular fame.

Throughout the course of the nineteenth century Highlanders and Scots in general fought for the Queen Empress throughout all of her far-flung dominions, completing the transition from handy cannon-fodder to heroes of the empire.

When the long Victorian and Edwardian twilight ended in 1914 Scotsmen flocked to answer Kitchener's call. Over half a million enlisted throughout the four unrelenting years of war, equal to some 23.7 per cent of the total male population and nearly half of all males between the ages of 15 and 49 years. Casualties were appalling: the Black Watch alone lost 565 officers and 9459 men.[4]

So many volunteers flocked to the imperial colours that even those considered too short for normal service were recruited into special or 'bantam' battalions, where the average height rarely exceeded 5 feet – at least one unit of Scottish bantams earned the fearsome sobriquet of 'demon dwarfs'.[5]

Despite the passage of the centuries and the array of distant battlefields the Highland regiments never lost sight of their seditious roots and, as late as the last decade at least six regimental pipers still played the old Jacobite air, 'Hey Johnny Cope, are ye wauken yet?' – popularly seen as a tribute to that general's flight from Prestonpans.[6]

> From such small battles was a Kingdom built,
> By such bold forays was a border held,
> By men in hodden grey or tattered kilts
> Who knew defeat, but know not to be quelled;
> And they that fell today were of our blood
> That cannot all be drunk by greedy earth,
> And who so fell in honour where he stood
> Fulfilled the purpose of his warrior birth.
>
> Bernard Fergusson

Notes on Sources

Preface

1 Prebble J.: *Culloden*, 1964, p.132.
2 Ibid: pp.135–136.

'WE ARE NOT YET SUBDUED': MONS GRAUPIUS, AD 84

1 Breeze D.J: *The Northern Frontiers of Roman Britain*, 1982, p.47.
2 Ibid: pp.28–33.
3 Tacitus: 'Agricola'.
4 'History of Rome' 76: Dio goes on to describe the north Britons in some detail, 'There are two principal nations of the Britons, the Caledonians and the Maeatae ... Both inhabit wild and waterless mountains and desolate swampy plains and possess neither walls, cities nor cultivated land, but live on their flocks, wild game and certain fruits ... They fight both in chariots with small, swift horses, and on foot, when they run very fast and also stand their ground with great determination.'
5 Tacitus's reference to a frontier line is the first suggestion of such a concept within the province, the first intimation that a complete occupation of the entire island may have been considered infeasible or impossible. At the time the Forth/Clyde Line may have been seen as the limit of expansion; see Breeze, *Northern Frontiers of Roman Britain*, pp.43–44.
6 Agricola was a favourite of the Flavian dynasty having supported Domitian's father, Vespasian, in his successful bid for the purple in the anarchic year of AD 69. His tenure of office extended to nearly twice the norm.
7 For example in N. Africa, N.W. Spain and the Alps; see Breeze, p.55.
8 There are seven or perhaps eight forts blocking the glens, stretching north-east from Drumquassie through Malling, at Menteith Bochastle at Callander, Dalginross at Comrie and Fendoch; see Breeze, pp.51–52.
9 Tacitus's account makes it clear that the Caledonian tribes had managed to, at least to a considerable degree, sink their internecine squabbling and unite in the face of the common foe, itself a compliment to the Governors' perceived mettle; see Breeze, p.58.
10 Of the legions present none was at full strength; detachments from each of the legions, probably at least two cohorts had been transferred to the Rhine

frontier where Domitian, thirsty for glory to match his late brother, was warring againt a Germanic tribe called the Chatti.

11 Tacitus: 'Agricola'.

12 Tacitus, 37.

13 Tacitus, 38.

14 See Maxwell G.: *A Battle Lost: Romans and Caledonians at Mons Graupius*, 1990.

15 Lynch M.: *Scotland: A New History*, 1991, p.3.

16 Agricola's unknown successor began to consolidate the ground, but events elsewhere in the Empire, particularly alarums amongst the mettlesome Dacians, necessitated the transfer of troops, particularly the veteran Legio II Adiutrix, and this diminution of military muscle made further expansion a logistical impossibility. A frontier may have been established along the Gask ridge; see Breeze, p.61.

17 Though only half the length of the southern bulwark the Antonine Wall was none-the-less a formidable border. Built of turves laid on a stone foundation, the base was some 15 Roman feet wide and perhaps ten feet in height, with possibly a wattle protection to the rampart. The wall was fronted by a ditch with the forts at regular intervals, some being planned at the inception and others added later. Between the forts lay mile-castles similar to those on Hadrian's Wall, though the intervening turrets appear to have been missed out. Alternative structures intended as signalling posts may have served instead; see Breeze, pp.102–112.

18 Five Antonine forts show traces of a legionary presence involving detachments of Legio II, VI and XX.

19 The Antonine Wall forts appear to follow the course of Agricola's earlier 'limes' and undoubtedly some of his forward outposts were refurbished at the same time. Excavations at Strageath have demonstrated two phases of Antonine occupation after the Primary Flavian. There are quite a number of unfortified hill forts dating from the late first and early second centuries. It would appear that refortification may have occurred after the abandonment of the Antonine Wall.

20 Scriptores Hist. Aug., Antoninius Pius, Ch.5.

21 c. AD 184 – Cassius Dio.

22 Dio.

23 Probably centred on the area from Stirling through Strathearn into Tayside and Angus.

24 Newstead near Melrose, recently excavated; there is an excellent small museum in the town.

25 Fraser G. MacDonald: *The Steel Bonnets*, 1971, p.15.

THE FOUR PEOPLES: NECHTANSMERE, 685

1 Marsden J.: *Northanhymbre Saga*, 1992, p.68.

2 Bede: *Anglo Saxon Chronicle*, trans. by G. N. Gormomsway.

3 Magnus Maximus was a fourth-century Roman Governor whose ill-fated imperial ambitions had stripped the province of troops. Rheged may have encompassed the north and west of present-day Cumbria and stretched into Galloway to the north and Northumberland to the east.

4 Nennius: *Historia Brittonum*; a Welsh scholar whose work appears in a ninth-century compilation.

5 Oswin of Northumbria subsequently married the princess Riemmelth, a descendant of Urien.

6 Aneirin, a sixth-century poet of the Welsh School, the 'Gododdin' forms part of the oral tradition and the first written version did not appear until some 250 years after the events it describes; see Chadwick N.: *The Celts*, 1970, p.285.

7 Lynch M.: *Scotland, A New History*, 1991, p.19.

8 Ibid: p.17.

9 See Hayes-McCoy W.A.: *Irish Battles*, 1958, p.52.

10 'Vita Wilfridi' Eddi was St Wilfrid's chanter and subsequent biographer.

11 Three fragments of the Irish Annals copied from ancient sources by Donald Mac Fibris, known as the Nechtansmere Victory Song, make reference to 'Bruide'. (MS.5301. fol.30 – Royal Library of Albert I, Brussels).

12 This is questionable and there is a view that the victory belonged solely to the Picts.

13 See Treece H. and Oakenshortt E.: *Fighting Men*, 1963, p.88.

14 Marsden J.: *Northanhymbre Saga*, p.130.

15 The Aberlemno Stones, Graeme Cruickshank – L942.01 Cr 957332A LRS 7337.

THE HOUSE OF CANMORE: CARHAM, 1018

1 See Treece H. and Oakenshott E.: *Fighting Men*, 1963, pp.78–104.

2 Lynch M.: *Scotland, A New History*, 1991, p.44.

3 The Picts suffered a particularly severe reverse in 839 and sporadic Norse incursions continued into the twelfth century when the Northmen burnt Aberdeen and sacked the priory on May Island.

4 Lynch M.: p.48. See also Brown D.: 'The Origin of Scottish Identity' in Bjorn C., Grant A. & Stringer K.J. (eds) *Nationalism and Patriotism in the European Past* (Copenhagen 1994).

5 The apparent triumph of Wessex did not mean that the Scots were by any means overawed. Malcolm I raided as far south as the Tees in 949 and, despite his subservience, Kenneth II campaigned vigorously in Northumberland twice during the 970s.

6 Sitwell, Brig. Genl. Wm.: *The Border*, 1927, pp.198–199.

7 The *mormaer* or 'great steward' was essentially a military function. In some areas, such as Moray, the office may have been hereditary. Moray, in particular, proved a troublesome province, stretching from the Mounth to Ross and from the western seaboard to the Spey, between the kingdom of Scots to the south and the warlike Norse Jarls of Orkney to the north the region resisted all attempts at establishing royal control. Four major initiatives by successive kings were repulsed; more than one lost his life in the attempt.

8 Means 'the expected one'.

9 MacBeth appears to have cultivated, in Thorfinn, the Norse earl of Orkney, a powerful ally who also fought, successfully, against Duncan. The first attempt to depose MacBeth was led by his dead rival's father, Crinan, the secular abbot of Dunkeld, whose house was related to that of Siward. The father, however, fared little better than the son, being defeated and killed in 1045. See Cowan, Prof. E. *The Historical MacBeth* in Sellas W.D. (ed.) *Moray Province and People* (Edinburgh 1993).

10 Norman A.V.B. and Pottinger D.: *English Weapons & Warfare 449–1660*, 1979, pp.29–34.

11 Oman, Sir Charles: *The Art of War in the Middle Ages*, 1924, pp.390–395.

12 Ibid: p.393.

13 See Stringer, Dr K.J.: *The Reign of Stephen*, 1993, pp.28–37.

14 See Cowan, Prof. E.J.: 'Norwegian Sunset – Scottish Dawn', Hakan IV and Alexander III' in Reid N.H. (ed.) *Scotland in the Reign of Alexander III*, 1990, pp.103–31.

15 Simpson W. Douglas: *Scottish Castles*, 1959, pp.6–10.

16 Norman A.V.B. and Pottinger D.: *English Weapons & Warfare 449–1660*, 1979, pp.44–49.

17 Hibbert C.: *Agincourt*, 1964, p.15.

'NOT FOR GLORY . . . BUT FOR FREEDOM': BANNOCKBURN

1314

1 Declaration of Arbroath, 1320.

2 Chronicles of Lanercost: pp.115–8; it could be that the chronicler may have exercised a degree of bias as the king was not generally excoriated for his licentiousness, see Reid: 'Alexander III; the Historiography of a Myth', in Reid (ed.) *Scotland in the Reign of Alexander III*.

3 The election of Baliol was recommended by an impressive body of 40 speaking for the Baliol/Comyn faction, 40 for Bruce and 24 chosen by Edward. The king behaved scrupulously, even adjourning for several months to allow consideration of an outsider's claim.

4 Lynch M.: *A New History*, 1991, p.62.

5 MacKay J.: *William Wallace*, 1995, p.76.

6 Ibid: p.81. 'Bon besoigne fait qy de merde se delivrer'; this remark was apparently made when the king handed the great seal to Warenne after Baliol's humiliation.

7 Ibid: pp.105–113; the unlucky bride was said to have been Marian Braidfute the young daughter and heiress of Hugh Braidfute of Lamington.

8 'At that time there was in Scotland a certain youth, Willelmus le Wallis, an archer who obtained his living by means of his bow and his quiver; of base descent, and mean birth and training.' (Cottonian M.S. in 'Wallace Papers', p.8) Though Wallace's origins remain, to a degree, obscure he appears to have been of gentle if not noble birth; his father was Sir Malcolm Wallace of Auchenbothie and Ellerslie. Much of what is known is derived from an epic poem compiled by Blind Harry some 150 years after the hero's death:

> 'Nine quarters large he was in length – no less;
> Third part in length in shoulders broad was he,
> Right seemly, strong, and handsome for to see.'
> See MacKay: *William Wallace*, pp.13–30.

9 Seymour W.: *Battles in Britain*, vol. 1, 1975, p.73.

10 Ibid: p.74.

11 Fisher: *William Wallace*, 1986, p.55.

12 Ibid: p.67.

13 The site of the battle is now totally built over, but a general view of the location may be had from the castle, one of the finest in the British Isles.

14 Seymour: *Battles in Britain*, p.75.

15 Ibid: p.76.

16 Fisher: *William Wallace*, p.81.

17 Seymour: *Battles in Britain*, p.79.

18 The horse were subsequently accused of treachery, but some later writers (Barrow: *Robert Bruce*) have been more inclined to favour panic over deceit; given their lack of experience and the imposing array of the English this is perhaps understandable.

19 Fisher: 'William Wallace', p.82 from Riley (ed.) William Rishanger: 'Chronica et Annales', London 1865.

20 Barrow G.W.S.: *Robert Bruce*, 1965, (revised) 1988, pp.206–208.

21 Ibid: pp.275–276.

22 Ibid: p.245.

23 Ibid: p.267–289.

24 Ibid: p.290–296.

25 Christison, General Sir P.: *Bannock Burn*, 1960, pp.9–10.

26 Ibid: p.10.

27 Ibid: pp.17–18.

28 Ibid: p.17.

29 Barrow: *Robert Bruce*, p.312.

30 Ibid: pp.313–314.

31 Christison, General Sir P.: *Bannock Burn*, p.19.

32 'My lord king, now is the time, if ever you mean to win Scotland. The English have lost heart; they are discomfited, and expect nothing but a sudden and open attack. I swear, on my head and on pain of being hanged and drawn, that if you attack them in the morning you could defeat them easily without loss.' (see Barrow: *Robert Bruce*, p.319).

33 Christison, General Sir P.: *Bannock Burn*, p.22. See article by Ashby McGowan in *Miniature Wargames* (May 1993) – the author has made an extensive study of the site and of the battle itself and has deeply researched both topographical and meteorological details.

34 Ibid: p.20.

35 Ibid: p.22.

36 Barbour of Aberdeen: *The Bruce*, 1375.

37 The field of battle is built up to a degree, but at least part of the site is now in the care of the National Trust for Scotland who have erected a visitor centre. There is also the Bruce memorial and Rotunda.

38 Lynch: *A New History*, pp.128–131.

39 Oman Sir C.: *A History of the Art of War in the Middle Ages*, vol. 2, 1924, p.103.

40 Ibid: p.103.

41 Ibid: p.106. The ground remains largely unchanged and the slope of the hill is plainly visible from the B6105; obviously the land is now drained and the morass which so impeded the Scots is no longer visible.

42 Oman Sir C.: *A History of the Art of War in the Middle Ages*, vol. 2, 1924, p.106.

43 Ibid: p.149.

44 The site is now largely built up, and the area of Neville's Cross forms a suburb of Durham itself – the line of the railway traverses the ridge upon which the English deployed and the A167 bisects the field.

45 Baliol finally resigned his right to Edward in 1356; after a quarter of a century spent in vying for the throne, the king had apparently decided that the captive David II was a more useful asset.
46 See Grant A.: *Independence and Nationhood* and Nicholson R. *Scotland, The Late Middle Ages*.

'A DOUGLAS, A DOUGLAS': OTTERBURN, 1388

1 Froissart, Sir J.: *Chronicles* (ed.) MacAulay, p.370.
2 Wesencraft C.: *The Battle of Otterburn*, 1988; this interpretation depends on an assumption that, before the battle, the Scots were besieging Cambo Tower rather than Otterburn Castle (now The Otterburn Towers Hotel).
3 Froissart, Sir J.: *Chronicles* (ed.) MacAulay, p.373.
4 Ibid: p.374.
5 Archibald, 4th earl of Douglas, son of Archibald the Grim and grandson of the 'Good Sir James'.
6 Bates C.J.: *History of Northumberland*, 1895, pp.188–189.
7 Douglas Simpson W.: *Scottish Castles*, 1959, p.16.
8 Kightly C.: *Flodden*, 1975, p.9.
9 Tabraham C.: *Scottish Castles and Fortifications*, 1986, pp.53–62.
10 Peterson H.: *The Book of the Gun*, 1963, pp.80–81.
11 Mons Meg is sympathetically displayed at Edinburgh Castle and remains a superb example of an early gun of the fifteenth century.
12 Peterson H.: *The Book of the Gun*, 1963, pp.17–18.
13 Norman A.V.B. and Pottinger D.: *English Weapons and Warfare, 449–1660*, pp.137–140.
14 Ibid: p.141.
15 Ibid: p.142.
16 Ibid: p.143.
17 Ibid: p.143.
18 Peterson H.: *The Book of the Gun*, 1963, p.47.
19 Blair C.: *European Armour*, pp.77–92.
20 Cauldwell D.A.: *The Scottish Armoury*, 1979, pp.14–15.
21 Ibid: p.27.
22 Ibid: p.28.

THE ROUGH WOOING: FLODDEN, 1513

1 Lynch: *A New History*, p.154.
2 Ibid: p.159.
3 Stewart-Black D.: *Scottish Battles*, 1936, pp.90–99.
4 Ibid: p.98.
5 Lynch: *A New History*, p.160.
6 Norman and Pottinger: *English Weapons and Warfare*, pp.195–197.
7 Peterson: *The Book of the Gun*, p.68.
8 Durham K. and McBride A: *The Border Reivers*, 1995, pp.13–16.
9 Norman and Pottinger: *English Weapons and Warfare*, p.185.
10 Ibid: pp.176–182.
11 Baldick R.: *The Duel*, 1965, p.40.

12 Ibid: pp.63–65.
13 Lynch: *New History*, p.159.
14 Ibid: p.160.
15 Kightly: *Flodden*, p.7.
16 Seymour W.: *Battles in Britain*, 1975, vol. 1, p.196.
17 Ibid: p.197.
18 Kightly: *Flodden*, p.11.
19 Ibid: p.12.
20 Seymour W.: *Battles in Britain*, p.201.
21 Kightly: *Flodden*, p.38.
22 Ibid: p.38.
23 Ibid: pp.33–34.
24 Ibid: p.36.
25 Ibid: p.41.
26 Seymour W.: *Battles in Britain*, p.205.
27 Kightly: *Flodden*, p.46.
28 Seymour W.: *Battles in Britain*, p.206.
29 Kightly: *Flodden*, p.48. The site is marked by a monument just beyond Branxton village and there is a clear view of the battlefield; in addition English Heritage have now mounted an excellent permanent exhibition at Etal Castle.
30 Mackie J.D. *History of Scotland*, 1969, p.133.
31 Lynch: *New History*, pp.161–168.
32 Fraser G.M.: *The Steel Bonnets*, 1971, pp.249–250.
33 Ibid: pp.250–252.
34 Ibid: p.251.
35 Lynch: *New History*, pp.205–206.
36 Ibid: p.204.
37 Ibid: p.208.
38 Seymour: *Battles in Britain*, p.213.
39 Ibid: p.213.
40 Ibid: p.214.
41 Ibid: pp.216–217.
42 Treece H. and Oakenshott E.: *Fighting Men*, 1963, p.203.
43 Ibid: p.203.
44 The site is now largely built over although a church still stands atop Inveresk hill and the Scots advanced over the ground now covered by the links.
45 Lynch: *New History*, p.197.
46 Fraser A.: *Mary, Queen of Scots*, 1969, p.263.
47 Ibid: pp.278–287.
48 Ibid: p.263.
49 Ibid: p.400.
50 Ibid: pp.400–401.
51 Ibid: p.401.
52 Lynch: *New History*, pp.225–226.
53 Ibid: p.232.

RAIDS AND REIVERS: ANCRUM MOOR, 1545

1 Durham K.: *The Border Reivers*, p.46. Kinmont was subsequently 'sprung' from within the seemingly impregnable walls of Carlisle by 200 of his compatriots, led by Walter Scott of Goldielands. Scrope appears to have

been ill-served if not actively betrayed by his subordinates, the Carleton brothers, by whose deliberate neglect the postern gate was left virtually unguarded.

2 Fraser: *The Steel Bonnets*, pp.154–168.

3 Ridpath G.: *The Border History of England and Scotland*, 1776. Most famous of the Armstrongs was Johnnie of Gilnockie whose splendid attire worn at a truce day before James V proved his undoing; the king was so incensed by the brigand's dazzling plumage that he went so far as to violate the truce and hang Johnnie and his followers on the spot.

4 Watson G.: *The Border Reivers*, 1985 edn, pp.99–120.

5 Tabraham: *Scottish Castles and Fortifications*, 1986, p.65. Smailholm, near Kelso, recently refurbished by Scottish Heritage, is a fine example and benefits from both its association with Scott and its splendidly romantic setting.

6 Watson: *The Border Reivers*, p.118.

7 Fraser: *The Steel Bonnets*, pp.248–249.

8 Ibid: pp.260–261.

9 Ibid: p.261.

10 Scott: *Minstrelsy*. The battle is commemorated in the ballad of 'Lilliard', a Scottish maiden who is said to have fought and fallen in the fight, having taken the field in vengeance for either family or lover killed by the English.

11 Durham K.: *The Border Reivers*, pp.13–16. There is a particularly fine and unique collection of border arms and armour at the Johnnie Armstrong Gallery at Teviothead. Some good pieces are also on view at the Border Museum in Hexham.

12 Seymour: *Battles in Britain*, p.222.

13 Fraser: *The Steel Bonnets*, pp.85–89.

14 Cauldwell: *The Scottish Armoury*, p.18.

15 Ibid: pp.42–43.

16 Fraser: *The Steel Bonnets*, pp.90–96.

17 Ibid: pp.309–312.

18 Ibid: p.312. The site lies a short way from the A696 where it crosses the border at Carter Bar and, in addition to the memorial, there is an epic panorama of the Border hills.

19 Fraser: *The Steel Bonnets*, p.175.

20 Ibid: p.176.

21 Ibid: pp.178–179.

22 Ibid: p.179.

23 Ibid: p.179.

24 Ibid: p.180.

THE PALADIN: DUNBAR, 1650

1 Wedgewood C.V.: *The King's Peace*, 1974 edn, pp.173–201.

2 Ibid: pp.221–246.

3 Lynch: *A New History*, pp.270–271.

4 Sadler D.J.: *Battle for Northumbria*, pp.137–138. The battlefield is now almost totally obscured by late development though the tower of Newburn Church still stands; however as mentioned the southward view is dominated now by the unappealing bulk of cooling towers.

5 Young P. and Holmes R.: *The English Civil War*, 1974, pp.34–59.

6 Haythornthwaite P.: *The English Civil War 1642–1651*, 1994, pp.26–30.
7 Ibid: p.36
8 Young and Holmes: *The English Civil War*, pp.44–46.
9 Ibid: p.40.
10 Ibid: p.46.
11 Ibid: pp.48–51.
12 Ibid: pp.54–57.
13 Hastings M.: *Montrose; The King's Champion*, 1977, pp.73–74.
14 Ibid: pp.80–81.
15 Reid S.: *The Campaigns of Montrose*, 1990, pp.16–19.
16 Ibid: pp.21–24.
17 Ibid: pp.24–27.
18 Hastings: *Montrose*, p.100.
19 Wedgewood C.V.: *The King's War*, 1958, p.289.
20 Haythornthwaite: *The English Civil War 1642–1651*, p.62.
21 Woodrych A.: *Battles of the English Civil War*, 1961, pp.63–64.
22 Ibid: p.71.
23 Ibid: p.80.
24 Ibid: p.79.
25 Hastings: *Montrose*, p.154. MacColla's intervention stemmed from the issue of the leadership of Clan Donald claimed by the Ulster McDonnells.
26 Hastings: *Montrose*, p.156.
27 Reid: *The Campaigns of Montrose*, pp.174–177.
28 Hastings: *Montrose*, p.163.
29 Reid: *The Campaigns of Montrose*, p.51.
30 Ibid: p.53.
31 Ibid: pp.55–56.
32 Hastings: *Montrose*, p.172.
33 Reid: *The Campaigns of Montrose*, p.62.
34 Ibid: p.63.
35 Ibid: p.65.
36 Ibid: p.68.
37 Hastings: *Montrose*, p.190.
38 Ibid: p.196.
39 Reid: *The Campaigns of Montrose*, pp.74–75.
40 Ibid: p.75.
41 Ibid: p.77.
42 Hastings: *Montrose*, p.201.
43 Ibid: p.218.
44 Ibid: p.224.
45 Ibid: p.225.
46 Ibid: p.225.
47 Reid: *The Campaigns of Montrose*, p.84.
48 Ibid: p.87.
49 Hastings: *Montrose*, p.227.
50 Ibid: p.235.
51 Ibid: p.239.
52 Reid: *The Campaigns of Montrose*, pp.106–107.
53 Ibid: p.108.
54 Hastings: *Montrose*, p.251.
55 Reid: *The Campaigns of Montrose*, p.114.
56 Ibid: p.116.

57 Ibid: p.118.
58 Ibid: p.119. Traditionally a feature called the 'Boath Doocot' stands where Montrose is said to have placed his standard. Though this tradition would seem questionable, the building is in the care of the National Trust for Scotland who have also provided a useful battle plan.
59 Ibid: p.125.
60 Ibid: p.125.
61 Ibid: p.128.
62 Ibid: p.129.
63 Ibid: p.130.
64 Ibid: p.131.
65 Hastings: *Montrose*, p.267.
66 Ibid: p.271. Most of the casualties appear to have been from the wives and female camp followers, a senseless slaughter of no tactical value.
67 Ibid: p.272.
68 Reid: *The Campaigns of Montrose*, p.138.
69 Ibid: p.140.
70 Ibid: p.142.
71 Ibid: p.143.
72 Ibid: p.142.
73 Ibid: p.144.
74 Ibid: p.146.
75 Ibid: p.147.
76 The battle site lies to the north of the present A803; part of the field now lies under a small lake, but there is a monument in the grounds of the Colzium-Lennox park – carved in the shape of an enormous curling stone, it stands to the rear of the royalist position and the main fighting took place towards the east and north-east.
77 Hastings: *Montrose*, p.284.
78 Ibid: p.284.
79 Ibid: p.290.
80 Reid: *The Campaigns of Montrose*, p.158.
81 Ibid: p.158.
82 Hastings: *Montrose*, p.295. The site lies north of Selkirk and can be viewed from the bridge over Ettrick Water, where there is a small monument. Though this is private ground, westward and on the south bank of the Yarrow stand the impressive remains of Newark Tower. It is said that Leslie had the male captives shot in batches and that a surviving section of the barnekin wall still bears the scars of gunfire. On a happier note one of the prisoners of rank, young Lord Ogilvy, with the aid of his mother, wife and sister, made a daring escape from St Andrews, where he was awaiting execution.
83 Lynch: *A New History*, p.276.
84 Ibid: p.277.
85 Woodrych: *Battles of the English Civil War*, p.162.
86 Ibid: p.169.
87 Ibid: pp.177–178.
88 Lynch: *A New History*, p.279.
89 Hastings: *Montrose*, p.334.
90 Ibid: p.334.
91 Ibid: p.334.
92 Ibid: p.335–336.
93 Ibid: p.336.

94 Ibid: p.339.
95 Ibid: p.341.
96 Ibid: p.341.
97 Ibid: p.351.
98 Ibid: p.351.
99 Lynch: *A New History*, p.279.
100 Young & Holmes: *The English Civil War*, p.302.
101 Ibid: p.304.
102 Ibid: p.305.
103 Ibid: p.304.
104 Ibid: p.305.
105 Ibid: p.305.
106 Ibid: p.306.
107 The site lies adjacent to the line of the present A1, some 2½ miles south of Dunbar. The ground is bisected by the main railway line and the aspect to the east is not aided by the untidy sprawl of the cement works. The battle monument is located just off the main road. The earlier Edwardian Battle of Dunbar (1296) took place just to the west of the civil war site, just below the eminence of Doon Hill.
108 Young and Holmes: *The English Civil War*, p.307.
109 Ibid: pp.313–314.
110 Ibid: p.314.

THE KILLING TIME: KILLIECRANKIE, 1689

1 Lynch M.: *A New History*, pp.287–291.
2 Ibid: p.282.
3 Ibid: p.288.
4 Ibid: p.289.
5 Ibid: p.290.
6 Ibid: p.293.
7 Linklater M. and Hesketh C.: *For King and Conscience*, 1989, p.73.
8 Ibid: p.31.
9 Ibid: p.31.
10 Lynch: *A New History*, p.294.
11 Linklater and Hesketh: *For King and Conscience*, pp.1–9.
12 Ibid: pp.43–48. Loudon Hill was, in fact, the site of a clash between Robert the Bruce and Aymer de Valence on 10 May 1307 when the future king won an early, and much needed, victory over the English.
13 Ibid: pp.5–6.
14 Ibid: p.45.
15 Ibid: p.45.
16 Ibid: p.50.
17 Ibid: p.51.
18 Ibid: p.53.
19 Ibid: p.53.
20 Ibid: p.54.
21 Ibid: p.54.
22 Ibid: p.55.
23 Lynch: *A New History*, p.296.

24 Ibid: p.295.

25 Ibid: p.297.

26 Linklater and Hesketh: *For King and Conscience*, pp.162–163.

27 Haswell J.: *The British Army*, 1975, p.20.

28 Young P. and Lawford J.P. (ed.): *History of the British Army*, 1972, p.26.

29 Ibid: p.54.

30 Ibid: p.54.

31 Barnes R.M.: *Uniforms and History of the Scottish Regiments*, 1950, p.47.

32 Rogers, Col. H.C.B.: *The Weapons of the British Soldier*, 1960, pp.77–79.

33 Ibid: p.65.

34 Barnes R.M.: *A History of the Regiments and Uniforms of the British Army*, 1950, p.29.

35 Ibid: p.30.

36 Young: *The British Army 1642–1970*, pp.50–51.

37 Barnes: *A History of the Regiments and Uniforms of the British Army*, pp.27–28.

38 Ibid: p.43.

39 Peterson: *The Book of the Gun*, 1963, pp.76–78.

40 Barnes: *A History of the Regiments and Uniforms of the British Army*, p.44.

41 Ibid: p.44.

42 Rogers Col. H.C.B.: *Artillery through the Ages*, 1971, pp.49–52.

43 Linklater and Hesketh: *For King and Conscience*, p.173.

44 Ibid: p.183.

45 Ibid: p.164.

46 Ibid: p.185.

47 Ibid: p.188.

48 Ibid: p.201.

49 Ibid: p.24.

50 Ibid: p.210.

51 Ibid: p.212.

52 Ibid: p.215.

53 Ibid: p.212.

54 Ibid: p.216.

55 The scene of Dundee's last triumph and death can still be clearly appreciated; the present course of the A9 lies through the pass of Killiecrankie and there is a visitor centre provided by the National Trust for Scotland; the steep ascent to the battlefield can be traced and there is a spot known as 'soldier's leap' – if the tale is true, a remarkable feat though the fleeing soldier clearly had a powerful incentive.

56 Smurthwaite D.: *Battlefields of Britain*, 1984, pp.192–193.

57 Lynch: *A New History*, p.301.

BLOOD ON THE HEATHER: GLENCOE, 1692

1 Murray W.H: *Rob Roy MacGregor*, 1982, pp.20–22. The story is that a pair of MacGregors, having been refused hospitality, had slaughtered one of Colquhoun's sheep for which they were duly hanged. The inevitable reprisal killed two of the laird's men and relieved him of a considerable quantity of stock. The pageant of the 'bludie sark' was enacted at Stirling, undoubtedly playing on the king's squeamishness.

2 Murray W.H.: *Rob Roy MacGregor*, p.18.

3 Ibid: pp.19–23.

4 Glenstrae surrendered on terms to Argyll, these being that he and his kin could seek exile in England. The MacGregors were indeed taken into England, under guard, and then immediately marched back to meet their fate – Glenstrae with five others was hanged at the Mercat Cross in Edinburgh on 20 January 1604. See Murray: *Rob Roy MacGregor*, p.22.

5 Bingham C.: *Beyond the Highland Line*, 1991, pp.52–58.

6 Ibid: p.64. MacTaggart may have been the heir of the secular Abbot of Applecross.

7 Ibid: p.66. Good examples are Dunollie, Dunstaffnage and Dunaverty.

8 Bingham: *Beyond the Highland Line*, p.68.

9 Ibid: p.68. Somerled was hailed by his Irish neighbours as 'ri Innse Gall' – 'King of the Hebrides'.

10 Ibid: p.74–76. For a full appraisal of Somerled's career, see Duncan A. A. M. Q. A. Brown: 'Argyll and the Isles in the Earlier Middle Ages', Proceedings of the Society of Antiquaries of Scotland XC (1956–57), pp.192–220.

11 See Bingham: *Beyond the Highland Line*, p.63. Lulach left a daughter who may have become connected to the House of Moray and whose descendents 'The MacHeths' had considerable support in the west. In 1130 a rebellion instigated by Heth's sons was defeated by the mailed knights of David I at Stracathro. The two surviving sons, Malcolm and Donald, were released in 1157, apparently as the consequence of a policy decision by Malcolm IV.

12 Grimble: *Clans and Chiefs*, p.49.

13 Ibid: p.50.

14 Bingham: *Beyond the Highland Line*, p.97. Brander M.: *The Making of the Highlands*, 1980, p.47.

15 Bingham: *Beyond the Highland Line*, p.78.

16 Lynch M.: *Scotland: A New History*, p.68. For a full assessment of the turbulent career of Alexander Stewart, see Grant A.: 'The Wolf of Badenoch', in W. O. H. Sellar (ed.), *Moray Province and People*, 1993.

17 Bingham: *Beyond the Highland Line*, p.80.

18 See Watt (ed.), Walter Bower, *Scotichronicon VIII* (Aberdeen 1987), p.75.

19 Bingham: *Beyond the Highland Line*, p.83.

20 Ibid: p.84.

21 Ibid: p.85.

22 Reid S.: *Like Hungry Wolves*, 1994, p.44.

23 Caldwell D.A.: *The Scottish Armoury*, 1979, p.19.

24 *Scottish Art Review*: 'Scottish Weapons', vol. 9, no.1, 1963, pp.16–22.

25 Ibid: pp.22–24.

26 Caldwell: *The Scottish Armoury*, pp.56–60.

27 Ibid: pp.53–56.

28 Ibid: pp.64–70.

29 Grimble I.: *Clans and Chiefs*, pp.216–217.

30 Bingham: *Beyond the Highland Line*, pp.102–103.

31 Ibid: p.103.

32 Prebble J.: *Glencoe*, 1966, p.27.

33 Lynch: *Scotland: A New History*, p.70.

34 Prebble: *Glencoe*, pp.165–171.

35 Ibid: p.172.

36 Ibid: pp.180–184.

37 Ibid: p.185.

38 Ibid: p.211–212.
39 Bingham: *Beyond the Highland Line*, p.107.
40 Tabraham C. & Groves D.: *Fortress Scotland and the Jacobites*, 1995, p.15.
41 Ibid: p.40.
42 Ibid: p.41.
43 Ibid: p.43.
44 Ibid: p.51.
45 Ibid: p.61.
46 Ibid: p.65. Enough of both the Ruthven and Bernera barracks exist to give a good impression of how they looked in the eighteenth century.
47 Ibid: p.70–76. Spectacularly unspoilt sections of Wade's roads still survive, driven over some of the wildest moorland in Britain.
48 Ibid: p.81. The fort has now almost entirely disappeared though a single bastion survives, tacked incongruously onto the nineteenth-century abbey building.

KINGS OVER THE WATER: CULLODEN, 1746

1 Lynch: *Scotland: A New History*, pp.300–305.
2 Prebble J.: *The Darien Disaster*, 1968, pp.30–54.
3 Ibid: pp.308–317.
4 Lynch: *Scotland: A New History*, p.310.
5 Ibid: pp.310–315.
6 Ibid: pp.315–317.
7 Seymour W.: *Battles in Britain*, vol. II, p.182.
8 Ibid: p.185.
9 Some recent opinion tends to be more charitable to Forster, pointing out that the Northumbrian rising was intended as a diversionary affair and that full-scale support was not anticipated – it is said that the people of Tyneside earned the sobriquet of 'Geordies' at this time as a result of their vociferous loyalty.
10 Seymour: *Battles in Britain*, vol.II, p.187.
11 Ibid: p.188.
12 Ibid: p.188.
13 Ibid: p.190,
14 Ibid: p.190. The town of Preston has obviously outgrown the bounds of 1715 – the present Harris Museum & Art Gallery in the centre may stand on the site where Forster established his headquarters.
15 Ibid: p.191.
16 Ibid: p.191.
17 Ibid: p.191.
18 Ibid: p.192.
19 Ibid: p.191.
20 Ibid: p.192.
21 Ibid: p.192.
22 Ibid: p.194.
23 Ibid: p.194.
24 The battle site remains unchanged, lying five to six miles north of Stirling and is traversed by the present highway from Dunblane to Blackford.
25 Lynch: *A New History*, pp.328–329.

26 Ibid: p.328.
27 Ibid: p.331.
28 Seymour: *Battles in Britain*, vol. II, p.197.
29 Ibid: p.198.
30 The castle lay ruinous for many years until it was totally and, as far as can be discerned, accurately rebuilt in the 1920s. Now open to the public it has become an enduring symbol of the romance of the Jacobites.
31 Seymour: *Battles in Britain*, p.199.
32 Ibid: p.199.
33 Ibid: p.200.
34 Ibid: p.200. Glenshiel today remains as widely majestic as ever and a fine view of the site can be had from the present road.
35 Baynes J. and Laffin J. : *Soldiers of Scotland*, p.163.
36 Ibid: p.136.
37 Hartman C. Hughes: *The Quest Forlorn*, 1952, p.8.
38 Recent accounts, particularly that of Stuart Reid in writing particularly of Culloden, have been kinder to O'Sullivan, who may have been less of a fool than many previous writers have suggested – his conduct may at times be construed favourably in comparison with that of Lord George Murray, generally regarded as the hero of the rebellion and who has been more fortunate in his biographers, see particularly Tomasson K.: *The Jacobite General*, 1958; see also Reid S.: *Like Hungry Wolves*, 1994, p.14.
39 Hartman C. Hughes: *The Quest Forlorn*, p.27.
40 Prebble: *Culloden*, 1964, pp.34–42.
41 This figure was based upon a considered calculation made by Forbes himself; see Tomasson K. and Buist F., *Battles of the '45*, 1962, p.26.
42 Tomasson and Buist: *Battles of the '45*, p.31.
43 Ibid: p.29.
44 Tomasson K.: *The Jacobite General*, 1958, pp.30–31.
45 Johnstone: *Memoirs of the Rebellion in 1745 and 1746*, 3rd edn, London, 1822, pp.32–33.
46 Tomasson and Buist: *Battles of the '45*, p.34.
47 Hartman C. Hughes: *The Quest Forlorn*, p.61.
48 Tomasson and Buist: *Battles of the '45*, p.46–47.
49 Ibid: p.57.
50 Seymour: *Battles in Britain*, p.206.
51 Tomasson and Buist: *Battles of the '45*, p.59.
52 Ibid: p.63.
53 Reid S.: *Like Hungry Wolves*, p.18. The author raises the question that the clans may have slaughtered more of the fleeing soldiery than the situation warranted and that this apparent bloodlust on the part of the rebels may go some way to explaining and indeed exploiting the horrors of the pursuit after Culloden. No contemporary accounts seem to dwell on this point, and Johnstone, admittedly partisan, stresses the care Lord George took to see the injured prisoners were decently treated.
54 Tomasson and Buist: *Battles of the '45*, p.64.
55 Johnstone: *Memoirs*, p.42. The battlefield now lies north of the A1 and the A198, the towns of Prestonpans and Port Seton have encroached on the field.
56 Hughes Hartman: *The Quest Forlorn*, p.83.
57 Tomasson and Buist: *Battles of the '45*, p.73.
58 Tomasson: *Jacobite General*, pp.70–73.
59 Ibid: pp.74–77.

60 Ibid: p.93.
61 Ibid: pp.105–106.
62 Reid S.: *Like Hungry Wolves*, p.21.
63 Tomasson: *Jacobite General*, p.126.
64 Ibid: p.127.
65 Ibid: p.128.
66 Tomasson and Buist: *Battles of the '45*, p.86.
67 Ibid: p.86.
68 It has been argued that Cumberland had done remarkably well and that the skirmish was, at worst, a draw, but in reality he had little to show for so many casualties. He had neither slowed nor prevented the retreat, whilst Murray had achieved his objective of deterring the pursuit and had disengaged largely unscathed.
69 Tomasson and Buist: *Battles of the '45*, p.87.
70 Ibid: p.87.
71 Ibid: p.90.
72 Seymour: *Battles in Britain*, p.210.
73 Ibid: p.210.
74 Seymour: *Battles in Britain*, p.212.
75 Tomasson and Buist: *Battles of the '45*, p.103.
76 Seymour: *Battles in Britain*, p.212.
77 Tomasson and Buist: *Battles of the '45*, p.105.
78 Ibid: p.97.
79 Ibid: p.106.
80 Ibid: p.107.
81 Seymour: *Battles in Britain*, p.214.
82 Tomasson and Buist: *Battles of the '45*, p.111.
83 Johnstone: *Memoirs*, pp.96–97. The battlefield today remains relatively unspoilt, though the city has spread to encompass part of the Hanoverian line. The monument stands at the head of the gulley that flanked the right of Hawley's position.
84 Reid: *Like Hungry Wolves*, p.26.
85 Tomasson: *Jacobite General*, p.164.
86 Tomasson and Buist: *Battles of the '45*, p.117.
87 Prebble: *Culloden*, p.78.
88 Reid: *Like Hungry Wolves*, p.51.
89 Prebble: *Culloden*, p.25.
90 The prince has received much opprobrium for this choice of ground though Reid argues that the site was no less suitable than that proposed by Murray and that O'Sullivan's observations on Drummossie Moor should be accorded more weight.
91 Murray must to an extent bear any accrued blame for this particular fiasco. To put it bluntly, he should have known better and certainly seems to have been driven more by hope than by common sense.
92 Prebble: *Culloden*, pp.67–75.
93 Seymour: *Battles in Britain*, p.220.
94 The exact position of Wolfe's has always been contentious. Stuart Reid undoubtedly gives the best analysis in his most detailed account; see Reid S. *Like Hungry Wolves*, pp.84–86.
95 The main disadvantage of the Moor, from the Highlanders' perspective, was the need to charge through such waterlogged terrain which, though it might impede cavalry, would quickly sap the cohesion and morale of charging infantry.

96 Tomasson: *Jacobite General*, p.225.
97 Reid again argues that the Jacobite guns were not totally ineffective and he attributes, from studies of the muster roles, a number of Hanoverian casualties to plunging roundshot. Equally he asserts that the Royal Artillery caused fewer casualties than traditionally supposed whilst not denying the psychological effect of the barrage on Highlanders unschooled in such horrors; see Reid S.: *Like Hungry Wolves*, pp.92–93.
98 Prebble: *Culloden*, p.64.
99 Tomasson: *Jacobite General*, p.235. There is some discrepancy as to when the battle actually began. Wolfe, the future hero of Quebec, and given to such precision, stated that the first Jacobite gun fired at around 1.00 p.m.
100 Prebble: *Culloden*, p.104.
101 Ibid: pp.112–113.
102 Ibid: p.106.
103 Despite any attempts at mitigation, most contemporary accounts testify to the bloodlust of the dragoons, though it is easy to imagine how soldiery, freed from the terror of defeat and death, might view civilians who had come to the moor as spectators.
104 Tomasson and Buist: *Battles of the '45*, p.180.

POSTSCRIPT: THE THIN RED LINE

1 Reputed to be the last words of the general before he was struck down by a French musket ball early in the afternoon of 18 June 1815. Picton commanded Wellington's 5th Division, which included the Black Watch (42nd), Camerons (79th) and Gordons (92nd). (Longford, Lady Elizabeth: *Wellington: The Years of the Sword*, 1969, p.542.)
2 Baynes J. and Laffin J.: *Soldiers of Scotland*, 1988, p.176.
3 Longford: *Wellington: The Years of the Sword*, p.542.
4 Baynes and Laffin: *Soldiers of Scotland*, pp.40–41.
5 The 18th Highland Light Infantry.
6 In fact 'wauken' means waking and refers to the general having overslept rather than to his having run away.

Select Bibliography

Anderson P.: *Culloden Moor*, 1920.
Armstrong W.A.: *The Armstrong Borderland*, 1960.
Bain J. (ed.): *Calendar of Documents relating to Scotland 1108–1509*, 1881–84.
Barnes R.M.: *A History of the Regiments and Uniforms of the British Army*, 1950.
Barnet C.: *Britain and the Army 1509–1970*, 1970.
Barrett C.R.B.: *Battles and Battlefields in England*, 1896.
Barrington M.: *Graham of Claverhouse, Viscount Dundee*, 1911.
Barrow G.W.S.: *Robert Bruce*, 1965.
Bates C.: *History of Northumberland*, 1895.
Black C. Stewart: *Scottish Battles*, Glasgow 1936.
Blaikie W.B.: *Origins of the '45*, 1916.
Blair C.: *European Armour*, 1958.
Borland Rev. R.: *Border Raids and Reivers*, 1898.
Brander M.: *The Making of the Highlands*, 1980.
Brousdsted J.: *The Vikings*, 1960.
Browne J.: *History of the Highland Clans*, 4 vols, 1838.
Buchan J.: *Montrose*, 1928.
Burnet G.: 'Memoirs of . . . the Dukes of Hamilton', 1747.
Caesar: *The Gallic Wars*, (trans. S.A. Handford), 1951.
Caldwell D.A.: *The Scottish Armoury*, 1979.
Chadwick H.M.: *Early Scotland*, 1949.
Christison Gen. Sir P.: *Bannock Burn*, 1960.
Collier G.F.: *Highland Dress*, 1948.
Cowan I.: *The Scottish Covenanters*, 1976.
Dalton C.: *The Scots Army 1661–1688*, 1909.
Douglas-Simpson W.: *Scottish Castles*, 1959.
Elliot F.E.A.: *The Battle of Flodden and the Raids of 1513*, 1911.
Fisher A.: *William Wallace*, 1986.
Forbes R.: *The Lyon in Mourning* (ed. Paton), 1895.
Frank A.: *The Clans, Septs and Regiments of the Scottish Highlands*, 1908.
Fraser A.: *Mary, Queen of Scots*, 1969.
Fraser G.M.: *The Steel Bonnets*, 1971.
Froissart Sir J.: 'The Chronicles of England, France and Spain'.
Gardiner S.R.: *History of the Great Civil War*, 1889 edn.
Hall E.: *Hall's Chronicles*, 1889 edn.
Hastings M.: *Montrose, the King's Champion*, 1977.
Hewison J.K.: *The Covenanters*, 2 vols, 1913.
Hughes-Hartman C.: *The Quest Forlorn*, 1952.

Hyde E., Earl of Clarendon: *The History of the Rebellion*, Oxford, 1826.
Johnstone: *Memoirs of the Rebellion in 1745 and 1746*, 3rd edn, London, 1822.
Jones G.: *A History of the Vikings*, 1968.
Keegan J.: *The Face of Battle*, 1976.
Kightley C.: *Flodden*, 1975.
Lang A.: *History of Scotland*, 4 vols, 1909.
Lindsay J.: *The Normans and their World*, 1977 edn.
Linklater E.: *Robert The Bruce*, 1934.
Linklater M. and Hesketh C.: *For King and Conscience*, 1989.
Lynch M.: *Scotland, A New History*, 1991.
Mackay-MacKenzie W.: *The Battle of Bannock Burn*, 1913.
Mackie E.W.: *Scotland, An Archaeological Guide*, 1975.
Mackie J.D.: *A History of Scotland*, 1964.
Moncrieffe Sir I.: *The Highland Clans*, 1967.
Mure Mackenzie A.: *The Kingdom of Scotland*, 1940.
Neillands R.: *The One Hundred Years War*, 1990.
Nennius: 'History of the British', ninth century.
Oman Sir C.: *The Art of War in the Sixteenth Century*, 1937.
Oman Sir C.: *A History of the Art of War in the Middle Ages*, 2 vols, 1924.
Peterson H.: *The Book of the Gun*, 1963.
Pine L.G.: *The Highland Clans*, 1972.
Powell T.G.C.: *The Celts*, 1958.
Prebble J.: *Culloden*, 1961.
Prebble J.: *Glencoe*, 1966.
Reid S.: *Like Hungry Wolves*, 1994.
Reid S.: *The Campaigns of Montrose*, 1990.
Reid S.: *The Clans, Septs and Regiments of the Scottish Highlands*, 1908.
Ridpath G.: *The Border History of England and Scotland*, 1776.
Rogers Col H.C.B.: *Battles and Generals of the Civil War*, 1968.
Rogers Col H.C.B.: *The Weapons of the British Soldier*, 1960.
Rothwell H.: (ed.) *Chronicle of Walker of Guisborough*, 1957.
Samford A.C.: *The Rising of 1745*, 1890.
Scott of Satchwells: *A True History of Several Honourable Families*, 1776.
Scott Sir Walter: *Minstrelsy of the Scottish Border*, 2nd edn, 1902.
Seymour W.: *Battles in Britain*, 2 vols, 1975.
Simkins M.: *Warriors of Rome*, 1988.
Sinclair-Stephenson S.C.: *Inglorious Rebellion: The Jacobite Risings of 1708, 1715 and 1719*, 1971.
Smellie A.: *Men of the Covenant*, 1909.
Stephenson D.: *Alistair MacColla and the Highland Problem*, 1980
Stephenson D.: *The Scottish Revolution 1637–44*, 1973.
Stewart Col D.: *Sketches of the Highlanders of Scotland*, 2 vols, 1977.
Tabraham C.: *Scottish Castles and Fortifications*, 1986.
Tacitus: *Annals of Imperial Rome* (trans. M. Grant), 1956.
Taylor C.: *Culloden*, 1965.
Tomasson K.: *The Jacobite General*, 1958.
Tomasson K. and Buist F.: *Battles of the '45*, 1962.
Treece, H. and E. Oakshott: *Fighting Men*, 1963.
Vasey N.: *Arms and Armour*, 1964.
Watson G.: *The Border Reivers*, 1985 edn.
Wedgewood C.V.: *The Great Rebellion: The Kings Peace*, 1974 edn.
Wedgewood C.V.: *The Great Rebellion: The Kings War*, 1958.

Wesencraft C.: *The Battle of Otterburn*, 1988.
Whitlock R.: *Warrior Kings of Saxon England*, 1977.
Wilkinson F.: *Arms and Armour*, 1965.
Young P.: *The British Army 1642–1970*, 1970.
Young P. and Adair J.: *Hastings to Culloden*, 1964.
Young P. and Holmes R.: *The English Civil War*, 1974.
Anglo-Saxon Chronicle (trans. G.N. Garmonsley), 1953.
'The Battle of Maldon', Anglo-Saxon epic poem.
'The Goddodin', Ancirin, British, sixth century.
Scottish Art Review: 'Ancient Scottish Weapons', vol. 10, no. 2, 1965.
'Tain Bo Cuailnge' Irish epic, dated eighth century, of earlier origin.

Index